Why There *is* a God

and why it matters

Regis Nicoll

FOR CLAIRE ROSE AND RENEE ELIZABETH

Why There *is* a God
and why it matters

CONTENTS

Preface

There was a time when it was nigh impossible *not* to believe in God. It wasn't because of man's irrational fears and superstitions, as atheist critics like to spin it, but because of nature's rational design.

For most of human history, the intelligibility of nature pointed to an inescapable fact: an eternal, uncreated source (the uncaused Cause, Yahweh, Logos, Nature's God) brought the universe into being with a rational structure that made knowledge possible.

By the 18th century that fact led to a methodological system of inquiry that liberated knowledge from the limits of natural philosophy and the errors of alchemy and astrology. Ironically, it also opened the way for disbelief in the thing that made true knowledge possible.

It wasn't long before the sweeping successes of the Scientific Revolution produced a shift in conviction from nature's God to man's mastery over nature. And with that, a certain script emerged: God is unnecessary, man is his own savior, and the unlimited powers of science and human reason will place civilization on the inevitable march to progress.

Over the last century, the story line, while having limited success over everyday folks (the vast majority of people today still hold religious beliefs), has exerted considerable influence over cultural-shaping institutions: the scientific establishment, the mainstream media, the arts and entertainment industry, education, and the courts and legal system.

The result has been an erosion of societal support for religion, making religious belief harder to maintain. Since 1960, the number of people who poll "no belief in

God" has risen over fivefold from 2 to 11 percent, and those with no religious affiliation have increased eightfold from 2 to 16 percent[1].

At the same time, Judeo-Christian norms have been eclipsed by a secular moral census; religious liberty has become ever more tenuous; and the social pathologies of divorce, out-of-wedlock births, non-marital sex, co-habitation, single parent homes, abortion, and sexually transmitted diseases have burgeoned.

How we view these developments and the world in general, ultimately hinges on our views about God: his existence, his character, and our relationship to him.

While most Christians know what they believe about these things, too few would be able to summon up anything more than a self-referential, "bible-says-so" if challenged. They may believe with all their heart that Jesus Christ lived, died, and rose from the dead 2000 years ago, but when pressed by a naysayer they withdraw or go silent because they have never examined the reliability of the historical record, nor considered how they would articulate a winsome response to someone who deems the bible a work of man rather than the word of God.

In the preface to his book, *The God Delusion*, atheist popularizer Richard Dawkins makes no bones about his goal: "If this book works as I intend, religious readers who open it will be atheists when they put it down."

In similar vein, my goals for this book are that 1) unbelievers who open it will be believers when they put it down, and 2) believers who open it will be more confident in their beliefs and in their ability to give them voice.

INTRODUCTION

In chapter 4 of *The God Delusion*, Richard Dawkins admits, ever so modestly, that he can't disprove the existence of God. He then proceeds to explain why God almost certainly does not exist. His argument, intended to expose the fallacy of intelligent design, goes something like this:

> The more complex a thing is, the more improbable it is (absent a Designer)
> God must be more complex than anything he created.
> Therefore, God is more improbable than anything in the universe.[1]

The argument (indeed, the entire chapter) can be reduced to the "zinger" fashionable among budding atheists testing their forensic chops, "Who created God?" It is the sort of thing that plays well to folks inclined to disbelief, who are either unaware of, or willfully overlook, fundamental errors in logic.

In this case, the first is the error of *category*. God, unlike the universe and its contents, is not a contingent object, but a non-contingent, necessary being; that is to say, God is not an effect, but a *cause* -- the ultimate Cause. If "God" demands an explanation, so does any ultimate cause whether material, immaterial, or intelligent.

Next, is question-begging. By insisting that anything presumed to exist, including a necessary being, was caused to exist, the argument presupposes naturalism, the very premise under question.

Then there's confirmational bias. By criticizing theism for its lack of empirical evidence, while ignoring the unproven and/or unprovable devices of naturalism (for starters, the multiverse, cosmic inflation, and macro-evolution) which, collectively, defy Occam's razor[2] and, individually, in some cases, defy known physical processes, the argument betrays a blinkered consideration of the facts.

Lastly, contrary to the underlying critique of theism, there *is* evidence, sufficient evidence, for the existence of God. The problem is, "The evidence hasn't been heard and found wanting; it's been unheard and ignored," to riff off of G.K Chesterton.

The challenge for Christians today, as in every era, is to be prepared in season and out of season to share the rational basis for faith. This is not foremost about defending truth, but about giving it voice. For as Charles Spurgeon once counseled, "Truth is like a lion. Who ever heard of defending a lion? Just turn it loose and it will defend itself."

A few years back, I was engaged in an online discussion with "Nigel" (not his real name).
Nigel was a self-described atheist and rising star in the *Brights* movement – a community of philosophical naturalists aimed at "illuminating and elevating the naturalistic worldview," as their slogan proudly states. Some of its more prominent luminaries include Richard Dawkins, Michael Shermer, and Daniel Dennett.[3]

After coming across an article I had written critical of naturalism, Nigel invited me to dialog with him on his open blog. I agreed and was quickly drawn into a protracted discussion.

Over a period of several weeks, we covered topics ranging from the origin of the universe and the nature of matter to the origin of morality and the nature of God. While Nigel betrayed no movement away from his atheistic position during the course of our exchange, a man who had been following our dialog left this remark:

> "I have truly been swayed by Mr. Nicholl's (sic) writings. There is a [lot] to think about in his reply. Somehow I think I've always known we were not a cosmic accident. And Nigel, you are a brilliant man. Am I to believe great minds are a product of evolution. It's not adding up any more. I'm not saying Christianity is right but I do now believe in a God. There, I said it. I'm on record. My curiosity is stoked for further responses from Mr. Nicholl (sic). Nigel, thanks for having this blog. I have some heavy things to think about now from both sides."

As I read those words my thoughts turned to Spurgeon. I realized that it wasn't me or my skill that moved this man; it was the truth turned loose upon him.

To equip the reader to do just that, this book is arranged around a collection of my essays that I have selected and revised to systematically address truth from the ground up: from nature of knowledge and the knowledge of nature to the competing narratives of naturalism and theism in explaining the origin of the universe, life, morality, the metaphysical questions of meaning, purpose, and significance, the role faith plays in all explanatory accounts, and how God -- in particular, the Christian God -- is the explanation that best fits the facts, notwithstanding the age-old problems of evil, suffering, and injustice.

Chapter 1

The Nature of Knowledge

"For I do not seek to understand that I may believe, but I believe in order to understand." -- St. Anselm

Two Men and Two Worldviews

Whether we realize it or not, each of us has a worldview -- that is, a basic set of assumptions that forms the bedrock of our beliefs about the world and human existence. But how do we decide which belief system to embrace among the dozens offered in the food court of ideas?

One side of the food court peddles an unsupervised cosmos where man is left to scratch out meaning from his otherwise meaningless existence; the other side offers a superintended creation imbued with meaning for man to discover. These are the non-theistic and theistic worldviews, respectively.

Evaluating their merits involves considering three things: coherence, correspondence, and conclusion.

Three "C's"

"Coherence" is about whether the tenets of a worldview are logically sound. For instance, the claim "there is no such thing as absolute truth," is itself a statement of absolute truth rendering it internally incoherent. Such logical incoherence is the syllogistic quicksand of transcendentalism and postmodernism.

"Correspondence" is how consistent a belief is with what is known empirically, scientifically, and historically. For instance, the conclusion of social researcher Gregory Paul that "The more secular, pro-evolution democracies" experience greater social health (than religiously-informed societies) ignored the history of ethnic, religious, and political atrocities committed by the secular, pro-evolution societies of the 20th century that he conveniently left out of his study.[1]

Lastly, there is "conclusion." If followed faithfully to its logical ends, would the worldview be livable? Our concern here is not primarily with what its proponents do, but what their worldview says they *ought* to do, recognizing that every belief system has its hypocritical, misguided, or weak devotees.

For example, the fact that Christians have been guilty of many of the same evils as non-Christians does not invalidate a worldview based on the Sermon on the Mount or the Ten Commandments. To the contrary--if only the second tablet of the Decalogue were universally and consistently observed, 99.9 percent of all the world's ills could be avoided.

Likewise, despite his utilitarian ethics that prescribe euthanasia for "useless eaters," Princeton professor Peter Singer spent large sums of money to care for his Alzheimer-stricken mother. However, what would society look like if it took seriously the "high moral position" of exterminating those who are a burden to society?

Only by passing a belief system through the filters of coherence, correspondence, and conclusion can we adequately judge its claims. Particularly instructive is examining a worldview through the lives of its champions.

In the book, *The Question of God—C.S. Lewis and Sigmund Freud Debate God, Love, Sex, and the Meaning of Life*, Harvard psychiatry professor, Dr. Armand Nicholi, has done exactly that.[2]

Two great men
Sigmund Freud and C.S. Lewis represent the polar ends of the worldview spectrum. Arguably, Freud stands as the 20th century's patron saint of scientific materialism[3]; and Lewis, as the most effective apologist for Christianity of the last hundred years.

Nicholi's choice of Lewis and Freud is uniquely valuable for many reasons: Among other things, each man was highly gifted intellectually, each became an atheist as a young man despite having early religious influences, both men had conflicted relations with their father, each experienced the rejection of peers and the tragic loss of loved ones, both were victims of malice by those in the religious community, and each was influential in shaping the moral ideals of Western culture.

The similarities, in nature and nurture, of Freud and Lewis are nothing less than eerie. Even the qualitative feature of their lives is remarkably similar. It's only after Lewis makes the hard turn from atheism that his life takes on a completely different character and begins to diverge significantly and irrevocably from that of Freud, who remained steadfast atheist.

By interweaving the views of Freud and Lewis into the narrative of their lives, Dr. Nicholi gives us an objective look into their respective belief systems. But first, what are the major tenets of those systems?

Two worldviews

To be complete, a worldview must address the big questions of life: *How did it begin? What went wrong? What is the solution? How should we live? And, how will it end?* Accordingly, we will examine what the worldviews of Freud and Lewis had to say about these fundamental questions.

How did it begin?

Freud admired Charles Darwin, applying his theory of common descent to his own theories about human drives and emotions. While Freud may not have had a full-orbed theory of cosmogenesis, he accepted the absurdity of human existence in an insensate universe. As a consequence, life had no inherent meaning for Freud. To the contrary, "The moment man questions the meaning and value of life he is sick, since objectively neither has any existence," Freud wrote Marie Bonaparte. As to the claim that man is created in God's image: "No," says Freud, "God is created in man's image."

Lewis held similar views before his conversion. But afterward he believed in a creative God who entered his creation at a particular point in history. Lewis also realized that if man is a creation, his existence has intrinsic meaning. What's more, Lewis believed, man was implanted with a longing to experience the purpose for which he was created.

What went wrong?

Freud considered the reality of human suffering one of the most powerful arguments against God. The losses of his childhood nanny and, later, his favorite daughter and grandson, combined with the bitter anti-Semitism he experienced throughout life, all worked to galvanize his conviction that man is alone in an dangerous, uncaring world.

Instead of a benevolent Hand guiding man along his hazardous journey, Freud concluded that "obscure, unfeeling, and unloving powers determine men's fate."

Although Lewis experienced many of the same life disappointments as Freud, he came to understand them in view of the Fall: Included in God's perfect creation were creatures with free will to choose good or evil; in time they went wrong, allowing the virus of sin to enter and begin its work of corruption and decay; and ever since, man has been living in "enemy-occupied territory."

What is the solution?
As a materialist, Freud trusted the omnipotence of science and the infallibility of reason. He also believed that men, educated to know good, would do good.

As for God: He was part of the problem--a universal projection of the "uneducated," a wish fulfillment, a childish fantasy. Freud's advice? "Grow up!" Seek not comfort in philosophy and religion; but accept reality and endure the vicissitudes of Fate "with resignation."

The mature Lewis came to realize that the cure for the human condition rested not in education of the human mind, but in transformation of the human heart. In contrast to Freud, Lewis exhorts us to "Wake up!" and realize we were designed to run on a certain fuel, God Himself. To run on any other means exacerbating our condition.

How should we live?
In Freud's view, ethics and morality are inventions of man. Even the Ten Commandments, Freud insisted,

derives from human need and experience rather than external Authority. Consequently, what is moral is what is self-evident. And, what is self-evident will govern the passions of the enlightened (and willing) masses.

Lewis, on the other hand, believed the moral law could no more be a product of invention than could the law of gravity. Lewis cited the similarities in what he termed the *Tao* between cultures of the modern and ancient worlds. For Lewis, the universality of the *Tao* was irrefutable evidence of its supernatural origin from which the most complete revelation was disclosed in the Bible.

How will it end?
Freud referred to death as the "end of the fifth act of this rather incomprehensible and not always amusing comedy." Death was not something to fret and obsess over, but something to accept and, even, will. For, in a Freudian sense, the end of conscious existence was the highest pleasure for those whose life had become too painful to endure.

In contrast, Lewis viewed death not as the end of a final act, but as the beginning of a new one. Neither was death an escape from pain, but an entry point to joy, inexpressible. In a letter to a seriously ill friend, Lewis wrote, "There are better things ahead than any we leave behind."[4]

As we will see later, the beliefs of these two men had a profound influence on their lives. But first, we need to embark on a metaphysical journey, starting with truth and knowledge, the stuff that beliefs are made of.

"Who gave us a sponge to wipe away the entire horizon? What did we do when we unchained this earth from its sun...Do we not feel the breath of empty space? Has it not become colder? – "The Madman" Friedrich Nietzsche

The Nature of Truth

If you've grown weary of vapid chatter about the price of gas, the latest guest on *Dr. Phil*, and the merits of cable versus DSL, try this with your friends while they are at their sherry: Ask, "Who believes in truth?"

After the room revives from the dead skunk you've tossed on the carpet, continue, "No, really, who believes that truth exists and that it is knowable?"

In my experience, whether you do this with co-workers, neighbors, or church members, the conversation will proceed something like this:

You're talking about absolute truth?

Yeah, that's what I mean.

That all depends.

On what?

On your viewpoint. Have you seen that sketch—the one that looks like a hag or a beautiful girl.

Yeah.

Well, which is it--a picture of a girl or a hag?

Maybe it's both, neither.

Exactly! It all depends.

Depends on what?

Okay. We're all products of nature and nurture which causes us to see things differently. As to the sketch--I may see a hag, but that gives me no right to claim that it IS a hag, or that others are wrong if they see something else. In the end, who's to say what it is, or if it's anything but a poor artist's scribbling?

The interlocutor reflects the prevailing sentiment of the day: truth is not an objective, overarching statement about reality; it is personal perception shaped by our genetic and experiential makeup. Among sophisticates, such relativistic thinking is all the rage. Yet few realize that their fashionable ideas are really quite old.

Nothing new
Nearly 2500 years ago, the Greek philosopher, Protagoras created quite a stir when he uttered, "Man is the measure of all things." It inspired a new wave of thinkers to correct those antediluvian misgivings about transcendent truth.

At the forefront was Gorgias who insisted, "Nothing exists; even if something exists, nothing can be known about it; and if something could be known about it, knowledge about it couldn't be communicated to others." With the myth of certain truth duly exposed, a new school of thought was born: sophism.

Like the modern-day hag/girl drawing, a favorite sophist illustration was the parable of the wind: One person feels the wind as cold, while another feels it as warm. And since the wind can't be both warm and cold, it's the individual--not external reality--that determines its properties. In fact, maybe it's the individual that determines the very existence of the wind. Maybe.

Further developments

By the 18th century, the relativism of sophistry was formalized by Immanuel Kant. Kant argued that the world as it really is hidden from us. All we have are sensory perceptions interpreted by the mind. In step with the sophists, Kant challenged the age-old assumption of objective reality with one sentence: "Mind is the law-giver to nature."

With all the force of six words, reality was dislodged from its sure footing to become an observer-dependent creation. It was nothing less than a Copernican revolution of thought, placing society on a journey in uncharted waters without map, compass, captain, or helmsman.

While we will address this further in Chapter 2, a Copernican Turn of physics followed that of metaphysics. At the macro-level, Albert Einstein found that measures of time and length were no longer fixed, but depended on movement; at the micro-level, Werner Heisenberg discovered that what we "see" depends on how we "look."

Relativity theory and quantum theory became the twin pillars of modern physics. Yet, little did the pioneers foresee how their theories would be seized as validating the "truth" the Eastern mystics had been telling us all along: objective truth is an illusion.

Examining the elephant

By the 1960's, East met West in the "The Blind Men and the Elephant." In the famous fable, six sightless investigators examine different parts of a pachyderm and find that it is like a tree, a rope, a wall, a branch, a fan, a spear.

The lesson? They were *all* right. The application? We, like blind men, have no privileged position to judge the perspectives of others. The conclusion? Given that all we have are our diverse experiences fumbling in the dark, practically speaking, there is no elephant!

Gorgias would be proud.

But if truth cannot be discovered and, if in fact, does not exist, then, it is our creation. No one takes that more seriously than those raised by parents who grew up in the 60's. Just ask Korey Rowe and Dylan Avery, two college students who co-produced the independent film, *Loose Change*.[5]

Counting "Loose Change"
Loose Change, say its young producers, "shows direct connection between the attacks of September 11, 2001 and the United States government." Which, according to Rowe and Avery, was not the work of Islamic terrorists, but a sinister act of our own government to justify the Iraq War. What's more, those weren't commercial airliners that crashed into the Pentagon on that fateful day, they were U.S. cruise missiles. I'm not sure whether to laugh or cry.

Amazingly, the film has gained currency, especially among college students, despite eyewitness reports, film footage, commercial jet debris, recovered black boxes and, oh yes, the fact that all the passengers on those flights were actually killed and buried!

Even better are the reasons given by young people for supporting the film: "We don't know the whole truth" (*So, we just make something up?*); "It's good to raise questions" (*Like whether 2 plus 2 really equals 4?*); "It stimulates critical thinking" (*Like entertaining Holocaust denial theories?*). But my personal favorite, *a la*

24

American Bandstand, is: "[it is] catchy, hip, with an upbeat soundtrack."

Loose Change marks the nadir of relativism, in which truth has devolved from what is "really, real"; to what I experience is real; to whatever I can manufacture and make you believe is real. And all of this with the support of modern science! Einstein and Heisenberg would have shuddered.

Back to Albert and Werner
While quantum weirdness convinced Heisenberg that the world of protons, positrons, and photons was a mysterium whose disclosures were observer-dependent, he never doubted the objectivity of pebbles, parks, and people. Even the strange goings-on in the micro-verse were the results of the *quantum potential* whose existence was absolute and universal. Despite the claims of transcendental science, the "elephant" exists, and not in a "Schrödinger's cat" spectrum of quantum states splitting off into parallel universes or waiting to materialize by the observation of a curious observer.

The same is true for Einstein. While he accepted that movement through space and time was subject-dependent, he believed in the absolute existence of *spacetime*. Einstein was so fully convinced in the objective existence of the universe--at all levels--that he could never embrace quantum theory because of its contingent implications.

Sadly, none of this prevented co-opting these great scientists as pioneers of modern relativism. Sadder yet, is that in our relativistic universe, we have lost the ability to distinguish truth from belief.

Unlike beliefs which depend on us and our minds for existence, truth is independent of us. It is not contingent on our acknowledgement or even our existence. As the philosopher, Bertrand Russell once put it, "[T]he truth of a belief is something not involving beliefs, or (in general) any mind at all, but only the objects of belief."[6]

Notwithstanding the claims of our modern sirens, truth is true regardless of our perceptions and beliefs, no matter how sincerely we hold them. Neither is it something we invent. To paraphrase C.S. Lewis, "We can no more create truth than we can create a new law of nature, like the law of gravity."

That's because truth is something we discover, beginning with our notions about knowledge.

"Belief consists of accepting the affirmations of the soul; unbelief, in denying them." -- Ralph Waldo Emerson

The Truth about Knowledge

It has become the default assumption among the smart set that there are two non-overlapping spheres of human understanding. One sphere is Nature where star fish, starlets, and stars are reducible to elemental forms of matter and energy. Here, direct observation and the powers of reason and science make knowledge certain.

The other sphere is Supernature populated by soul, spirits, God, and everything else originating from human imaginings, needs, and yearnings. Beyond the reach of empirical examination, knowledge here is tenuous and uncertain.

The former is the realm of Facts, the latter the realm of Faith, and betwixt them, there is no connecting thoroughfare. Such was not always the case.

The early Greeks believed in a primal source of harmony that made the universe, in its diversity, a coherent whole. (The word, "universe," contains the idea of "in the many, one.")

Accepting a common rational structure for the mind and the universe, they supposed that nature *and* knowledge were unified. Even "things unseen" were thought to be knowable through the powers of unaided reason. That presumption held sway until the arrival of "hard" empiricism.

From unification to bifurcation

Reliance on reason alone led the Greeks to many false conclusions about the universe – aether, geocentrism, and spontaneous generation, to name a few. Corrections to those errors were held back for well over a millennium until the scientific method was introduced adding experimentation to rational analysis.

The new, empirically-based approach enabled the discovery of laws and mathematical relationships that described the workings of the universe with breathtaking accuracy. And with that, came a new theory of knowledge.

Inspired by the smashing success of the Scientific Revolution, John Locke and George Berkeley concluded that the only reliable source of knowledge was empirical. Unlike the ancient and medieval rationalists who believed that the cognitive powers of the mind were sufficient for discovering the true nature of things, Locke and Berkeley insisted that knowledge stems from sensory experience. They insisted that the mind is a blank slate with no in-built organizing architecture. It is our senses that inform our mind, not the other way around. With each new game-changing discovery of science, rationalism fell deeper into the shadow of empiricism, until fully eclipsed by the "hard" empiricism of David Hume.

Undergirding the empiricism of Locke and Berkeley was the presumption that *true* knowledge was possible, even for things not directly accessible by sense perception, like physical laws and abstract mathematical concepts like infinity. But David Hume said, "No!"

According to Hume, we have no access to physical laws -- they are not implanted in us from birth, or writ large in the sky for all to read. All we have is a continuing stream of experiences from which we construct associations and relationships that have no necessary bearing on what is really, real. We may have experienced a sunrise every morning, but that does not guarantee the sun will rise tomorrow. Without access to the true nature of things, we are left to form working assumptions to help us order our lives. Hume's "hard" empiricism jolted Immanuel Kant out of his dogmatic slumbers.

To rescue knowledge from the onslaught of Hume, Kant synthesized rationalism with empiricism, proposing that the mind is endowed with faculties that give meaning to our experiences. This led to Kant's observer-dependent reality which he compartmentalized into two-tiers.

In the lower tier, the realm of nature, knowledge of physical *phenomena* was possible through reason and science. In the upper tier, whatever lies beyond or beneath the sensible realm of nature (things Kant termed, *noumena*), knowledge was "soft," subjective, and apprehended through intuition, instinct, and sentiment.

Kant argued that his synthesis made possible the identification of laws, even the moral law. However, it wasn't long before his bifurcated view of knowledge resulted in a fact-faith split that pushed the moral law into the upper tier, along with the rest of Supernature.

This had a tremendous influence on the gatekeepers of science. Caught up in the anti-clericism of the times, they sought to liberate science from the fetters of faith by reducing its scope to "natural" explanations under the rubric of methodological naturalism. The result was scientific materialism.

But as we will see, materialistic science is far from faith-free.

Faith all the way down
The materialist operates on the belief that "nature is all there is." The word "belief" signifies something that is

not scientifically proven. In fact, this founding proposition is not scientifically proven or provable because, given that only natural explanations are allowed, materialistic science depends on the very premises it is trying to demonstrate. Like all worldviews, scientific materialism is founded on a faith statement. But faith is not limited to its groundwork -- it comprises its superstructure, as well.

Consider one of the most familiar, and basic, features of nature: gravity. Like angels, heaven, and God, we can't see, smell, taste, or touch gravity. Sure, we feel a downward pull toward earth, but we also "feel" an upward pull toward heaven. Even the most successful theories of gravity are not explanations, but descriptions that are wildly different.

In one pitch, gravity is an invisible force, associated with matter, mediated by who knows what? – some say, gravitons, which, by the way, have never been isolated, observed or measured, but, nonetheless, are a convenient placeholder for our ignorance. And talk about matter -- no one knows why gravity is fond of *it* and not other things, like photons.[7]

In another depiction, gravity is not a force but, rather, the topography spacetime shaped by the presence of matter. Again, why does matter, and nothing else, have this effect? No one knows. More fundamentally, which came first, matter or space? If space, did it have no shape? If matter, did it occupy no space?

That is not to take anything away from the *formulations* of these theories. Indeed, they have led to many space-age advancements. Yet the gravitational phenomena we observe, and the laws and equations that describe them, are independent of their explanation or ultimate cause.

Whether the orbit of the earth is the result of an invisible force, a spacetime warp, or the guiding hand of God, our observations and mathematical descriptions are unaffected. The explanation we accept is an exercise of faith, not a demonstration of fact. That's why, as we will see later, everyone has faith. But now a look at two (supposed) competing sources of truth.

"There are two books laid before us to study, to prevent our falling into error; first, the volume of Scriptures, which reveal the will of God; then the volume of the Creatures, which express His power." --Sir Francis Bacon

Science and Religion: adversaries or allies?

For the better part of the last century, science and religion have had a rocky relationship. The source of their tension, which has intensified in recent years, can be traced to Enlightenment thought that held unaided reason omnipotent.

From the sixteenth to nineteenth centuries, an explosion of scientific discoveries convinced thinkers that the cosmos was a grand machine that could be analyzed without reference to its Designer. By the twentieth century, the overwhelming success of science in modern medicine and technology strengthened the conviction that the universe was a self-contained mechanism.

Although trust in the explanatory power of science soared, faith and religion were allowed a voice, as long as that voice was restricted to man's spiritual needs. The late Stephen Jay Gould called this bifurcated view, "non-overlapping magisteria" (NOMA).

Today, naturalistic science and NOMA are reigning paradigms in the scientific establishment. But for the pioneers of science, the study of nature was inextricably linked to nature's God — specifically, the God of Christianity. But first, a little background.

The lens of nature
In primitive history, man found himself in a world of

both regularity and capriciousness. Diurnal periods, seasons of the year, moon phases, the cycle of life and the like, formed a seabed of predictability that enabled man to function in his day-to-day existence. But superimposed on that seabed were earthquakes, floods, droughts, pestilence, and disease—things that came unexpectedly and without warning.

These vagaries caused man to view himself as a victim of mysterious forces that ruled the earth and skies. For him, order and chaos, fate and fortune, or warring gods were in perpetual clash, making any systematic understanding of the world impossible.

But by the fifth century B.C., the Greeks acknowledged a "cosmic principle of order," they called the *Logos*, which gave rise to a rational, comprehensible universe. This was the seed of natural philosophy--a system of observation and logical analysis. The most influential figures of the period were Plato and Aristotle who approached the study of nature from two different starting points.

For Plato, the world consisted of matter and forms. Matter was the stuff of sense perception--concrete objects that exist for a time, undergo change and finally vanish. Forms, on the other hand, were eternal, immaterial ideals which defined the qualities and purposes of matter.

In Plato's universe, matter and forms were separate and distinct, with the material world but a shadowy projection created by the real world of forms. From this dichotomous perspective, Plato studied nature not to understand it, but to unravel the metaphysical mysteries of meaning, purpose, and the essence of the good life.

Aristotle, in contrast, held that the material world was real and that nature—its material existence and immaterial forms--were a cohesive, integrated whole. Consequently, Aristotle studied nature for its own sake becoming a prodigious investigator, especially in the classification of flora and fauna.

Although both men applied logic and deductive analysis to their observations, their failure to incorporate experimentation caused them to reach a number of invalid conclusions. For example, Aristotle believed in a geocentric universe and in the celestial substance, aether. He also declared that heavier objects fell faster than lighter ones—a conclusion that, in testament to Aristotle's enduring influence, would go unchallenged for nearly 2000 years!

Experimentation was shunned because it was associated with physical work—the duty of servants and slaves. For citizens and persons of standing, the only commendable work was the high exercises of the intellect: art, politics and philosophy.

Natural philosophy was further hampered by a tendency toward dualism. Even Aristotle, despite his belief in nature's wholeness, reasoned that there were two sets of laws governing the universe: one for the heavens which were pure and eternal, and another for the earth which was corrupt and fleeting.

This led to an emphasis of the heavenly over the earthly, causing the advance of science to languish centuries after Aristotle's death. Although there was alchemy, astrology and medicine, the deeper understandings of chemistry, astronomy and medical science would have to await nearly two millennia for a new paradigm.

The lens of scripture
The low view of nature held by the ancient philosophers stood in stark contrast to that in scripture.

In the opening chapter of Genesis, the Creator declared creation, all of it—material and immaterial, seen and unseen, celestial and terrestrial—good! Included, were a pair of co-*workers* who, in contradistinction to Greek dualism—were "living souls" comprised of a material body and immaterial spirit. Their job assignment: to manage, care for, and enrich the Creator's handiwork.

But it's in the gospel account we find the supreme statement of nature's value. There we read of the Creator assuming corporeality for an earthly visitation to redeem and restore a world wobbling on its axis from sin.

The significance of the material world, as evidenced in God's dazzling display of love, couldn't be further removed from that reckoned by the ancient philosophers. Through the lens of scripture, the physical world is of inestimable worth in the Divine calculus.

In the 13th century a Dominican scholar used that lens to refract the blurry image of the *Logos* into that of the living God. Like the apostle Paul who stood in the Areopagus calling out the identity of the "UNKNOWN GOD" to the Athenian seekers,[8] Thomas Aquinas declared that the God of Abraham, Isaac, and Jacob was the "cosmic principle of order" of the Greek philosophers.

Aquinas argued that the universe is intelligible not because it is a product of an impersonal uncaused Cause, but because it is a creation of a rational God. This God, though separate from his creation, sustains it and values it, and destines it for a glorious makeover.
In the meantime, He has endowed a special creature— man-- with intelligence, giving him the responsibility to exercise his rational powers in caring for creation. For Thomas, this was the God of scripture.

Thomas Aquinas was pivotal in changing the prevailing

sentiment that nature was inherently corrupt. As nature became restored to its proper place, interest in the material world grew and the study of nature became viewed as a noble pursuit. This laid the groundwork for cultural and technological advances that would come later.

The birth of science

Roger Bacon was a Franciscan monk and a contemporary of Aquinas. Bacon and, later, William Ockham, another Franciscan, introduced the ideas of induction and verification into what would become the backbone of the scientific method. But it wasn't until the sixteenth century that the crawl to discovery took a sudden, upward lurch.

It was then that another devout believer named Bacon— Francis, this time—amended the venerable Aristotelian method with hands-on experimentation. By synthesizing observation and hypothesis with experimentation and validation, Bacon sired a method of investigation which would be a template for all who followed.

Within a few decades, man's understanding of the world was turned on its head by Kepler, Galileo, and Newton -- all men of faith, men whose Christian worldview gave them confidence in a rational, comprehensible world; men who considered the study of nature a sacred calling. They were the vanguard of something that had been held back for millennia by pagan philosophy and mysticism: Science.

After mid-wifing science, Christian thought catalyzed the Scientific Revolution and sustained it for the next two hundred years. As historian Alvin J. Schmidt remarks in his book, *Under the Influence*, "[V]irtually all the scientists from the Middle Ages to the mid-eighteenth century—many of whom were seminal thinkers—not only were sincere Christians but were often inspired by biblical postulates and premises in their theories that sought to explain and predict natural phenomena."[9]

Well into the nineteenth century, Christian thinkers dominated the scientific frontier with groundbreaking discoveries in the fields of electro-magnetism, microbiology, medicine, genetics, chemistry, atomic theory, and molecular motion.

It is noteworthy that despite the technological and engineering marvels produced by ancient Egypt, China and India, true science did not come out from those civilizations. Because of their transcendental worldview, the workings of Nature were thought to be beyond the grasp of mere mortals. Consequently, scientific advancement went so far, but no farther.

Neither did science emerge from Islamic culture which, after its Golden Age, has been in free fall since 1200 AD. It was then that Muslims embraced a more orthodox Islam in which Allah was a capricious puppeteer beyond reason and logic, and man his fatalistic marionette.

Granted, these cultures made some great technological achievements, but it is the unique Christian understanding of God and his creation that made modern science possible. And the scientific materialist who insists that religious faith is an argument from ignorance has it quite the other way around.

"Every unbiased mind must admit that the age in which the chief development of the science of mechanics took place was an age of predominately theological cast."
German physicist, Ernst Mach[10]

Arguing From Ignorance or Evidence?

According to religious critics, a believer lumbers to the edge of every frontier of knowledge, poised to retire his investigations with "God did it!" contentment. The reality is that the scientist who approaches the world as a product of intelligence, rather than of matter and motion, is less likely to stop short of discovery. Instead of dismissing a feature that, at first glance, appears inert, unnecessary, or superfluous, he is more inclined the push the envelope of investigation to unravel its function and purpose.

Instead of obstructing science, Christianity, with its emphasis on a personal Creator, inspired an age of discovery that opened the way *for* science.

Speculations about a sun-centered universe had been around for some time, but challenges to the Aristotelian model refined by Ptolemy, didn't gain serious attention until the "Copernican Turn" in the 16th century.

Nicolaus Copernicus was a Christian who understood the universe as an intelligible creation that operated according to mathematically-coherent principles. His initial attraction to heliocentrism was not the result of new observational data, but of his notion that the sun -- symbolic of God as Light and Lamp – seemed a fitful center of divine activity.
He, along with other early researchers, believed that the elegant structure observed in creation should be

describable in an elegant fashion. Thus, when heliocentrism proved more mathematically simple than the reigning earth-centered model, it gained a slow following.

Like Copernicus, Johannes Kepler believed that the mysteries of nature could be unlocked with the key of mathematics. Kepler put it this way, "The chief aim of all investigations of the external world should be to discover the rational order and harmony which has been imposed on it by God and which He has revealed to us in the language of mathematics."

Kepler's belief in the mathematical precision of the universe led to his discovery of three fundamental laws of planetary motion--the foremost, that the planetary orbits are elliptical, rather than circular, as modeled by Copernicus.

While the discovery of mathematical elegance was the product of faith for these pioneers, it has been the source of faith for others. In his book, *Truth Decay*, Douglas Groothuis, shares the account of a Russian physicist: "I was in Siberia and met God there while working on my equations. I suddenly realized that the beauty of these equations had to have a purpose and design behind them, and I felt deep in my spirit that God was speaking to me through these equations." In that moment, the young scientist stepped over the chasm from atheism to theism and, ultimately, Christianity. [11]

Copernicus and Kepler published their paradigm-shifting theories without much controversy. It was a different story for Galileo, who drew the full ire of the Catholic Church.

The Galileo affair
To hear the secular elites tell it, Galileo was a hero-martyr in the enduring struggle of free inquiry against the

tyranny of Religion. But the truth is that the Roman Curia did not object to his heliocentrism on religious grounds, but on scientific ones.

Despite the ground-breaking work of Copernicus and Kepler, the Catholic Church, and the general populace remained thoroughly Aristotelian. Resistance to heliocentrism was due to three things: 1) it was contrary to the common sense perception of a static earth, 2) there was no accompanying physical mechanism to account for it, and 3) it lacked a sufficient body of evidence to overturn a model that had proven quite successful for centuries (for example, stellar parallax was not observed until the 19th century)[12].

Compounding the problem, Galileo published his work in Italian, the language of common folk, rather than in the scholarly language of Latin. It was attempt to mainstream his theory, by bringing the force of public acceptance to bear upon the scientific establishment. Galileo added to his troubles by writing scathing satires intended to embarrass his clerical critics.

For his offenses, Galileo was sentenced to a short prison stay followed by house arrest in his own villa until his death in 1642. While the Church's punitive actions were overly harsh, its reluctance to accept novel theories in the absence of scientific vetting was reasonable.

Nevertheless, secular elites summon Galileo from the grave as star witness in the ongoing case of *Science v. Religion*. Much overlooked is that while the Catholic Church was resistant to the new theories, not all Christians were. Specifically, Lutherans and Calvinists encouraged, and even helped fund, Copernicus and Kepler in the publication of their works.

A clockwork
The modern charge against religion would have been

summarily dismissed by the vanguard of science, including the father of the mechanical worldview, Isaac Newton.

Isaac Newton was a gifted polymath whose three laws of motion and law of gravity were the crowning achievements of the Scientific Revolution. Newton's law of universal gravitation gave Kepler's planetary laws a physical explanation that validated heliocentrism. But most significantly, Newton's discoveries led to the notion that the universe was a giant "clock-work" – a cosmic mechanism reducible to its constituent parts, operating autonomously according to inwrought universal laws.

For some, the clock-work universe allowed for a Creator, but not a Tinkerer. For others, it allowed for neither. For many, it led to brimming confidence in science as a wellspring of knowledge that would enable man to harness and manipulate nature.

It is a great irony that Newton's theories became the foundation of scientific materialism – a worldview that excludes, *a priori*, any supranatural causation. Newton was a devoted Christian who was motivated, in part, by a desire to prove the existence of God through the design of creation.

Against those who were eager to embrace the machine model, Newton warned "Gravity explains the motions of the planets, but it cannot explain who set the planets in motion. God governs all things and knows all that is or can be done." This was no "God-of-the-Gaps" argument from ignorance but, rather, a design inference from evidence. Although Newton has been co-opted by the scientific materialists, in truth, he was a forerunner of the Intelligent Design[13] movement.

In his footsteps followed men like John Dalton, Andre

Ampere, Georg Ohm, Michael Faraday, Louis Pasteur, William Kelvin, Gregor Mendel, and George Washington Carver -- believers whose achievements were the outworking of their Christian faith.

Scientists in the truest sense of the word, they were investigators who doggedly followed the evidence wherever it led, approaching the gaps of understanding not with "God did it!" resignation, but with "God created it" expectation.

Every scientist, whether he realizes it or not, stands on the shoulders of these giants. And, as we will see, his beliefs, whether he realizes it or not, are based on faith in something or someone.

"Did you ever notice that all machines are made for some reason?" – Hugo Cabret

Losing Faith

It's a familiar story, Margaret Wheeler Johnson's account about losing her faith. As Johnson tells it, the personal integrity that religion instilled in her, "made it impossible to maintain faith" in religion.[14]

A while back, Columbia University professor Mark Lilla made a similar disclosure; namely, the truth that led him *to* faith was the very thing that led him "out of faith."[15]

In Johnson's case, the turn was sparked by doubts concerning her denomination's teaching about the sacrament of Communion; in Lilla's case, it had to do with the interpretation of a particular Bible passage that he found disagreeable. (The scriptural text in question, and its reading, Lilla does not disclose.)

Margaret Johnson and Mark Lilla are in the growing company of individuals who have left Christianity not because of core doctrines—like the Nicene Creed—but because of a sectarian peculiarity, a disagreeable scriptural interpretation, or what they deem as hypocritical practices.

Yet they wouldn't think of abandoning their pet political party over an isolated plank in the platform, a questionable policy proposal, or the misdeeds of a member in the ranks.

What folks like Johnson and Lilla often don't realize (or admit) is that they don't lose their faith; they merely shift it from one object to another. Otherwise, they would quickly learn that without faith in something, life itself would be impossible.

What we don't 'know'
Faith is the bridge between what is known and what remains unknown; and that, it so happens, is a gap of cosmic proportions.

Although the scientific enterprise has led to discoveries that have been phenomenally successful in man's manipulation of nature, it has done little to advance our understanding of nature. In some ways we are like the car owner who believes that he really knows how cars works, because when he turns the ignition key and presses the gas pedal, his car moves. Truth is, very few owners know how a car works; even among trained mechanics, few understand, much less could explain, all of the underlying physics.

And while the physics of auto mechanics could be learned, albeit with a great deal of effort, a comprehensive understanding of nature is unlikely, if not impossible.

That's because only four percent of the universe is made up of things that we can see, probe, and measure. The rest (96 percent) consists of dark matter and dark energy that remain hidden from our investigative tools.[16] What's more, what we know about that accessible "four percent" is precious little.

For example, what we "know" about matter is that it is made up of atoms consisting of elementary particles which are (take your pick): localized excitations in the ubiquitous quantum field, or (as we'll see in chapter 3) Planck-sized "strings" of energy whose "vibration patterns" produce the sensations of mass associated with matter.

But whether they are quantum blips or vibrating strings, the inescapable conclusion is that there is no "there," there—at least, any "there" that we could recognize as such.

In short, the sum-total of our knowledge is infinitesimal in comparison to our ignorance, making some kind of faith an indispensible part of human existence. So the question is not *whether* we base our convictions and actions on faith, but on *what* faith do we base them.

Bad faith, good faith
For example, Margaret Johnson, in eulogizing her loss of religious faith, expresses a faith that is every bit as religious as the one she left behind:

> I could no longer honestly claim that the marvels I had always named as proof of the existence of a benevolent, omniscient creator—the human body, spring—are examples of anything but the order into which, marvelously indeed but following to no master plan, *evolution channels entropy.*" (My emphasis.)

Evolution channels entropy? You mean that the mind-numbing marvel of the human body, from the complex organization of the DNA macromolecule to the integrated functionality of physiological systems, is the end product of a trial-and-error process of chance and adaptation?

Accepting that proposition requires faith of high order—so high, that everything known about the origin of functionally complex systems must be discarded for a process that is unproven and, indeed, has been shown repeatedly to exceed the creative resources of the entire universe (as we will see in Chapter 7).

This is faith, derived not from reason but, rather, an

"escape from reason" (as the late Francis Schaeffer might have put it), leaving belief to the whims of non-rational influences (e.g., personal desire, popular opinion, or emotional affinities or aversions). It is faith that is blind to the facts, like that of the parent who believes her child will become a nuclear physicist despite his difficulty mastering his multiplication tables. Such is *bad faith*.

On the other hand, accepting that the highly organized structures of life (the simplest, which far exceed the complexity of the most advanced machines man has made) derive from an intelligent source—even if beyond our understanding—is to stand upon what is known to be possible. It is following the evidence and its trajectory to where it leads, weighing all explanations in the light of reason and accepting the one that best fits the facts. Based on established knowledge and exercising reason, this conclusion is the product of *good faith*.

Parts & purpose
Bad faith deems the machine-like features of nature beneficial, useful, or detrimental, but bereft of any intended purpose. Good faith sees it differently, like Hugo Cabret, the title character in the 2011 Oscar-winning film *Hugo*.

Hugo, a young mechanical savant, lives alone in a secret hideaway of a train station. There, unbeknownst to anyone, save his friend Isabella, Hugo services and maintains the elaborate station clock.

One day while working on the intricate clockwork, Hugo turns to Isabella and poses,

> "Did you ever notice that all machines are made for some reason? They make you laugh, like Papa Georges' toys, or they tell time, like the clocks ... Maybe that's why broken machines always make me

sad, because they can't do what they're meant to do…Maybe it's the same with people. If you lose your purpose … it's like you're broken."

Hugo presses his insight further as he takes Isabella to a majestic overlook of the bejeweled Paris nightscape:

> Right after my father died, I would come up here a lot … I would imagine that the whole world was one big machine. Machines never have any extra parts, you know. They always have the exact number they need. So I figured if the entire world was a big machine I couldn't be an extra part, I had to be here for some reason… And that means you have to be here for some reason, too.

In two short passages, Hugo turns the tables on materialism. For the materialist, broken parts (think: vestigial organs and junk DNA) are evidence that the "machine," however, complex and functional is merely the unguided, unintentional product of atomic collisions. But for Hugo Cabret, the "machine" is evidence of intention, such that parts, no matter how deformed and defective, point to purposes which are intrinsic, if obscured in the present by their condition.

Heart matters
With each passing year, the pile of surplus parts used to bolster the claims of Darwinian evolution has been dwindling, as researchers continue to discover functions, previously hidden. For example, inert segments of DNA dismissed as "junk," are increasingly being found essential in gene expression, either through direct action as a chemical "switch" or indirectly as a "space" or "punctuation mark" in a molecular command string.

In 2012 the ENCODE Project, a five year study involving 30 peer-reviewed papers, concluded that 80 percent of the human genome has a biological function.[17]

The Human Genome Project, completed in 2003, put that number at 2 percent.

Good faith, in light of nature's architecture, would lead us to expect that trend to continue.

And yet, there is no denying the brokenness of nature, as evidenced in "parts," which while not superfluous, cannot, or cannot completely, fulfill their intended purpose: the blighted tree that can't bare fruit; the omega wolf that can't find a mate; the defective appendage or organ inimical to health and well-being… or the collective "we," who, because of varying degrees of bad faith, are weighed down from ascent to our supreme end--communion with God. And Margaret Johnson seems to know that.

After describing her former life as one of "magical thinking," she closes with some telling disclosures.

She describes her current life (that committed to reason) as a "wasteland in comparison, a frolic in the land of false idols"—upscale bistros, fine cuisine, and a tribe of urban professionals; she admits to a gnawing emptiness that she "can't name and can't begin to fill" and, she confesses, "When I'm at my wit's end, I find myself sending up a plea for help. And afterwards, in the face of all reason, I sometimes feel relief."

Margaret Wheeler Johnson has not lost faith. She is just oscillating between two faith objects: one, pulling her further into the wasteland, and the other nudging her gently out. One, autonomous reason; the other, reason's Source.

"It isn't just that I don't believe in God... I hope there is no God!... I don't want the universe to be like that."
Thomas Nagel

There are No Agnostics

Agnostic Ron Rosenbaum wants to clear something up: "Agnosticism is not some kind of weak-tea atheism," but the stout ale of "radical skepticism, doubt in the possibility of certainty." In fact, his belief system is as distinct from atheism as it is from theism. It is important that you know this.

In "An Agnostic Manifesto" Rosenbaum takes great pains to explain that God-deniers, like God-believers, have childlike faith: faith that reality is nothing but the sum-total of the physical world; faith that science is the sole source of knowledge; faith that the materialistic quest will unravel the deepest mysteries of the universe, including the ultimate questions about human existence; faith that their beliefs are not based on faith, but are settled beyond rational argument.[18]

For example, atheists believe that the universe is the product of some materialistic process. For the moment, a cosmos-birthing fluctuation in the *quantum potential* is a popular one.[19]

They believe this, not because it is proven or even provable, but because it *must* be true to keep their worldview from collapsing like a dying star.
God-deniers dismiss God-believers for their dogmatic claims, while, as Rosenbaum rightly notes, never "consider[ing] that it may well be a philosophic, logical impossibility for something to create itself from

nothing." Not to mention the impossibility of nothing creating everything!

But agnostics, Rosenbaum proudly points out, refuse to believe what is not or cannot be verified as true and, thereby, stand against the dogmatism of both theism and atheism. When faced with the question of cosmogenesis – what "banged" and who, or what, caused it -- the agnostic shrugs, ever so humbly, "I don't know."

It is a response calculated to let you know that he occupies an elevated plain of intellectual integrity, where lives are directed by facts not faith. What the agnostic doesn't realize, or willfully ignores, is that he is just as much a person of faith as those he tries to distance himself from. It begins with what he really knows.

What he knows
What he, or anyone, *knows,* is what he accepts as true, starting with *personal experience.*

Children learn about the dangers of a hot stove not from their mother's warnings, but from the smarting of their curious finger tips. Adults will stubbornly insist that a ball, swung over the head on a string, will follow a curved path when released, until they try it themselves and discover that it continues on a straight one.

In cases where personal experience is no help – like, questions about the origin of the universe, the existence of heaven, the soul, the meaning of life, etc. – human beings depend on non-experiential sources for knowledge.

One source is *intellectual predisposition*. This was best expressed by Harvard biologist, Richard Lewontin who once said: "We take the side of science in spite of the patent absurdity of some of its constructs, in spite of its failure to fulfill many of its extravagant promises...

because we have a prior commitment, a commitment to materialism." [20]

Note that Lewontin's faith in science as the ultimate source of knowledge is based on his intellectual preference to a particular worldview, not on science's proven explanatory power in answering ultimate questions.

Another source is our *non-rational sensibilities*. For instance, astrobiologist Paul Davies believes that a yet-to-be-discovered principle is woven into the cosmos that makes biological life inevitable.[21] He believes this, not because he has any evidence to substantiate it, but because, as he says, he is "more comfortable" with it than the alternatives -- presumably, those that include a necessary, omnipotent Being.

More to the point is NYU law professor, Thomas Nagel, who, in a moment of admirable candor, admitted, "It isn't just that I don't believe in God... I hope there is no God!... I don't want the universe to be like that."[22]

For Davies, and particularly Nagel, knowledge is determined neither by empirical proof nor observational data, but by emotional aversion and affinity.

Lastly, there is *authority*.

At the individual level, knowledge is limited. No one can directly verify every claim that is trotted out as fact. For that reason, much of what "we know" depends on the word of others: journalists, scientists, historians, teachers, parents, pastors, peers. The existence of subject matter experts means that a person need not have lived in nineteenth century France to know that Napoleon existed, nor bounce a laser beam off the moon to know that light travels at 186,282 miles per second, nor contract syphilis to know that extramarital sex can lead to an STD.

Obviously, authority-derived knowledge requires faith -- faith in the expertise and trustworthiness of other people. It is by faith that a non-chemist knows that arsenic is poison (as experiential knowledge would be fatal), that a person knows the identity of his biological parents (unless he has settled the matter with a definitive DNA test), or that anyone knows anything about the lives of Alexander the Great, Julius Caesar or Jesus Christ.

It is even by faith that we know that the law of gravity will remain valid tomorrow.

Despite mathematical relationships that describe the *effects* of gravity with astounding precision, there is no consensus about the nature of the thing. Is it a distortion of space-time, an attractive force of tiny, mediating and, as of yet, hypothetical particles (gravitons?) that act like a gigantic rubber band, a mysterious "action-at-a distance" between bodies having mass? All of the above? Take your pick. The lack of consensus indicates that we know neither the *what* nor the *why* of gravity.

Without such knowledge, belief that the tide will go out in the morning is nothing more than belief that the future will be like the past. But if the universe is the fluke product of random collisions, as atheists contend, that belief requires faith of a high order – faith not only in the unwavering regularity of nature but, more fundamentally, that our sensory experiences correspond to reality, and that our minds and intellects have the ability to discern the true nature of things.

If, on the other hand, the universe is the product of an Intelligence that wanted to make it intelligible by intelligent beings, the lawful, orderly, and predictable behavior of nature is a logical and reasonable expectation.

Three thousand years ago, Solomon penned a thirty-two chapter lesson listing all he had learned about wisdom. First on his list was this: "The fear of the Lord is the beginning of knowledge."[23] Indeed, more important than *what* we believe, is *whom* we believe.

The claims of Ron Rosenbaum notwithstanding, the agnostic, like everyone else, exercises faith. What's more, his belief in "uncertainty" is an expression of faith in the certainty that answers to "ultimate" questions are uncertain. So, in reality, his faith is not in uncertainty at all. And that applies to his practiced faith, as well as, his professed faith.

Practical belief
Faith is confirmed not in what we say (our beliefs), but in what we do (our behaviors).

A child standing nervously at the edge of the pool, being coaxed by his father in the water, must either plunge in or remain, feet firmly planted, at water's edge. There is no middle way. The child may believe with all his heart that his father won't let harm come to him, but until he jumps, his fear holds him captive in *functional* unbelief. When the "rubber" of belief meets the "road" of decision, doubt defaults to unbelief.

To the question, "Does God exist?" a person can answer, yes, I don't know, or no. But in practice, a person must live as if He either does or doesn't exist; there is nothing else to do, but oscillate schizophrenically between the two.

Agnosticism is a statement, a mood, a posture. It thrives in the intellectual oxygen of coffee houses and cocktail conversations. But outside of those habitable zones, in the real world where life is lived, the atmosphere supports only belief and unbelief.

"The world is charged with the grandeur of God."
Gerard Manley Hopkins

From Doubt to Belief

Have you ever felt like a fish in an aquarium? After surveying our cosmic home and noting how well equipped it is with everything we need to survive and flourish, seeming perfectly suited for us—maybe too perfect—have you wondered, "Is everything staged; am I one of countless players on a set monitored by some unseen Observer?" Truman Burbank did.

In *The Truman Show* (1998), Truman Burbank is the unwitting star of a continuous-running reality show telecast from *Seahaven*. Hermetically sealed from the outside world, *Seahaven* is a virtual community where everything, from traffic to weather, is under the omnipotent control and supervision of its televisionary-creator, Christof.

Placed in *Seahaven* at birth, Truman accepts things for what they seem to be: his family, his best friend, the oversized moon, a community that revolves around him. But despite his tightly controlled existence, Truman eventually suspects that there is something odd about his white picket fence world.

For instance, why do complete strangers address him by name? Where did that light fixture come from that dropped out of the sky? And that strange voice broadcasting his every movement over the radio--what was that all about? It all adds up to something more.

Determined to find out, Truman "sea-jacks" a vessel and

heads for the horizon until his craft slams into the cyclorama wall of the *Seahaven* set. At that point Christof, in a Yahwehic voice from the "heavens," booms, "I'm the creator...of a television show...you're the star."

Like Truman Burbank, many of us question whether things are as they seem. Is reality only what I perceive with my senses? Or is there a truth "out there," something beyond the fish bowl of my spatio-temporal existence? Is there an Attendant who is watching, caring? And how can I know?

Archimedes once said that he could move the earth with a long enough lever and a leverage point at a suitable distance from the earth. To gain knowledge a similar *Archimedean Point* is required. For it is only from a transcendent point of reference that our perceptions and understandings can be tested against objective truth.

The truth that Truman learned about his home did not come from his unaided reason. It came from the *Archimedean Point* of the real world beyond: an unintended control room transmission, an actor's miscue, a discovered mini-cam, and finally, the confession of Christof himself. In fact, as the lead-in quote indicates, the handprint of *Seahaven's* "creator" was everywhere for Truman to see. Absent that handprint, Truman would have been as helpless as a fish in an aquarium trying to learn about the world outside.

The universe is also covered with the handprint of its Creator, as Gerard Manley Hopkins informs us.[24] All the same, the absence of bullet-proof evidence can be a stumbling block for those struggling with God's hiddenness.

A "conversation"

Mr. Johnson, could I bother you for a moment?

Sure, Nathan. What's on your mind?

Well, lately I've been wondering, uh…how we can know God exists. Ever since Kevin was killed in that car crash last year…then the Nepal earthquake and all the senseless stuff going on in the Mideast…it's just, I don't know, if God's around, there doesn't seem to be much evidence of him. Am I wrong?

I understand what you're saying.

I mean, what do we know about God, really? All we have are a few scraps of ancient texts, written by ancient people who claimed to have heard or seen something… just other people's word, not certain truth, not a one-plus-one-equals-two kind of thing. How can I believe in something that's so uncertain?

You make a good point. It's an issue that a lot of people have struggled with at one time or another. Like St. Augustine.

Really?

That's right. Augustine concluded that if we only believed and acted on what can be proven with absolute certainty, we'd believe and act on very little. In fact, nothing in life would be stable.

Hmm.

Nathan, let me ask… does your mother love you?

Sure she does. But…

Can you prove it?

No, but…

How do you know that your father is really your father?

What?

How do you know that your dad is not someone your mother married just to give you a father figure?

I don't really see how…

Isn't your belief about your dad based on your mother's word? Isn't your certainty in her word based on your faith in her character, and your faith that she loves you--a faith, I might add, for which you have no "certain" proof?

I guess so.

Like "Nathan" we would all like certain knowledge to remove every lingering doubt. But we live in a twilight interim of which the apostle Paul writes "Now I know in part."[25] And though our knowledge is neither complete nor conclusive, it is sufficient for belief and action in the shadow time.

Such is the nature of faith—as Tom Skinner, former gang leader turned chaplain for the Washington Redskins, realized: "I spent a long time trying to come to grips with my doubts and suddenly realized that I had better come to grips with what I believe. I have since moved from the agony of questions that I cannot answer to the reality of answers I cannot escape...and it's a great relief."[26]

Despite uncertainty, self-doubt and a paralyzing fear of water, Truman Burbank also was gripped by an answer he couldn't escape--that there was more to life than his

Seahaven existence. In an act of raw faith, Truman braved a perilous voyage that almost claimed his life, but ultimately landed him on the threshold of something truly stunning—not another community or even an exotic island, but another world. And for those of us in that world, an even more marvelous destination awaits.

"No eye has seen nor ear heard, or mind conceived what God has prepared for them who love him."[27]

"Can a person who flunks the test to the most basic question in life, 'is there a God?', be considered intelligent?" Jeff Clinton

A Matter of Intelligence

Are religious believers intellectually challenged? According to a raft of studies popular in free-thinking circles, yes.

After compiling dozens of surveys conducted over a 50-year time span, researcher Burnham P. Beckwith concluded in 1986, "Among American students and adults, the amount of religious faith tends to vary inversely and appreciably with intelligence."[1] According to a 2008 Gallup survey 73 percent of college-educated individuals profess belief in God, compared to 88 percent of those with no college.[28]

Among scientists, religious belief is much lower. In 2009, Pew Research reported that 41 percent of scientists believe in God.[29] Other studies found that belief in God was held by 7 percent of *National Academy of Science* members and only 3.3 percent of UK *Royal Society* fellows. [30]

What this means to religious skeptics, like Richard Lynn, is that really smart people (like him) don't believe in God. Lynn, a professor of psychology, believes it is "simply a matter of IQ" – the higher the IQ, the greater immunity to religious belief.[31] That puts the burden upon bright folk to "break the spell" of religion by lighting a candle in the "demon-haunted world" of superstition.

A while back, a friend asked me, "Can a person who flunks the test to the most basic question in life, 'is there a God?', be considered intelligent?" It's good question, because what we "know" about our world, human nature, life's purpose, moral ethics and just about everything else hangs on what we believe about their origin.

But what *is* "intelligence?" Surprisingly, there is no unanimous agreement on what it is, except, as someone once quipped, "intelligence is whatever intelligence tests measure."

From a survey of standard dictionary definitions, intelligence is associated with the ability to learn and use knowledge. The *American Psychological Association* calls it, "[The] ability to understand complex ideas, to adapt effectively to the environment, to learn from experience, to engage in various forms of reasoning, to overcome obstacles by taking thought."[32] But perhaps the most comprehensive definition is found in "Mainstream Science on Intelligence," endorsed by 52 researchers:

> *"Intelligence is a very general mental capability that, among other things, involves the ability to reason, plan, solve problems, think abstractly, comprehend complex ideas, learn quickly and learn from experience. It is not merely book learning, a narrow academic skill, or test-taking smarts. Rather, it reflects a broader and deeper capability for comprehending our surroundings—'catching on', 'making sense' of things, or 'figuring out' what to do."* [33]

Defined that way, intelligence is inextricably connected with worldview: the mental model we use to understand the world and our place it. Problem solving and affecting our environment depend on the rational *ability* of our mind to make "sense of things," but they also depend on the non-rational *capability* of our heart to apply the "sense" our mind has "made."

Consequently, a person who orders his life according to a worldview that aligns with the way the world really works, could be said to possess *true* intelligence, while a person who orders his life after an incongruent worldview, could be said to demonstrate *artificial* intelligence.

In a lengthy discussion I had with a self-proclaimed atheist, I was informed that, unlike the "God hypothesis," naturalism is free of untestable, unfalsifiable placeholders. To which, I politely pointed out that naturalism brims with placeholders, whimsical theories sustained by nothing other than the will to believe.

I went on to explain that these theories grew out of the unsettling recognition that we inhabit a Goldilocks planet, one in which life teeters on the edge of non-existence. Scrambling to account for these "just right" conditions, desperate theorists trotted out the *multiverse,* an infinite manifold of universes that guarantees the existence of our hospitable home, and every conceivable (and inconceivable) one as well. But that's not the half of it.

The very existence of the multiverse depends on the *quantum field* – a gossamer fabric of reality comprised of neither matter nor energy, but "potentiality."

In this wraithlike realm *virtual particles* continuously pop in and out of existence in such a way that the universal laws of conservation are not violated -- except, that is, in a singular event that occurred over 14 billion years ago. By a process called *inflation,* one of those "particles" defied the sacrosanct laws of physics by materializing, then exploding at such an expansive rate that it gave birth to all the matter and energy that would become our fledgling universe.

Even the baloney-detectors of laymen should peg out when leading researchers like Alan Guth present this narrative beaming, "It is said there is no such thing as a free lunch. But the universe is the ultimate free lunch."[34] Sad to say, such cognitive dissonance among authorities is far from the exception.

Indeed, when other gap-fillers like *emergence, memes* and *macro-evolution* are added to account for biological life, thought, and the encyclopedic information in the genome, the narrative of naturalism reads more like a Brothers Grimm tale than Newton's "Principia Mathematica."

My interlocutor responded, "Regis, but the speculative theories about the multiverse are there for a reason... We can either try to work out what's going on by proposing bold new ideas about the construction of the entire universe... Or we can say: "God did it." I mean, what is the alternative?"

Precisely, what *is* the alternative?

A whiff of jitteriness oozed from his question -- for the inescapable answer is "There is no alternative." Either the universe is the thoughtful creation of an intelligent Designer, or the fluke product of some pre-cosmic, unintelligent essence. If we reject the Designer because he is unyielding to our empirical methods, we are left with a scenario that depends on a host of things that are, likewise, unyielding -- not to mention the task of explaining the existence of art, music, literature, poetry and language as creations of our neuron impulses.

Discussing his re-conversion after a 20-year sojourn in atheism, English writer A.N. Wilson confesses "I was drawn, over and over again, to the disconcerting recognition that so very many of the people I had most admired and loved, either in life or in books, had been believers." What's more, the complexities of our humanness forced him to reassess, on an intellectual basis, the materialistic dogma that love, music, and language are artifacts of unguided, unintelligent evolutionary processes.

Wilson recounts a conversation with a fellow materialist that underscored the uncritical, unexamined tenets of the "faith."

After chatting about their common difficulty in remembering people's names, Wilson's friend offered "It is because when we were simply anthropoid apes, there was no need to distinguish between one another by giving names." Wilson writes "This credal confession struck me as just as superstitious as believing in the historicity of Noah's Ark. More so, really."[35]

Turning back from the sirens of atheism, Wilson returned to the faith he had left decades ago, with the conviction "that we are spiritual beings, and that the religion of the incarnation, asserting that God made humanity in His image, and continually restores humanity in His image, is simply true. As a working blueprint for life, as a template against which to measure experience, it fits."

After years in the wasteland, A. N. Wilson rediscovered the one worldview that lines up with the way things really are. In his words, "it fits!" It is an intelligent discovery that begins with considering the true nature of things.

To that, we now turn.

Chapter 2

The Nature of Reality

"Everything we know about Nature is in accord with the fundamental process of Nature that lies outside of space-time." Henry Pierce Stapp

---

"Our task is not to penetrate into the essence of things, the meaning of which we don't know anyway, but rather to develop concepts which allow us to talk in a productive way about phenomena in nature." – Niels Bohr, on the task of physics

Paradigms in Upheaval

A question that has occupied the thoughts man from the earliest times is the nature of reality. Is reality, at its root, the cosmic stew of matter and energy, the ethereal stuff of mind and spirit, or some combination thereof?

As early as the 6th century BC, Heraclites and Parmenides took opposing positions on this age-old question. Heraclites believed that reality consisted of those things that change; that is, things whose ephemeral manifestation is in the physical realm. This concept formed the basis of *materialism,* the naturalistic view that the physical world of matter and energy is all there is.

Parmenides, on the other hand, argued that what was real was that which didn't change and, therefore, was eternal. He considered the material world, being in flux and transitory, as unreal, and our sense perceptions of it, illusionary. The Parmenidian paradigm is the foundation of *idealism*; the view that reality is grounded in the non-physical realm of mind, thought, or spirit.

The metaphysics of Parmenides greatly influenced the philosophy of Plato. In his *Allegory of the Cave,* Plato depicted the material world as a shadow pointing to the real world of ideas and "forms."

But by the 17th century, Rene Descartes, influenced by the early Greek philosopher Pythagoras, proposed that reality was not of one, but two separate essences; one, mind, the other, body. The Cartesian concept – formally called, "substance dualism" – held that the mental and physical were so substantially different, that neither could be shown to be a form of, or be reduced to, the other.

A few years later, Benedict De Spinoza presented a twist to substance dualism, suggesting that the body and mind are different manifestations of a more basic and ubiquitous substance, like Spirit, the universal force, the divine mind, cosmic consciousness, or the transcendental self. This view of reality became known as "property dualism."

Although Spinoza has been called the first modern pantheist, the germ of property dualism has commerce with some Pauline concepts, as reflected in Paul's depictions of Christ who "fills everything in every way," and God "who is over all and through all and in all." [1]

You may be thinking that each of these views has some good points and some not so good. Or maybe you've concluded that they all fall short of describing reality. Interestingly, contrary to Niels Bohr's lead-in quote, modern science holds some important clues.

The Commonsensical World

Everyday experience tells us that the world is made up of physical things: things that occupy a definite position in time and space; things that possess actual properties like size, shape, color, texture, mass, and velocity. Our experience also tells us that the law of cause-and-effect is alive and well: a pot boils when heated; a soccer ball moves when kicked; my eardrum rings with the sound of the cymbal crash. Conversely, we "know" that any effect on an object requires an action, or force, on that object.

During the Scientific Revolution, this commonsense knowledge received a shot-in-the-arm, in no small measure, due to Isaac Newton and his laws of motion and gravity. The intuitive concepts of physicalism and cause-and-effect became so entrenched that by the 19th century, scientist Marquis de Laplace boldly asserted that the universe was completely deterministic.

According to the clock-work model of Laplace, the future state of any object could be fully determined if its initial state, and all of the forces acting on it were known. Laplace went so far as to suggest that the deterministic laws of science governed everything from falling apples to human behavior. (Laplace presaged modern-day philosophical naturalists who believe that materialistic processes are responsible for every phenomenon from eye color and the Aurora Borealis to human spirituality and sexual identity.)

As long as investigators were content in examining the macrocosm of the sensible world, all appeared well. But as researchers delved into the underlying microcosm, a shift of tectonic proportions began shaking the halls of scientific inquiry.

First tremors
The first seismic movement occurred in 1900, about one hundred years after light was found to behave like waves.[2]

Max Planck was investigating the energy distribution of radiating heat when he discovered that electro-magnetic radiation (including heat and visible light) was comprised of infinitesimal packets of energy called quanta.

Five years later, Albert Einstein reinforced Planck's finding when he demonstrated that those tiny packets of energy also exhibited particle-like behaviors, like a spray of ordnance from a sub-atomic assault rifle.

In 1924 another startling discovery was made when French nobleman Louis de Broglie pondered the implications of Einstein's theory of relativity. The mass-energy equivalence of special relativity ($E=mc^2$), together with the wave-like properties of light, led de Broglie to theorize that material "things," like electrons, also have a wave-like character.

DeBroglie's hunch was validated three years later by a couple of experimenters at Bell labs. After directing an electron beam though a double-slit grating, Clinton Davisson and Lester Germer observed an extraordinary phenomenon on the electron-sensitive screen behind the grating: an interference pattern, the signature of wave interaction.

It is provocative that, similar to the mind-body *dualism* proposed by the 17th century metaphysicists, early modern physicists were unraveling a dualistic character of the physical world. The discovery of wave-particle duality suggests something both ethereal and material about physical nature. It could also hint to a more basic essence of matter and energy. But more on that later.

What was waving?
Let's go back to the Davisson-Germer experiment. If Davisson and Germer were correct – that particles behave like waves -- what was "waving?" The earliest clue came in 1927 after Werner Heisenberg discovered the "uncertainty principle."

Contrary to the assertions of Laplace, Heisenberg discovered that inside the microcosm of nature, the exact states and positions of quantal entities, like the electron, cannot be fully known. In other words, the innermost stratum of nature was opaque to human investigation. That was a staggering blow to classical physics because it shattered the causal underpinnings of a clock-work universe.

Even more stunning was what unfolded when Heisenberg's principle was combined with the quantum formulations of Erwin Schrödinger. That partnership led to the discovery that the electron does not occupy an exact location at any given time, but is instead spread out over time and space according to a probability function.

It turns out that what is "waving," is the electron itself according to the probability of its being in a given position. As a result, the interference pattern of the Davisson-Germer experiment is the result of the electron passing through *both* slits at the same time!

Now if you are thinking, "This goes against everything I know about the real world," take comfort -- you are in very good company. It was such findings that caused early quantum theorist, Niels Bohr, to remark, "If someone says that he can think about quantum physics without becoming dizzy, that shows only that he has not understood anything whatever about it."[3]

But hold onto your seats, because the nature of reality gets "curiouser and curiouser."

"Numerous assaults on our conception of reality are emerging from modern physics… [But] I find none more mind-boggling than the recent realization that our universe is not local." --Brian Greene, physicist

More Upheaval

As we saw, the conception of reality underwent a seismic shift when investigators popped the lid on the quantum world. Instead of finding a substructure consisting of orderly, well-defined building blocks, early pioneers peered into a microcosm of wraithlike objects that were fuzzy and erratic. On the forefront was Werner Heisenberg.

Heisenberg discovered that in nature's deep regions our investigative probes have a pronounced effect on what we actually observe. For example, if we measure the velocity of an electron, we will disturb its position, and if we measure its position, we will alter its velocity. The result is that we can know where it is, but not what it's doing, or we can know what it's doing, but not where it is.

But here's the real kicker: We can refine our experiment so that the disturbances are reduced, but there is a point beyond which, no matter how skillful and meticulous we are, the precision of our measurement cannot be improved. Indeed, there is an inbuilt limit that is neither the fault of the experiment, the experimenter, or his experimental apparatus, a limit that forms a boundary to what can be known.

This imprecision, popularly known as the "uncertainty principle," was a main feature of the *Copenhagen Interpretation* (CI) associated with Werner Heisenberg and Neils Bohr. Wave-particle duality and wave function probability were also a part of CI.

All of this was so alien to prevailing understanding that Neils Bohr remarked, "The quantum world cannot be fully understood nor can physical meaning be applied to its wave-function description… quantum mechanics only explains the external observations. It tells us nothing about the internal structure."

Bohr's sentiment reflected a growing unease with the quantum world, a world whose secrets appeared locked to human investigation, leaving final explanations a mystery never to be solved.

We'll see just how much a mystery, shortly. But for now let's examine some more mind-numbing repercussions of the Copenhagen Interpretation.

According to the Copenhagen Interpretation, the description of a particle is handled entirely by its wave function, a mathematical formulation of all the potential states of a particle (including its position, speed, and direction). When a particle is "observed," the wave function "collapses," thereby transforming one of its potential states into an actual one. In essence, the particle is *created by* the observer *in* his act of observing!

The suggestion of an observer-created reality was reminiscent of the Kantian Turn in philosophy, which regarded nature and nature's laws as mind-dependent. Expectedly, critics were quick to challenge this fantastic claim with some creative thought experiments. One of the most famous being, *Schrödinger's Cat*.

The thought experiment involves a hypothetical feline confined in a box with a sealed vial of poison. Inside is a contraption that will the release the poison and kill the cat if a sensor is struck by an electron traveling in random flight.

Following the logical consequence of CI, until an observer takes a peek in the box, the cat is neither dead nor alive, but in a superimposed state of life-death! Schrödinger's Cat demonstrated the absurdity of observer-created reality. Or did it?

Einstein and Co.

CI advocates were quick to suggest that large, complex objects -- like a cat -- are subjected to constant bombardment of subatomic elements in their environment. The continual impingement of light waves, cosmic rays, and a host of other fundamental particles amounts to billions of "observations" that cause the wave state to promptly coalesce into a single value. Thus, well before an anxious observer checks in on the cat, it is either dead or alive, not in some limbo of half-existence.

But what about simple, micro-sized objects like an electron? Einstein and a couple of his colleagues, Boris Podolsky and Nathan Rosen, proposed another thought experiment in which a sub-atomic particle splits off into two smaller particles of equal mass.

According to the laws of conservation, the total spin of the "daughter" particles must equal that of the "parent." For example, if the spin of the parent was 0, then the spin of one daughter must be +1 and the other -1.

Einstein and company reasoned that if daughter A was measured with a spin of +1, the spin of daughter B could be determined as -1 without actually measuring daughter B. But according to CI, daughter B has no spin until *it* is measured. And if daughter B *was* affected by the measurement on daughter A, the measurement would generate an instantaneous signal to daughter B in violation of special relativity (which sets the cosmic limit of travel at the speed of light.[4])

This was sufficient in the minds of Einstein, Podolsky, and Rosen to invalidate CI. But where they right?

A non-local universe
The thought experiment of Einstein and company (known as EPR) was rooted in classical thinking; namely, that objects possess real properties whether we observe them or not, and that actions cannot proceed faster than the speed of light -- the latter defining what is called *local action*. But were these conditions operative in the innermost region of nature?

In 1964, Irish physicist John Bell devised a theorem whereby such speculations could be tested. In the 1970s and 80s, investigators applied Bell's theorem to a range of experiments, and what they found was nothing short of breath-taking.

Contrary to the contention of Einstein, the experimenters discovered that a particle "over here" *does* care about what happens to a particle "over there." And not only does the particle "care," but it responds in an instantaneous – that is, non-local -- manner.

Also remarkable is what they did not find. They did not find that quantum-space consists of objects with actualized properties, as was argued by Einstein. Their findings confirmed the notions of a fuzzy, ethereal – some would say, "spooky"--realm of nature.

The astonishing verification of Bell's theorem suggests a substructure of nature that is vastly counter-intuitive. In contrast to the familiar macroworld of physical things governed by orderly laws, the obscure and unexpected microworld appears populated by spectral objects exhibiting chaotic behavior -- objects that are lawless, operating "on their own," and yet maintaining a visceral connectedness.

In short, the staggering revelation at the edge of nature's horizon, it is that there is something not quite natural about the "natural" world.

C. S. Lewis insinuated this over 50 years ago when he remarked, "If the movements of the individual units [of Nature] are events 'on their own', events which do not interlock with all other events, then these movements are not a part of Nature."[5]

"Feynman, I know why all electrons have the same charge and the same mass… because they are all the same electron!" John Wheeler

The Answer that Fits

When we plunge down the rabbit hole of reality and enter the realm of photons, electrons, and quantum wave functions, what we discover is weirder than we ever could have imagined.

Among the things that strike us peculiar are things in identity crisis -- things that act sometimes as particles and sometimes as waves. And try as hard as we may to discern what they really are, their schizophrenia thwarts our every effort.

What's more, if we fine tune our looking glass, we find not a solid assortment of detached and distinct particles, but a murky lattice of objects that defy precise description. To be sure, quantal objects and their behaviors upturn everything we thought we knew about the world and how it works.

In the world we know, the laws of Newton reign, allowing us, for instance, to determine the complete trajectory of a baseball once we know its initial conditions and all the forces acting on it. But that's in the world we know.

Quantal space
Once we cross the quantum threshold, Newton's laws are useless in telling us anything about an electron in that same baseball. If we try to zero in on its location, its speed can have any value from zero to infinity. And if we try to dial in on its speed, quantum uncertainty allows

the particle to exist anywhere in the universe!

Such is the nature of quantal space -- the innermost region of nature where properties like energy, position, and speed do not possess explicit values at any moment in time, but fluctuate wildly and unpredictably.

Because of quantum uncertainty, an electron associated with the baseball may exist, in any instant, inside the baseball, at the edge of the cosmos, or any point in between. Maddeningly, and against all reason, common sense, and everyday experience, the further in we drill, the less clarity and more turbulence we encounter.

But if we are not so greedy in obtaining precise knowledge, we can guesstimate the position of the electron within a fuzzy shroud around the nuclear structure of the baseball. We only need to back off and examine it a bit removed.

A seething sea
Imagine taking a sky-diving plunge 10,000 feet over the ocean.

In your initial glance down, you would see the "big picture" -- a textureless stretch of blue with shorelines, contours of landmasses, and small footprints of ocean vessels. As you descend, you would eventually distinguish the features of large waves and white caps.

Further down in free fall, you would make out smaller waves and currents. And, finally, after you pop your chute and approach the surface, what appeared as a serene body of water from 10,000 feet, becomes a tumultuous seascape of activity.

If you were to take a gnat's eye-view on a small patch of water you would lose all perception of the "big picture." You would only see the wild undulations of water creating waves, bubbles, and foam as it is pummeled by wind, tidal forces, and subsurface currents.

The innermost stratum of nature is much the same. Up-close-and-personal, the quantum world is a seething sea of energy and particles, where exotic things like muons, mesons, neutrinos, positrons, and electrons incessantly "foam up" and dissipate in harmony with the quantum potential. However at the 10,000 feet level, the quantum foam smoothes out, allowing the "big picture" of books, leaves, keyboards, and SUVs to be apprehended by sentient beings.

The quantum potential is conjectured by many theorists as an all-pervasive force field that energizes the entire quanta-sphere. Provocatively, the theory suggests of some sort of inter-cosmic region of creative activity.

It is a suggestion bolstered by established principles of quantum physics which show that the strength of this field is colossal. So colossal, that physicist David Bohm once noted, "If one computes the amount of energy that would be in one cubic centimeter of space... it turns out to be very far beyond the total energy of all the matter in the known universe."[6]

What all this implies is that there is something within the infrastructure of the cosmos that is creative, omnipresent, and omnipotent. But there is another provocative feature of this mysterious entity.

An integrated fabric
Remember that things, as we think of them in a classical sense, do not exist in the quantum realm, and what is apprehended by our senses depends on how we conduct our observation.

If we use particle accelerator (or "atom smasher") in a certain way to probe this realm, we see electrons -- if in another way, we see muons. But in the end, our effort to understand what is really going on is frustrated.

It is like trying to figure out how a Swiss watch works by strafing it with an Uzi and examining the flying debris. In each case, the reductionism upon which our experiment is founded is flawed, because the quantum world, like the movements of a Swiss watch, is more than the sum-total of its parts, or the material that comprises it.

Indeed, the non-local behavior of quantum phenomena gives evidence of a fundamental interconnectedness. Recognizing the logical end of this implication, physicist John Wheeler once remarked to Richard Feynman, "Feynman, I know why all electrons have the same charge and the same mass... because they are all the same electron!" [7]

Accordingly, many theorists conceptualize electrons (and other quantal entities) not as separate and distinct, but as localized excitations of the infinitely extended quantum field where "wholeness" shatters our usual conceptions of space and time. In essence, this field is thought to be the gossamer-like threads of a cosmic fabric.

The otherworldly features of quantal space once prompted Lawrence Berkeley physicist, Henry Pierce Stapp, to remark "Everything we know about Nature is in accord with the fundamental process of Nature that lies outside of space-time." [8]

So what is it that lies outside of space-time?

Implications at quests end

Pulling back the layers of nature and peering deep into its interior, we encounter a substructure of infinite potentials rather than infinitesimal particles. Instead of discovering details about things "in there", we are left pondering the deep mysteries of Something in, and beyond, "there."

At the end of our investigative quest is the hint of an interface between space-time and *beyond* space-time, between the material and immaterial.

The border region between the natural and supra-natural appears to be an interstitial well-spring supercharged with Something, which -- as it pours into space-time -- fuels the cosmos with matter and energy arranged in simple and complex forms according to Its organizing principles.

The answer that fits
So what does this all tell us about reality? It tells us that reality consists of both the physical and non-physical, of things seen and unseen. It also suggests, in line with Spinoza, that ultimate reality is of a more basic substance than either mind or matter.

Although the ardent scientific materialist might associate this with the quantum potential, he is challenged to explain how an impersonal, non-conscious entity displays the extraordinary creative power and genius that is rife in the universe.

The only thing befitting the data emerging from the new science is not something, but Someone. Someone who is unbounded by space-time, and yet is able to penetrate space-time to shape it and sustain it. Perhaps, Someone whose self-description, "I AM!", conveys all the omnipresence, omnipotence, and omniscience apprehended by science.

Chapter 3

The Holy Grail of Science

"Do you know the laws of the heavens?"[1]

A Theory of Everything

Man's success in harnessing nature has convinced many investigators of a grand principle underlying all phenomena—a Theory of Everything (TOE)-- that will help us unravel all of the "hows" and "whys" of the world we live, including the very meaning of our existence.

As Stephen Hawking wrote in *A Brief History in Time*, "if we do discover a complete theory... [we would] be able to take part in the discussion of why it is we and the universe exist. If we find the answer to that, it would be the ultimate triumph of human reason—for then we would know the mind of God."[2] Hawking is surely onto something. If we knew the mind of God, I imagine he'd look a lot like the guy in the mirror.

Little wonder that the TOE has been called the Holy Grail of science.

Early notions

As early as the sixth century B.C. various thinkers supposed that everything in the universe was reducible to some primary substance like water, air, fire or earth. For example, Heraclites foreshadowed modern field theory[3] and relativity[4] , as we will see in a moment, when he declared fire as a material substance and a motive force. Others, like Empedocles and Anaxagoras, argued that an immaterial agent -- whether "Love and Strife" or an incorporeal Mind -- gave rise to the universe.

Over the next 2500 years, investigators would traverse the inner depths of matter to the outer reaches of the cosmos, yielding theories of the atom, space-time and the fundamental forces of nature. But over the last century, their discoveries have been as stunning as they have been confounding -- perhaps no more so than those concerning the structure of the universe.

Beyond space and time

The world we are familiar with has three dimensions. By specifying latitude, longitude and altitude, one can uniquely locate anything on the planet – anything stationary, that is. But many things we interact with are not fixed in location, they move in the fourth dimension of time. For example, if I want to meet a friend in New York City, it won't do to say I'll meet him on the 50th floor of the Chrysler building on Lexington Avenue at 42nd Street – I must also specify a date and time for our meeting.

Until the 20th century, time was considered a convention rather than a dimension. The reigning paradigm was that time was a measure of change independent of one's position and movement. In the classical understanding, time ticked at a uniform rhythm whether in the bowels of

Carlsbad Caverns, on the pinnacle of the Andes Mountains, or in the Challenger space shuttle.

Then, with his theory of Special Relativity, Albert Einstein jolted the scientific community by introducing time as a dimensional aspect of the cosmos. Although most people associate Einstein's theory with the relative nature of time, it is really about the invariance of the speed of light. What Einstein showed was that regardless an observer's motion, light will always appear to travel at 300 million meters per second. However, for a traveler racing through the cosmos at near light speed, perceptions of time and even physical dimensions, *do* change.

Consider Captain Kirk accelerating his starship to warp speed. For him, time will slow and lengths will contract relative to measurements taken by a stationary observer. As he approaches the speed of light, Kirk experiences a fundamental relationship between space and time -- namely, how he moves in space affects how he moves in time.

Moreover, an even more provocative implication of Einstein's theory is that *everything* moves at light speed in *spacetime*. Although you may feel like couch potato watching a *Law and Order* marathon in a catatonic stupor, you are actually moving at the speed of light through the time dimension. In contrast, once the *Enterprise* hits warp speed in the space dimension, the adventurous Kirk becomes a couch potato in the time dimension (that is, he doesn't age!). It's enough to make your head throb.

Einstein's paradigm-shattering science revealed how space and time, once considered separate and unrelated, were interwoven in a cosmic tapestry now known as *spacetime*. But, as we saw in chapter 1, Special Relativity also revealed the equivalence of matter and energy.

Although Heraclites may have been the first to speculate the unity of matter and energy, it wasn't until Einstein's equation of $E=mc^2$, that the hunch of this ancient had any scientific basis.

In thinking beyond a three-dimensional universe to a four-dimensional one, Einstein discovered unity between space and time and also matter and energy. But the question that plagued Einstein until his death was whether *spacetime* and *matter-energy* were similarly related in some fundamental way. It was an important puzzle piece missing in the Theory of Everything.

Clumps and crinkles
A decade after the achievement of Special Relativity, Einstein worked out what many consider his greatest triumph: General Relativity, the revolutionary theory of gravity which established the connection between space and matter.

In the 200 hundred years leading up to Einstein, Newtonian physics had explained gravity as an attractive force between bodies having mass. According to Newton, the strength of gravity depended on the masses of objects and the distance between them. What's more Newton insisted, this force was transmitted instantly. For example, an exploding supernova ten million light-years away would have an immediate, if unnoticeable effect on Earth.

But Newton's "action-at-a-distance" violated the cosmic travel barrier: the speed of light. This greatly troubled Einstein and motivated him to seek an alternate explanation consistent with relativity theory.

In a thought experiment Einstein imagined an elevator accelerating in outer space. Einstein reasoned that the forces experienced by an elevator occupant would be the same as those for a passenger in a stationary elevator. Thus, if there were no windows to betray movement, neither occupant could tell whether he was motionless on Earth or accelerating in space. Being equivalent in effect, acceleration would produce the same sensations as gravity.

Einstein further imagined someone shining a beam of light across the cabin of the accelerating elevator. Because of the upward acceleration of the elevator, the light beam would bend toward the floor. Einstein concluded that because of equivalence, gravity would produce a similar distortion. For instance, light traveling near a massive object -- like the sun -- would move in a curved, rather than straight trajectory.

In contrast to Newton's motive force between material objects, gravity could now be understood as the geometric influence of matter on spacetime. In Einstein's universe, matter told spacetime how to bend and spacetime told matter how to move. *Matter-energy* comprised the clumps and crinkles in the spacetime fabric.

With the connection between *matter-energy* and spacetime established, it seemed that Holy Grail of science was well within reach.

Trouble afoot
Over the past century Einstein's theories have been repeatedly verified and shown to be accurate to a high degree. They depict an intricately woven fabric bending and twisting in the presence of galaxies, stars, and planets. And despite all of their mind-boggling implications, their mathematical expressions are beautiful in their simplicity.

The simple elegance with which relativity describes the

intimate associations between matter, energy, space and time, makes the theory just "seem right." But even before Einstein broadcasted his theory to the scientific community, other researchers were unearthing the seeds of something that would confound Einstein and all who would follow in quest of the Grail.

"Who has understood the mind of the Lord, or instructed him as his counselor?"[5]

Fits and Starts of a Theory

Who could have guessed it? By visualizing the universe in four dimensions, Albert Einstein revolutionized the reigning concepts of space, time, matter, and energy. Space and time, long considered independent of each other, were revealed as interconnected threads in the cosmic fabric, *spacetime.* Not only did movement in space affect movement in time, but spacetime itself was shaped by the presence of matter and energy.

This intimate association convinced Einstein that any final theory of the universe included the union of physical forces as well. While emerging developments would frustrate Einstein in his unification efforts (as we will see), relativity theory was the high water mark of classical science.

Law and order

Like many ancients, Aristotle believed in an orderly universe discernable through human reason. Confident in a rational world, Aristotle developed scientific teachings that remained virtually unchallenged for nearly two millennia. But derived from logic rather than experimentation, Aristotle's insights, as we've seen, were not always consistent with reality.

During the next 300 years, the marriage of experiment with theory enabled a new breed of investigators to develop models with predictive, as well as descriptive power. Empirical support for Kepler's planetary orbits, Isaac Newton's classical laws of motion, and James Clerk Maxwell's equations of electromagnetism bolstered faith in the universe as a comprehensible place.

On the pinnacle
Albert Einstein came on the wave of these developments. Like his predecessors, Einstein believed in a cause-and-effect world operating according to physical laws. Not only was Nature comprehensible, but unraveling her mysteries was only a matter of human ingenuity and resolve. At the same time, Einstein was awed by this, remarking, "The most incomprehensible thing about the world is that it is at all comprehensible."[6]

His frequent references to God and "the Great One," have led some to conclude that Einstein was a believer, but at best he was agnostic about a theistic God. At one point he claimed that his was the God of Spinoza--a pantheistic deification of Nature—which, for Einstein, was a sort of cosmic principle of order, as opposed to a Grand Tinkerer who kept his hands on the dials.

Nevertheless, his theory of relativity placed investigators on the penultimate step toward a Theory of Everything. Or so it seemed.

Without warning, a new wave of researchers arrived with some very unwelcome news: In the innermost regions of nature, the cosmos was not the smooth, quiescent landscape described by Einstein; it was a frothing sea of chaotic activity. And that had monumental implications.

Back to mystery
The advent of twentieth century saw the birth of quantum theory. Physicists with strange names, like DeBroglie, Bohr, Heisenberg and Schrödinger, told of an even stranger world beneath the atomic horizon, where physical reality is not actualized until it is "observed." And what *is* observed are tiny *Lego* blocks behaving sometimes like particles and sometimes like waves in a cloudy microcosm. What's more, these edgy

schizophrenics and their murky environment defied all attempts at physical description.

The bad news for unification theorists was that the small-scale structure of the cosmos looked hopelessly concealed. It was like opening a Matryoshka doll only to find a smaller doll, which houses another until the innermost one is reached with nothing deeper to reveal. At the frontier of reality, the pioneers had peeled away the skin of the onion, only to find a sphinx sitting stubbornly silent.

It wasn't that this "phanta-sphere" was beyond the reach of current science but, rather, that hiddenness was an intrinsic feature of it. Which is exactly what one would expect of divine Agent working in a supernatural realm. As one ancient voice put it, "His glory covered the heavens and... rays flashed from his hand, where his power *was hidden*."[7]

Over sixty years ago, C.S. Lewis realized that "if this theory is true all our confidence that Nature has no doors, and no reality outside herself for doors to open on, would have disappeared." In other words, if true, quantum theory reveals something beyond Nature and a portal through which "events may by fed into her" by... the Supernatural.[8]

Of course most scientists chafe at such *mystispeak*, confident that naturalistic answers await those who refuse to surrender to supernatural dead ends. And, by turning their attention to other aspects of the final theory, they avoid the disquieting implications at the quantum horizon...at least for a while.

A merry merger
Central to a Theory of Everything is an account of the forces of nature--one that goes beyond identifying and describing the forces, to explaining why they are the way

they are. To date, these are gravity, electromagnetism, and the weak and strong nuclear forces.

While everyone is familiar with the first two of these, the last two are esoteric to all, but the nuclear specialist. Briefly, the "strong" force is responsible for holding the atomic nucleus intact and the "weak" force governs radioactive decay of some atomic nuclei.

Because of the success of relativity in describing the relationships between space, time, matter and energy, there was (and is) a strong feeling that these four forces must also be related in some fundamental way. By the late 1970s, that hunch proved right -- at least for two of the four forces. It was then that a group of researchers received the Nobel Prize for showing that at extremely high temperatures -- like those of the universe within moments of creation -- the electromagnetic and weak forces merge into what has been coined, the "electroweak" force.

Later calculations, at even higher temperatures, suggested the unity of the electroweak and strong forces. And although experimental verification is unlikely (particle accelerators with sufficient power to test the theory require a track the size of our Solar System!), there is good reason to believe that at the moment of the Big Bang three of the four known forces were indistinguishable from one another. The puzzle yet to be solved by theorists is how gravity fits into this merry merger.

Trouble on the horizon
According to General Relativity, gravity is responsible for the shape and texture of the universe at large (that is, visible) scales. And while the theory has been extremely successful in describing what happens in the macroscopic range, at sub-atomic distances the theory self-destructs, yielding meaningless results.

Although speculations abound about black holes, worm holes and time tunnels, the actual effects of gravity at the sub-atomic horizon are unknown. Again, the vexing transition at the classical-quantum divide is proving to be an impassable chasm for scientific frontiersmen.

All of modern physics rests on two pillars scientific achievement: General Relativity and Quantum Theory. Each enjoys a vast amount of experimental validation. Yet, their disjuncture at the quantum threshold indicates there is a problem with one or both of these theories. And that spells T-R-O-U-B-L-E for theorists afflicted with supernatural glaucoma.

> *"For, in the end, what is man in nature? A nothing compared to the infinite, an everything compared to the nothing, a midpoint between nothing and everything, infinitely removed from understanding the extremes: the ends of things and their principles are hopelessly hidden from him in an impenetrable secret."* – Blaise Pascal[9]

"Science sometimes pretends to answer questions in these domains, but the answers are often so silly that we are not inclined to take them seriously." Erwin Schrödinger

Got the World on a String

We live in an age of unprecedented progress, in which advances in knowledge and technology have accelerated from an evolutionary scale to a revolutionary one. In less than one hundred years, telegraphs and adding machines have been replaced by the marvels of cell phones and microprocessors—thanks, in no small part, to quantum theory.

Although the quantum theory is rightly credited with much of today's high-tech wizardry, many scientists believe its crowning achievement is the Standard Model of physics.

The Standard Model describes the universe at the subatomic level. With outstanding experimental validation and exceptional success in terms of technological application, the model, in the minds of many, is foundational to a Theory of Everything—the Holy Grail of science that holds the answers to man's pressing questions about the universe and himself. Notwithstanding its success, the Standard Model has some troubling snags.

The particle zoo
First off, the model is rather messy. With experimental evidence for hundreds of subatomic particles from exotic baryons and mesons to more familiar protons and neutrons, and with three types of force carriers, the

Standard Model amounts to what some have called, a "particle zoo."

Although many of these particles can be reduced to combinations of more fundamental quarks and leptons, even they come in various "colors" and "flavors." As a result, the zoo's "basement" is cluttered with nearly twenty fundamental species, not including those needed to form antimatter[10].

Next, the model is silent on how these elemental components came to be and how nature "selected" the values for the dozen or so parameters (like particle mass, force strength, and electronic charge) needed to describe them.

Finally, the force responsible for the large-scale structure of the cosmos, gravity, is excluded, leaving a gaping hole in any comprehensive theory.

However, some theorists believe that a serendipitous find by a budding young researcher could hold the key to these and other snags.

It's all about strings

In 1968, while doing research for his physics fellowship, Gabriele Veneziano came across a two centuries-old mathematical formulation that described the strong nuclear force in astonishing detail. For a time no one knew why this old algorithm worked, until it was realized that it applied to a vibrating string. It was the seed of what would become String Theory.

In the Standard Model of physics, the building blocks of matter are represented as point-particles of vanishingly small size. In string theory, by contrast, they are modeled as "strings" of finite (although extremely small) size. This finite dimension gives the universe a minimum grain structure—that is, a size below which, matter, space and time cannot be further divided.

Imagine taking a human hair and breaking it in half; and repeating the process over and over until there is nothing left to divide. According to string theory, your hair-splitting task could not go on *ad infinitum*, but would end once you reached the dimension of a string--an unimaginably tiny 10^{-33} centimeters.

Despite their extremely small dimensions, strings are just large enough to eliminate those pesky calculation problems encountered by gravity at subatomic scales. That is, a string is sufficiently big to mend the cosmic rip created when General Relativity meets quantum theory in the innermost stratum of nature. At the same time, strings are not inert threads that fill the universe--they are continuously vibrating fibers that *make up* the universe. In essence, everything--matter, energy, space and time— is composed of strings.

What we observe experimentally—particles with material properties like mass, charge and magnetic spin—is determined by the vibrational pattern of the string. Think of a guitar string that can produce a range of notes and sounds by varying the string tension and plucking technique.

In similar fashion, the tension of a cosmic string determines how it will resonate to produce the material properties we associate with quarks, photons, electrons and the like. And yet we know that Eddie Van Halen is not doing the "plucking." So who is? We'll get back to that.

To account for the full assortment of species in the particle zoo, strings must vibrate in at least ten rather than three dimensions. You're probably thinking the same thing that crossed the minds of many early theorists: That can't be right!

Or could it?

A world in hyperspace

In his book, *Hyperspace*, physicist Michio Kaku writes, "the laws of nature simplify and unify in higher dimensions." Recall that by considering the universe in four, rather than three dimensions, Einstein demonstrated the unity of matter and energy and of space and time. It is an example, notes Kaku, that what is impossible in three dimensions is child's play in higher dimensions.[11]

Consider a person living on Platter Boulevard -- a two-dimensional neighborhood where there is no height or depth, only length and width. Imagine our character trying to enter a locked house without a key. Confined to a pancake existence, he is faced with an impossible task — absent discharging a Chuck Norris-style sidekick against the door. However, if our little guy could move in the third dimension (of height and depth), he could step effortlessly over (or under!) the door, creating quite a stir, no doubt, to his flat neighbors inside.

When limited to three dimensions, it is difficult to see how the laws of the cosmos can be reduced to a unified principle. But in ten dimensions, string theory suggests that everything is a consequence of some overarching phenomenon of strings. As to what that phenomenon could be: for now, it's anyone's guess.

One obvious question is why these extra dimensions are not observed in our everyday experience. The answer is that they are tightly enfolded into the three dimensions of the observable universe. It is like a kite string that appears to be a one-dimensional object when seen from a distance. At closer inspection, a second dimension of thickness comes in view. But it's not until we take a gnat's eye-view on the surface, that its three-dimensional nature becomes apparent.

Unfortunately, the size of these extra dimensions is so small that even the most ardent supporters of string theory concede we will never have probes powerful enough to detect them. But if we could, emeritus professor Timothy Ferris says, we would find that strings "are just curved space." [12]

So the world is one unplumbed product of pure geometry? That's right, says Princeton physicist David Gross: "To build matter itself from geometry—that in a sense is what string theory does."[13] So matter is a product of geometry, which is a measure of space which, according to relativity, is shaped by matter which?

Despite such "gerbil-run" logic and a bevy of unanswered questions, there is a belief among researchers that string theory holds the brightest promise for a Theory of Everything. Among those thorny questions are: What physical principle underlies the theory?; What is the source of a string's unending supply of vibrational energy (that is, what or who is "plucking" it?); and Where do strings come from in the first place?

That could be why Harvard researchers Paul Ginsparg and Sheldon Glashow characterize string theory as an activity "to be conducted at schools of divinity by the future equivalents of medieval theologians," and why others are looking elsewhere for answers.[14]

Others weigh in
Astrobiologist, Paul Davies believes that the laws of physics are embedded in nature. In Davies' formulation, mind and matter are melded into a kind of cosmic consciousness that has encoded the blueprint of life in the fabric of the universe.[15] As to how that came to be…well, that's a "matter for future research."

As for Stephen Hawking, he believes that our universe is

a product of quantum processes. In every moment of time, infinitesimal changes in the sub-nuclear stratum of nature cause whole worlds to branch off into separate realms—each with its own "history."

At the moment of the big bang, the universe had no unique history; instead, there was a superimposition of histories for all possible universes. According to Hawking, the job of the investigator is to select a "history" from the mix. This amazing feat is accomplished by examining the conditions that now exist, and working backward to discover what the initial conditions must have been. In effect, the present determines the past.

If that's not enough to make you squirm, Hawking resorts to some mathematical prestidigitation with "imaginary time" to avoid the absurdities encountered with big bang and black hole singularities.[16]

Hawking's theory is one of several variations on the "multiverse" — a supercosmos containing an infinite number of universes, trotted out by theorists in an attempt to account for our finely-tweaked world as neither a creation nor accident, but as an inevitability. But here's the rub: An infinite cosmos in which everything (and anything) is inevitable, is one in which even God must exist in one of its branches.

I'm reminded of what quantum pioneer, Erwin Schrödinger, once said: "Science sometimes pretends to answer questions in these domains, but the answers are often so silly that we are not inclined to take them seriously."[17]

Back to the future
The notion that string theory, cosmic consciousness, the multiverse, or any other naturalistic principle will lead to a theory of everything is flawed from the get-go. Should

experimental research eventually verify one such model, it will merely describe how, rather than explain why, the cosmos conforms to it.

Indeed, the most vexing questions of man: Why is there something instead of nothing? What is the meaning and purpose of life? What does it mean to be human? and What is the "good" life? will be left unanswered.

Realizing that their noble quest is leading them back to where their journey began, physicists Ginsparg and Glashow remarked, "For the first time since the Dark Ages, we can see how our noble search may end, with faith replacing science once again."[18]

Chapter 4

In the Beginning...

"[Science] can only explain later events by earlier events, but it can never explain the beginning." Werner Heisenberg

Word or Quantum?

In 2006, a whiff of smoke from the world's largest and oldest blast wafted into view last year.[1] After reviewing data from a satellite probe, a team of NASA scientists reported tiny irregularities in the cosmic microwave background radiation—that faint relic of energy from the primordial explosion that gave birth to the universe: the Big Bang.[2] Although the pattern of the relic was first mapped in 1992, the sensitivity and resolution of the latest measurements provide the map with much finer detail.

Why is that important? Because it could hold the key to some very puzzling questions, like: What banged? Why does the universe look so uniform in all directions? And why is it "flat," sitting on the balance between eternal expansion and eventual collapse?

The Word or the quantum?
For investigators, there are two ways to approach this. The first way is to begin with a theistic presupposition:

> "In the beginning was the Word, and the Word was with God, and the Word was God. □□ He was with God in the beginning. Through him all things were made; without him nothing was made that has been made."[3]

The other way, making but the slightest word change above, is to begin with a materialistic premise:

> "In the beginning was the Quantum, and the Quantum was with God, and the Quantum was God. □□ The Quantum was all there was in the beginning. Through the Quantum all things were made; without the Quantum nothing was made that has been made."

In the latter account, the Quantum can be anything from the quantum vacuum of scientism to the Void of Buddhism. In all cases, the Quantum is an immaterial (and impersonal) well-spring of limitless power from which the material world materializes. What's more, insist its apologists, unlike the Creator-God of religious superstition, the existence of the Quantum has been validated by modern physics. Enough said.

It all goes back to Heisenberg who, as we learned earlier, found that the microcosm was a fuzzy mysterium whose operating principles were hopelessly veiled from human inspection. Despite the initial repulsion to Heisenberg's "uncertainty principle," the scientific establishment eventually embraced it, with later scientists recognizing its application for cosmology.

From out of nowhere

Recall that if we look at the universe on a cosmic scale, most of it appears a tranquil wasteland devoid of matter and energy. But due to "uncertainty," if we could peer deep into its inner structure, we would see the serene spacescape turning increasingly turbulent.

Thus, in the "vacuum" of space, at large scales, the amount of energy is very close to zero; but at sub-nuclear scales, it fluctuates violently, causing elementary particles to pop into and out of existence! "Say what?" you object, "Wouldn't that defy the sacrosanct law of physics saying neither matter nor energy can be created or destroyed?"

It would, *if* all this popping in and popping out occurred over measurable time lapses. But in the tiny quantum realm, creation and annihilation are happening so quickly that the ledgers kept by the energy conservation accountants always sum to zero.

Inflation to the rescue
Now if that makes you wonder how the Quantum could lead to the creation of the universe, just follow this story line...

Before time and space, there was only the quantum vacuum. Then, some thirteen or so billion years ago, a succession of extraordinary events occurred:

Out of the ineffable nothingness, a colossal amount of energy suddenly appeared in a space much smaller than that of an atom. Instantly, the sub-atomic nugget exploded, spewing forth all the matter and energy of our soon-to-be universe.

But before the growing newborn was overcome by gravitational collapse, another strange thing happened: inflation. Inexplicably, something akin anti-gravity kicked in to take cosmic expansion into hyperdrive. The expansion was so rapid that if the tiny nugget had been a piece of sand, it would have grown to the size of the known universe within a trillionth of a second.

At the same time, the rate and strength of inflation were in perfect pitch to keep the Big Bang from becoming either a Big Crunch or a runaway explosion. By this exceptional process, the universe was placed delicately on the razor's edge between immediate annihilation and unending expansion, allowing it to become the birthing center of quarks, electrons, and muons--seeds of what would become stars, planets and galaxies.

In short, the raw ingredients of the universe were created *by* something that consisted *of* nothing-- instantly!

Such is the story of how the Quantum became Creator. After learning about the latest NASA findings, Columbia University physicist Brian Greene reflected: "Galaxies... are nothing but quantum mechanics writ large across the sky."[4] It's like the magician's trick of pulling a rabbit out of a hat, without the hat. Or magician.

A few stubborn facts
To date, the foregoing (albeit brief) sketch is the best that science has to offer to explain the universe. Although stellar "red-shift" data and General Relativity support the notion of a primordial bang with subsequent expansion,[5] the rest is speculation "writ large" about phenomena that have never been observed, are untestable, and oft-times in conflict with known laws of physics.

For example, the quantum vacuum is precisely that: a vacuum. It consists of neither matter nor energy, but is something that mysteriously gives rise to such things. However, in a world operating under strict materialistic principles, the first law of thermodynamics (that you can't get something for nothing) is inviolable.

Somehow that doesn't bother many theorists who blithely accept the universe as one grand exception, a "free lunch" as cosmologist Alan Guth put it.[6]

Then there is the phenomenon of inflation. Not only does inflation rely on a process (i.e., anti-gravity) that has neither been observed nor replicated; to generate the universe as we know it, inflation has to be finely-adjusted—so fine, as astronomer Hugh Ross notes, that if it had been different by one part in 10^{55}, the conditions necessary for life would not have evolved![7]

Such "just-so" precision is eerily *un*-natural, causing scientists to recoil from the logical and reasonable implications. When one considers that our "goldilocks" universe emerged out of the infinite variety that could have emerged, it seems as if the Quantum "knew" we were coming.

In a bygone time, the universe was rightly accepted as a creation—a miraculous and intended work. But today, all that can be admitted is that it is a product of a "singularity:" a one-in-a-time "natural" occurrence in which the fundamental laws of physics broke down.

Yet, even with the raw materials of matter, energy, minerals, and chemicals in place, there is the problem of organizing them in a functional matrix necessary for biological life.

"Something we cannot see, touch, or get our hands around is out there, organizing life."[8] -- Margaret J. Wheatley

The Problem of Biological Life

One the most vexing and long-standing mysteries of science is the origin of life -- that is, how did the building blocks of matter (atoms and molecules) lead to the building block of life: the biological cell? Even Dawkins admits that no one knows.

Up until the 19th century, leading scientists generally assumed that an organizing Intelligence was involved. But after the popularization of Darwinian Theory, origin-of-life researchers began narrowing their investigative scope to unintelligent causes.

For a time, explaining life as the unplanned effect of natural forces went rather swimmingly. Then, in 1953 James Watson and Francis Crick unraveled the architecture of DNA, the now famous double helix "molecule of life." With that breakthrough scientists soon learned that the instructions for life came from a code within the DNA molecule. What's more, they found that the tiny double helix structure governed a whole range of cellular functions from DNA replication, repair, and data transmission, to feedback looping and self-correction processes for transcription errors. Such complexity led Bill Gates to remark, "DNA is like a computer program, but far, far more advanced than any software we've ever created."[9]

According to modern evolutionary theory that complexity arose from an unsupervised process of random variation and natural selection. There's just one catch. Before the selection process can begin, there has to be something to "select." And that something is genes. If evolution can be thought of as manufacturing process whose product is increasingly complex life forms, then genes are its raw materials.

Genes are regions of DNA that consist of thousands to hundreds of thousands of base molecules arranged in a precise sequence. Needless to say, producing such a highly organized structure from a random, undirected process is a tall order.

Consider a simple one-celled organism made up of 250 proteins of 150 amino acids each. Using the experimental findings of protein scientist Douglas Axe, intelligent design theorist Stephen Meyer calculated that the probability of producing such a cell by chance is $10^{41,000}$. [10] Low odds for sure. But what if chance had an opportunity in every moment of time?

For a 15 billion year-old universe, there has been about 10^{17} seconds for chance to get the arrangement right. According to quantum theory, each of those seconds can be divided into 10^{43} moments of time (known as Planck time), giving Nature a whopping 10^{60} chances to produce a single simple cell. Unfortunately, that is far short of the $10^{41,000}$ needed.

And none this accounts for the time it would take for the building blocks of matter (quarks and leptons) to form atoms; and atoms to form the molecules necessary to create something to shuffle.

But didn't researchers Harold Urey and Stanley Miller demonstrate how this could all happen way back in 1953? While it is true that Urey and Miller produced some amino acids in a highly controlled laboratory setting, their success depended not on an undirected and unguided process, but on an intelligently designed experiment that was meticulously controlled to ensure "just-right" conditions for producing the necessary chemical components.

What's more, their experimental conditions, as it was later learned, did not reflect those of early earth which were hostile to, not "just-right" for, amino acid production. Had those conditions been faithfully simulated, their much-heralded life-building chemicals would not have survived, intelligent intervention or not.

In light of all of this, even atheists like Sir Fred Hoyle have admitted, "The idea that life originated by the random shuffling of molecules is as ridiculous and improbable as proposing that a tornado blowing through a junkyard would cause the assembly of a 747!"[11]

Hoyle is among many who now concede that the universe is neither old enough nor large enough to produce even the most elemental cell. And without cells, evolution is like a factory assembly line without anything on the conveyor belt.

But if the laws of nature cannot account for life, and God didn't create it, then how did life come about? Over the last 30 years, there has been a growing conviction about a creative process encoded in the cosmos. First a little background.

A cosmic blueprint
It is a fundamental principle of physics that in any closed system—one isolated from energy input—things inexorably decay. Take your house, for example. Unless you regularly expend energy into its maintenance and upkeep, your domicile will eventually collapse into a pile of rubble.

This principle is also true for the universe. As the

universe expands, it moves ever further from its original ordered state of pure energy into an increasingly differentiated and disordered configuration of matter and energy.

While on the cosmic level, the "arrow of time" always points from order to disorder, on the local level that arrow can be reversed. On an intra-cosmic scale, a system can borrow energy from its environment to organize matter, turning disorder into order.

Consider the formation of a star. When a disorganized collection of atoms combines to form a clump of matter, it can join with other clumps through gravitational attraction. If the clumping continues, the gravitational energy of the growing mass will be eventually converted into self-sustaining nuclear reactions, giving birth to a new star.

On the other end of the spectrum is the development of biological life. By way of a process not completely understood, a hodgepodge assortment of molecules arranges itself into a conscious, living organism.

In his book, *The Cosmic Blueprint*, astrobiologist Paul Davies marvels at the development of the human embryo. From a single fertilized egg, a variety of highly specialized cells emerge, governing host of functions and hereditary traits. Davies wonders how these cells "know" whether to be a brain cell or bone cell. He also wonders how, at the molecular level, a cell "figures out" where it is supposed to go in the finished product. It's as if each cell is programmed with zip code and routing instructions.

Without question, the production of independent action, thought, language, rationality, and creativity from a single cell is nothing short of miraculous. It suggests to Davies, a "blueprint" and a "global supervising agency" that guides the organism to its final state.[12]

Self-organization

Lest you think that an endorsement of theistic creation, Davies is quick to state otherwise. Rather than a Creator or some mystical principle operating behind the scenes, Davies believes in the "organizational properties of complex systems." Life, according to Davies, is "written in" material processes at work in the cosmos—processes that Davies believes are "likely to be forthcoming as result of new approaches in research." That's as strong a faith statement as any to be heard from theists.

For Davies, our existence is not accidental, but fundamental to the cosmos. And that gives Davies, what he calls, "a deep and satisfying basis for human dignity."

Paul Davies is one of a growing number of researchers who have concluded that neo-Darwinism is insufficient to account for the full complexity of the universe. They have come to realize that complex systems, like the mind, are more than the sum of their parts—and more than what can be explained by gradual adaptation and selection. Yet they attribute that difference not to Omnipotence, but to "emergence."

According to emergence theory, evolution is just one epiphenomenon of a grand and inexorable process of self-organization hard-wired into matter itself. As the meta-process of Nature, emergence "explains" the existence of things that do not impart a distinct evolutionary advantage--things like multi-cellularity, sexual (versus asexual) reproduction, and intelligence.

For those uncomfortable with the idea of an omnipotent Creator, emergence imparts hope in an omnipotent creation—all without any moral baggage.

But self-organization overlooks some very inconvenient

facts: To self-organize, there first has to be a "self"— a coherent assemblage of matter and energy functioning under the direction of a mind. There also has to be a blueprint and a set of assembly instructions for a "self" to follow in creating the inevitable end-product, a self. It's actually all a bit circular.

What's more, the belief that the instructions for life are deeply embedded in the cosmic matrix of matter and energy, is like believing that the information in this essay originates from the chemicals in the ink and paper on which it is written.

The chemicals on this page neither create information nor are, themselves, information. Rather they are the tools used to form letters that make words and sentences, according to pre-designed conventions of language and grammar to communicate something originating outside of those chemicals: my thoughts—vaporous cerebrations that can be right, wrong or indifferent, but certainly not material.

The same is true for the instructions for life. The atoms and molecules in DNA are not those instructions, they are building blocks used to form the chemical sequences that direct a host of cellular functions including data replication, repair, transmission, feedback looping and self-correction—all according to a "language," blueprint and design originating elsewhere: the mind of God.

Admittedly, that is a faith statement. But those who criticize it have a faith statement all their own -- like Richard Dawkins who stated, "I believe, but I cannot prove, that all life, all intelligence, all creativity and all 'design' anywhere in the universe, is the direct or indirect product of Darwinian natural selection."[13]

As to how, well, there are some interesting ideas about that.

"We can dismiss it as happenstance. We can acclaim it as providence, or w can conjecture that our universe is a specially favored domain in a still vaster universe."[14] -- Sir Martin Rees, royal astronomer, United Kingdom

Extraordinary Claims

For some time now, scientists have known that our life-friendly cosmos depends on the delicate balancing of a host of universal constants: Newton's gravitational constant, the mass and charge of the electron, and the strengths of the weak and strong nuclear forces, just to name a few. If the value for any one of these constants was slightly different, questions about the universe couldn't be asked—intelligence, and biological life itself, would have never come about.

All this makes scientists edgy, because conditions that depend on coincidence and fine-turning suggest something of a "set-up" job. But that is against the "rules of play," so modern scientists have been churning out alternate accounts for over half a century.

In his critique of intelligent causation, the late Carl Sagan famously challenged, "Extraordinary claims require extraordinary evidence." What bypassed the critical filters of the science popularizer, is that the extraordinary theories concocted by materialistic scientists not only lack extraordinary evidence, but *any* evidence, and in some cases, *any possibility* for evidence.

Take one floated by the late Sir Fred Hoyle.

Panspermia
Hoyle, a mathematician and astronomer, confessed that his atheism was shaken by research into the carbon atom.

After realizing that the energy levels of carbon were precisely those required for carbon-based life, Hoyle remarked, "A common sense interpretation of the facts suggests a superintellect has monkeyed with the physics." [15]

Regrettably, such common sense was insufficient to turn Hoyle away from naturalism. Faced with our "against-all-odds" existence, Hoyle, along DNA co-discoverer Francis Crick, posited that refuse from an extraterrestrial civilization containing the seeds of life were distributed throughout the cosmos on the "wings" of comets. Of course, how those super seeds and their master producers came into existence is left to anyone's imagination.

While Hoyle's "panspermia" is a fringe scientific theory, there is another that has gained a growing following over the last couple of decades.

The Multiverse
Turning rationality on its head, modern investigators start with a bit of Sherlockian logic: "When you have eliminated the impossible, whatever remains, however improbable, must be the truth." Then, after defining the "impossible" as anything supra-natural, they conclude that life is not improbable, it's inevitable. Our existence is Exhibit "A." Clever.

In one pitch, the delicately-tweaked features of our universe arose from a supercosmos called the "multiverse." As the name implies, the multiverse contains not one, but an infinite number of universes, ensuring that the intricate network of coincidences necessary for life will be actualized in one of them. The theories for how these universes were produced rival anything imagined by H.G. Wells or Gene Roddenberry.

Many-worlds
As early as 1957, Princeton's Hugh Everett III proposed

111

the "many-worlds" theory. "Many-worlds" starts with a controversial interpretation of quantum theory in which sub-atomic particles are thought to continuously split into separate quantum states. Everett imagined that each split created a parallel universe in which particles exist as mirror images of themselves. As a result, every possible state of a particle is realized, somewhere!

Problems with this theory are many, including where all of these parallel universes exist, how an entire universe can be created by an infinitesimal change in a particle's state, and the endless stream of universes created by every object in the cosmos at every moment in time. Then you've got folks like Marcus Chown, cosmology consultant for *New Scientist*, who takes "many-worlds" to its logical conclusion. Betraying no hint of sarcasm, Chown opines, "Elvis didn't die on that loo eating a burger but is still alive in an infinite number of places."[16]

Nevertheless, many-worlds finds appeal with those having a transcendental view of reality. For them, alternate states of existence and parallel universes follow naturally from belief in mind-creating omnipotence. For rank-and-file scientists, somewhat less mystical models are being embraced.

Chaotic inflation
In 1981 Stanford cosmologist André Linde reasoned that the universe could have been created by an "inflationary" phenomenon. Through a set of mathematical gyrations, Linde showed that a sudden fluctuation in a sub-atomic vacuum could become a "bubble" of intense energy ballooning into a whole universe. While Linde's inflation showed how a universe could be generated, it did not explain how a single bubble could lead to a world meticulously configured for life.[17]

But what, Linde mused, if the initial "bubble" quickly disintegrated into a constellation of bubbles, much like the fizz created after opening a bottle of soda? And, what if inflation is a continuing process? (Anyone counting the number of "ifs" here?) Then, Linde concluded, an infinite number of bubbles would be created leading to an unending variety of universes...and we just happen to live in the one that makes our existence possible. How fortunate for us.

Despite its highly contingent nature, Linde's "chaotic inflation" (as it's been called) resonates with many in the scientific community. Notwithstanding, the lack of empirical support relegates his theory--even under the most liberal scientific standards--to little more than hopeful speculation. As a result, some disquieted investigators have turned elsewhere: Those mysterious objects called black holes.

Cosmic cannibals

Black holes, it is conjectured, are insatiable cannibals gobbling up everything in their cosmic neighborhood. Stephen Hawking is among those who have proposed that black holes are birthing centers for *Star Trek* phenomena like wormholes, time-tunnels and multiple universes.

Early in the life cycle of a star, the heat released from nuclear reactions in its interior produces an outward pressure that balances the inward gravitational pull of the stellar mass. As the star ages and its nuclear reactions diminish, gravity takes over upsetting this fine balance and stellar collapse begins. Eventually gravitational attraction becomes so intense that any object (including light) entering its "event horizon" becomes helplessly lost in its fearsome grip. It is at that point a black hole is created.

But what actually happens inside the dark gourmand? While no one knows for sure, it is thought that deep in its recesses, a black hole becomes increasingly violent until it causes a rip in spacetime—a cervical opening, if you will, for its "digested" contents to burst out into a baby universe of its own.

For all its charm and appeal, "black hole creation" has a major problem. Unlike chaotic inflation in which matter disappears over the microscopic time scales allowed by quantum uncertainty, in "black hole creation" matter disappears over macroscopic time scales, thus violating the law of conservation. And that has plagued researchers for over three decades.

Nonetheless, Stephen Hawking was so confident in the theory that he made a bet with a fellow physicist in 1997 that black hole creation would be proven right. Then, in 2004, Hawking made a startling announcement.[18]

A dramatic reversal
Speaking at an international conference in Dublin Ireland, Hawking said that he was wrong about his 30-year assertion that material entering a black hole leaves our universe.

Reversing his previous position, Hawking conceded that black holes are not cosmic birthing centers, nor mystical portals to some parallel universe—theories that gained currency through his best-selling book, *A Brief History of Time* and his later book, *Black Holes and Baby Universes and Other Essays*.

Dr. Hawking said his new calculations debunk what he and others have speculated. In a dream-squashing conclusion Hawking emphasized, "I'm sorry to disappoint science fiction fans, but if [mass and energy] is preserved [as required by the laws of physics] there is no possibility of using black holes to travel to other universes."

His peers were unsettled. Reflecting the thoughts of

many in the audience, University of Chicago physicist Robert Wald responded, "He's running away from what we still believe." The angst in Wald's remark is palpable.

A theory in trouble

Stephen Hawking's announcement is but the latest sign that the multiverse and, with it, philosophical naturalism is in trouble. Added to its technical difficulties, the theory fails to do what it sets out to do; namely, to explain how our universe turned out the way it did. Instead, it asserts that our world *has to* exist, because in an infinite number of universes, all configurations are possible and we're here, so that proves it! Such contrived reasoning leaves some researchers cold. A theory in which anything is possible, is a theory that explains nothing.

Stanford physicist Leonard Susskind is among those who understand what is at stake. Susskind admitted that without some alternative "explanation of nature's fine-tunings we will be hard pressed to answer the ID critics. One might argue that the hope that a mathematically unique solution will emerge is as *faith-based* as ID."[19] (Emphasis added.)

At least Susskind is forthright. When a theory depends on "extraordinary claims" about fantastic quantum behavior, imaginary singular events, and principles defying known physical laws, all that remains is unwavering faith in naturalism.

What's more, for a scientific theory, the multiverse makes no predictions, has no technological cash value, holds no promise for the betterment of man or the planet, and defies Occam's Razor, a cardinal principle of science which holds that when various solutions are offered to a problem, the simplest is the preferred.

But what should raise the least skeptical eyebrow about

this extraordinary account is that it is not derived from evidence or even the possibility of forthcoming evidence, for even *i*F another world DID exist with its own unique set of physical parameters, it would be undetectable with instruments constrained by the distinctive parameters of our universe.

Rather, the multiverse and other materialistic accounts are based on the necessity of their story-tellers to avoid considering the Impossible. As cosmologist Bernard Carr warned his colleagues, "If there is only one universe you might have to have a fine-tuner." And, just in case they missed his point, Carr added, "if you don't want God, you'd better have a multiverse."[20] Check.

Carr tipped the hand on the "dirty little secret" of cosmology: the object is not to follow the evidence wherever it leads, but to follow our wishes and boldly go, hoping they're so. And this, promoted by folks who are proud to say that, unlike believers in the Impossible, their beliefs are not based on faith or wish-fulfillment, but hard evidence.

Sci-fact or sci-fi
Those of more sober mind will sense there is more of metaphysics than physics going on here. Indeed, the notion that nothing became everything, instantly, is magic not science; that it happened (or is happening) ad infinitum is more befitting sci-fi than sci-fact.

Science writer and journalist John Horgan agrees: "Multiverse theories aren't theories," Horgan writes, "they're science fictions, theologies, works of the imagination unconstrained by evidence."[21]

David Gross, Harvard particle physicist and multiverse skeptic, urges his colleagues to not quit on fundamental science by settling for theories that can explain anything. As he well knows, a theory in which anything is possible, is a theory that includes the possibility that some of those unsettling philosophical and theological conclusions might also be true.[22]

Then there's Steven Weinberg again, who in a theoretical physics conference at Stanford learned that British cosmologist Martin Rees was so confident in the multiverse that he would he bet his dog's life on the theory and that inflationary theorist Andrei Linde would bet his own life on it. To which, Weinberg quipped, "As for me, I have just enough confidence about the multiverse to bet the lives of both Andrei Linde and Martin Rees's dog."[23]

But perhaps the harshest critic of inflation and the multiverse is Paul Steinhardt. Since receiving the 2002 Dirac Medal in theoretical physics for his work on inflationary theory, Steinhardt has turned on the theories.

Steinhardt explained, "For the last 400 years, most people would say the key thing that distinguishes science from non-science is that scientific ideas have to be subject to tests. Some people are nowadays thinking, no, that doesn't necessarily have to be the case. That's a mega-issue [for me]." He went on to say that these theories are unfalsifiable and can be made to fit any possible set of experimental observations.[24] And that's a deal-breaker for him.

Lately, some scientists are turning attentions to an even more novel theory – that our world is a simulation.

A Virtual World
In one version of the theory, the virtual universe is an inevitable outcome of the multiverse: with an infinite number of universes, there are necessarily some, even many, with advanced civilizations possessing the technological wherewithal to create universe-sized simulations.[25]

In fact, given the astronomical odds against our material existence, say proponents, it is more probable that we are "artificial intelligences" in an ET's computer simulation than intelligent beings in a world of matter and motion. They're not kidding.

In a hat tip to the Wachowski brothers, Britain's royal astronomer and multiverse believer Sir Martin Rees weighs in, suggesting it is quite likely that we're "in the matrix rather than physics itself."

Well, we shouldn't be surprised. Hollywood "science" is the science you get when you buy into a sci-fi concoction unsupported by scientific experiment, empirical data, or physical necessity. Nevertheless, to its credit, the virtual world theory does share the one merit of panspermia: it presumes the need of intelligent causation to account for the informational complexity of the universe.

According to other theorists, our universe is not *The Matrix* of an ET gamer, but a virtual reality created by the quantum world – the *real*, real world. As they see it, a number of scientific conundrums, like the flexibility of time, the bending of space, and quantum entanglement, that make no sense in a physical cosmos, become explicable in a virtual world produced by *information processing* in the quantum world.[26]

Consider the "twin paradox" of Special Relativity, in which a man leaves earth at near light speed and returns one year later to find that his twin brother has aged decades. As Brian Whitworth explains,

"A virtual reality would be subject to virtual time, where each processing cycle is one 'tick.' Every gamer knows that when the computer is busy the screen lags—game time slows down under load. Likewise, time in our world slows down with speed or near massive bodies, suggesting that it is virtual. So the rocket twin only aged a year because that was all the processing cycles the system busy moving him could spare. What changed was his virtual time."[27]

I would add that every gamer also knows that behind every program is a programmer. Whitworth, when asked about the identity of the programmer, writes, "Perhaps God is the programmer, or advanced aliens, or as [philosopher Nick] Bostrom suggests, ourselves from the future!"[28]

Whatever one thinks about the virtual universe theory, it reflects an ancient notion – one that goes as far back as Plato and Paul who were fond to call the things of this world "shadows" (projections, virtual representations, creations?) of the true and real.

Maybe these new theorists are on to more truth than they know.

From a higher dimension
With a pinch of theoretical physics and a heap of mathematical prestidigitation, a trio of scientists at Canada's Perimeter Institute argue that the universe isn't the product of a big, physics-defying, bang in the pre-cosmic vacuum; rather, it is the three-dimensional "event horizon" of a black hole created from a dying star in a four-dimensional universe.[29]

What's more, the wave of their mathematical wand has convinced them that the horizon (our cosmic home) is something of a hologram of its higher dimensional "parent."

Now I have to confess, when I first read this my "baloney detector" went off scale. Just another sci-fi fantasy, I thought, built on the same empirical quicksand as the multiverse and virtual world. With a sigh and shrug, I dismissed it out-of-hand, not giving it a second thought.

A few days later, my wife, peering over her iPad, asked, "Hon, did you see the piece about the universe coming from a four-dimensional black hole?"

"Yeah, I did. So?"

"Well, how about that?"

"How about what?"

"That our universe was produced by *higher* dimensional one."

"Uh, uh … Oh, yeeahhh! Heck, I missed that altogether! Thanks, dear."

An ancient narrative tells of a higher dimensional Being in a hyperspatial realm that brings a three-dimensional world into existence. It also tells of Him operating within that world to sustain it and, on occasion, interfere with the "natural" course of events.

If a hyper-dimensional region is woven into the fabric of the three-dimensional cosmos, as string theorists propose, it would account for how the "Impossible" could do the "impossible." Let me explain.

Recall that in hyperspace things become more simple, unified, and interconnected, and what is difficult-to-impossible in lower dimensions is easy in higher ones. For example, as we saw in the previous chapter, in a 2-D world, a 3-D being can gain access to spaces that are closed to 2-D beings.

Also recall that one of the provocative implications of Einstein's theories of relativity is that space and time form the warp and woof of the cosmological "fabric" known as *spacetime*.

If we follow Einstein's insight a step farther and imagine a hyperspatial realm filling and interlocking with the interstitial spaces of that fabric, we can understand how an ultra-dimensional Being can "violate" the inviolable laws of nature, and do so in an unseen realm.

We could also understand how the material (3-D) body and the immaterial (ultra-dimensional) spirit co-exist and co-operate to form the self, or "living soul," as that ancient narrative puts it, and how things like consciousness, thought, creativity, moral agency, will, shame, and guilt are not reducible to neural impulses produced from chemicals triggered by external stimuli, but are immaterial properties of the self enabling it to interact with the world, seen and unseen.

Remember, no black holes!
The bad news for those raising their cups to the creative power of black holes comes from Stephen Hawking. Like a skunk wandering into a garden party, the much-revered physicist reminded the partiers of something that was sure to make them gag on their sherry: the announcement he made a decade earlier that black holes, conventionally conceived, don't exist.[30] And Hawking is not alone.

According to UNC-Chapel Hill physicist Laura Mersini-Houghton, when a dying star collapses under its own gravitational attraction, it doesn't produce a cosmos-creating singularity; it sheds mass in the form of Hawking radiation, "so much so that as it shrinks it no longer has the density to become a black hole."[31] Mersini-Houghton's end-of-star-life scenario has three important things to commend it.

First, it preserves the sacrosanct laws of conservation;

second, by discrediting the possibility of stars compressing down to a quantum-sized dimensions, it resolves one of the thorniest problems in physics: the conflict between General Relativity and quantum mechanics for super massive objects at sub-atomic scales; third, it renders the wonky theories of quantum gravity and string theory, along with its tarted-up sister, M-Theory, superfluous.

Now to the notion that our world is a hologram of a hyper-dimensionality. Crazy? Maybe not.

A Hologram World
A hologram is a two-dimensional medium, created by laser light, which conveys three-dimensional information. As told in scripture, the visible 3-D world was created by Light, and also conveys ultra-dimensional information: "God's invisible qualities--his eternal power and divine nature --have been clearly seen, being understood from what has been made."[32] But that's not all.

One of the head-spinning features of a hologram is that, unlike a conventional photograph, every part of a hologram contains *the whole* image. For example, if you tear off the corner of a photograph and throw the rest away, you lose most of the image. If you do the same thing to a hologram, you lose nothing, as the corner retains the entire image.

One hyper-dimensional reality contained in every part of our 3-D world is the Trinity. In fact, the Trinitarian essence of the Godhead is reflected in every stratum of nature.

At the cosmic level, the universe consists of *three* things: space, time, and matter—each, having *three* integral components.

Space exists in *three* dimensions: length, width and height. Time has *three* aspects: past, present, and future. Matter is made up of *three* sub-nuclear ingredients: quarks, leptons, and bosons, each uniquely defined by *three* parameters: electronic charge, mass, and magnetic spin. What's more, atoms contain *three* things: protons, neutrons, and electrons. And, if that's not enough, all protons and neutrons are made up of *three* quarks.

And that's not all.

At the chemical level, water—the major molecule of life—is an example of matter with distinctive triune qualities. Consisting of *three* atoms (two hydrogen and one oxygen), water can exist in solid, liquid, or gas forms without changing its chemical makeup. *Three* forms, the same essence.

But wait! As explained by Einstein—in his $e=mc^2$ relation—matter is energy and energy, matter. And, you guessed it, energy comes in *three* varieties: the strong-nuclear, the electro-weak, and gravitational.

Finally, each of these grand components—space, time, and matter—are intricately woven and interconnected in the unified fabric of spacetime. A single, integrated essence. Just like the Trinity.

What's more, at the human level, the tripartite composition of mind, body, and spirit mirrors the triune partnership of the Godhead.

Yet, there's nothing new in all of this. The knowledge that our universe came from a higher dimensional realm is recorded in the opening verse of scripture, "In the beginning God"; that it reflects a higher dimensional reality is recorded a couple of dozen verses later, "Let us make mankind in our image."[33]

It seems the late physicist and astronomer Dr. Robert Jastrow sized things up pretty well when he mused,

"For the scientist who has lived by his faith in the power of reason, the story ends like a bad dream. He has scaled the mountain of ignorance; he is about to conquer the highest peak; as be pulls himself over the final rock, he is greeted by a band of theologians who have been sitting there for centuries."

Last best hope

For the scientific materialist, these theories are last best hope to keep the flames of the Enlightenment burning. The very notion that the Impossible could be true is an existential threat to science that could end discovery and technological progress, hurling civilization back into a new Dark Age of superstition, ignorance, and fear. Serious stuff.

But here's the thing: the whole question of why we're here is not a scientific question; it's a theological one. Whether the explanation is God, the multiverse, or some yet to be discovered mechanism of cosmic Darwinism, it will always be tentative and unprovable, because no matter how reasonable and robust the theory, there is no way of knowing that it's in fact the way it happened. Thus, our favored explanation will always be a matter of (yet, again!) faith, faith in our presuppositions of how the world is.

At the same time, the answer has no effect on the scientific enterprise or our ability to study and harness nature for the good of nature and man.

To the contrary, our ability to detect, measure, and analyze the light spectra from a distant quasar is independent of whether the star was produced from the Big Bang or the command of God. The study of the human genome – its functions and similarity with other species – is independent on whether it is a product of common descent or common design. Advances in medical science do not depend on whether microevolution is a phenomenon of mud-to-man Darwinism or was front-loaded by an intelligent Designer. The recent confirmation of the Higgs boson (the "God Particle")[34] didn't hang on whether the Higgs was produced by a random fluctuation of the quantum field or from a Divine pronouncement. No, all of these things and more are there to be discovered and studied irrespective of their ultimate origin.

All the same, methodological naturalists keep scrambling for answers, with some even looking to the heavens, hoping to hear from their sky gods.

"For the time will come when men will not put up with sound doctrine. Instead, to suit their own desires, they will gather around them a great number of teachers to say what their itching ears want to hear. They will turn their ears away from the truth and turn aside to myths." [35]

Searching for Wisdom in the Sky

The search for extraterrestrial intelligence (SETI) is over 50 years old. In 1960 astronomer Frank Drake aimed a radio telescope at a nearby star in hopes of detecting an intelligent signal. A half century and thousands of stars later, the only sign of intelligence has remained at the near end of the telescope.

SETI hopefuls are quick to point out that absence of evidence does not mean evidence of absence. Like SETI research director, Jill Tarter, who says all the research to date amounts to sampling "*A SINGLE GLASS OF WATER FROM THE OCEANS.* And no one would decide that the ocean was without fish on the basis of one glass of water." Tarter adds teasingly, "The 21st century now allows us to build bigger glasses, much bigger glasses." [36]

Dr. Tarter and the seti folks also want you to know that if you'd like to help with those "glasses," your donations are fully tax deductible. Yes, the seti institute is a 501 (c)(3) organization.

Bigger glasses
Problem is, they don't need *BIGGER GLASSES;* they need a pitcher the size of Texas. It is estimated that there are over 100 billion galaxies in the universe, each containing over 100 billion stars. That puts the number of stars in the universe roughly equal to the number of grains of

sand on all the beaches on earth. But even with a state-sized jug, the physics is against it.

Given the size of our Milky Way galaxy, a message sent within it, traveling at the speed of light, would take on average ten's of thousands of years to reach us. A message sent from our nearest neighboring galaxy (Andromeda) would take over two million years! And that's for a civilization that is highly advanced, desires to be found, and has pin-pointed its beacon at our tiny "blue dot."

Unbothered by the infinitesimal probability of success over, hmm, say, the next few million years, the SETI Institute is soliciting a $100 million endowment from private interests (its federal funding was terminated in 1993). Oh, and don't forget, all contributions are tax deductible.

Gaining respect

Early on, SETI was viewed by mainstream scientists in much the same light as *UFOlogy*. But that has been changing in recent decades as researchers have been wrestling with one of science's most maddening mysteries: the origin of life.

Over the last few decades, the discoveries about the complexity of life and the host of delicately-balanced conditions that make it possible have led researchers, turned off by the contrivances of the multiverse and anxious to keep a Director off the set, to one of two conclusions: One, planet earth is a fluke of nature in a universe that is hostile to life; or two, earth is one of many life-friendly habitats in a cosmos brimming with life.

For those uncomfortable with the first alternative, astrobiologist Paul Davies floats an idea.

Paul Davies is a curious fellow. Davies believes there is a "deep life principle" embedded in the cosmos, making it intrinsically habitable. He believes this, you'll recall, not because there is any supporting evidence for it, but because he is "more comfortable" with it than the alternatives. At the same time, he acknowledges that SETI is nothing less than the search for "wisdom in the sky."[37]

Consider this stirring appeal on the SETI website from Frank Drake:

> "Ponder these questions for a moment: Would the discovery of an older cultural civilization out there inspire us to find new ways to survive our increasingly uncertain technological adolescence? Might it be the discovery of a distant civilization and our common cosmic origins that finally drives home the message of the bond among all humans? Might the revelation that we are not alone, but one species in a universe of possibilities, alter the course of human history forever?"[38]

The messianic hope is clear: If we can but tap into ET's vast warehouse of knowledge, we will escape the trajectory of certain doom, and join the *brotherhood of being* propagating throughout the universe from cosmic shore to cosmic shore. ET will save us from ourselves… if we can only find him. The good news is that *you* can help, with that *tax-deductible* donation.

An old yearning
One of man's oldest yearnings is to find "his place" in the universe. It's the quest of Ellie Arroway, a SETI researcher in the 1997 film *Contact*. Near the end of the film, Ellie is transported to an alien world and reports what she found to a governmental panel:

> "I was given something wonderful. Something that

changed me. A vision of the universe that made it overwhelmingly clear just how tiny and insignificant -- and at the same time how rare and precious we all are. A vision... that tells us we belong to something greater than ourselves... that we're not – that none of us -- is alone."

If you want to "belong to something greater" but not too great, with a cosmic companion not a cosmic Authority, who will give you the sense of transcendence without the burden of moral duty, SETI is the ticket.

A warning

Added to the technical problems of contacting aliens, are some practical concerns. For example, there is no reason to expect that aliens would have any interest in us and, if they did, that their interest would be benign, much less, benevolent. In fact, if the materialistic narrative is true, it is possible – perhaps, likely -- that an advanced civilization surviving long enough to out-pace our technology, has done so not by helping its neighbors, but by dominating and exploiting them, or by serial extermination and colonization.

Physicist Stephen Hawking would agree. In his jaundiced view of SETI, Hawking warns, "If aliens ever visit us, I think the outcome would be much as when Christopher Columbus first landed in America, which didn't turn out very well for the Native Americans."[39]

His warning is well taken. For if all biology, behaviors and beliefs are Darwinian, as materialists contend, the greatest universal harmony will be achieved when the universe is populated by replicates of "me" -- people who look like me, act like me, and think like me. And that can only happen if the "me" is the smartest and strongest specimen around, as well as the one most willing to exert his superiority over the underlings.

New strategies

Over fifty years of silence from all our stellar eavesdropping has convinced Paul Davies that new strategies are needed in our search for cosmic neighbors.

Given the age of our solar system, Davies believes there is a good chance that an advanced civilization visited earth in the distant past; most likely, well before the appearance of homo sapiens. If so, it could have left behind clues: long-lived nuclear waste, geological scars from mining operations, space probes adrift in the solar system, or a message in a "bottle"; specifically, in the biological cell.

Davies is certainly on to something. As we'll see in Chapter 5, the living cell houses a vast library of highly specialized instructions that govern cellular production, quality control, transportation and delivery; molecular machine assembly, maintenance and repair; and even communication and networking between cells.

One of those instructions tells an organism to replicate "after its kind," a message, as it were, from an extraterrestrial that was later recorded in written format with the added note, "And it was very good."[40]

Chapter 5

Breaking the Spell of Materialism

"I think only an idiot can be an atheist. We must admit that there exists an incomprehensible power or force with limitless foresight and knowledge that started the whole universe going in the first place." -- C.B. Anfinsen, 1972 Nobel Prize for Chemistry.

"The ontology of materialism rested on the illusion that the kind of existence, the direct 'actuality' of the world around us, can be extrapolated into the atomic range."[41] -- Werner Heisenberg

Under the Spell

To the enlightened class it is unthinkable to cede any limit to human understanding. If some poor fellow should suggest the unintelligibility of the universe absent an Intelligence, he'll quickly find himself banished from polite society for committing the unpardonable sin of invoking the "God of the Gaps." Yet those who dismiss him as a glassy-eyed fundamentalist trapped in the "demon-haunted world" of religious superstition are fundamentalists of a different sort: materialism.

Materialism is a worldview based on a naturalistic understanding of reality, for which "nature" is all there is. There is no supernatural, neither spirit, soul, nor God. There is only the cosmic matrix of matter and energy operating according to physical laws. Reality is what is objective, observable and reproducible. For the materialist, everything is a product of physical processes. On the surface of things, this would seem correct.

Our everyday experience is one of matter and energy: we operate iPads, plant gardens, drive cars, and marvel at stars; we struggle against an unseen force as we climb the stairs; we are stung by a hidden power after touching the door knob; and an invisible, intangible force guides our compass needle to true North.

But what are these things, really, these things of matter and energy? What do we even mean by a "material" world?

The vacuous desk
As I write this I am setting at a desk made of composite wood material. It is no Chippendale, but it is amply sturdy to support the weight of a computer, printer, and peripheral gadgets, not to mention a pile of reference books. Its appearance and feel lead me to believe that in a fundamental way it is solid. After all, wood is composed of chemicals, which are made of atoms, which are rock solid, right? Not by a long shot.

Consider one the carbon atoms in my wooden desk. Surrounding a compact nucleus of six protons and six neutrons is a cloud of six electrons. Although the physical size of the atom is infinitesimal, the relative distance between the nucleus and its electrons is enormous.

It is like our Solar System on a microcosmic scale. The

Solar System contains a huge amount of material in the sun, planets, and interplanetary media, yet physical matter makes up less than one part in one trillion of its volume. With all of that empty space, the Solar System is one gigantic vacuum that contains a few impurities.

Now imagine if Rick Moranis entered my computer room and stumbled into a "Honey, I Shrunk the Kids" mishap on a subatomic scale. What the incredibly-shrinking Rick would find is that each of those gazillion atoms in my desk is a tiny micro-void that mysteriously gives rise to our perceptions of color, texture, and hardness. But that is only the tip of "material world" weirdness.

The quantum potential
We know from experience that when an object, like our car, absorbs energy by crashing into another object, it suffers damage. If we want our car repaired, we don't expect it to return to its original condition by itself. Rather, we take it to a body shop, where it will be restored by the skillful hands of trained technicians.

Now this is strange. When one of my desk's atoms is damaged by bumping into one of its neighbors, it quickly returns to its original condition, all on its own.

Equally strange is the phenomenon of the electronic "orbit". Unlike the Earth whose orbit is slowly spiraling toward the sun, the electrons in the atom are held in fixed regions. But the real stumper is why, with a positively charged nucleus and a negatively charged electron, the atom doesn't quickly self-destruct. In fact, according to the laws of electrodynamics, atomic annihilation should occur in less than a microsecond.

The stability (and very existence) of the atom suggests a... a Hand that guides it and holds it together. But in materialism there can be no such Hand; there is only physical matter and physical processes, which leaves these mysterious phenomena to be explained mechanistically.

In the mechanistic account, atomic weirdness arises because tiny particles, like the electrons in my desk, do not exist in any objective sense. Rather they are observer-dependent products resulting from our investigative disturbance of that ubiquitous cosmic force field, the "quantum potential."

Neither matter nor energy itself, the quantum potential is, as its name implies, "potentiality"-- an invisible substrate that permeates the whole cosmos and provides the *potential* of being. Thus, when physicists talk about an electron, what they are really talking about is a scientific construct described by mathematical formulae and probability functions. As quantum theory pioneer Werner Heisenberg once wrote, "elementary particles… form a world of potentialities or possibilities rather than one of things and facts."[42]

So despite its appearance, my cheapo desk is a vacuous object comprised of a vast throng of "potentialities" materialized by physical disturbances in the quantum mist, giving my desk the sensible properties of color, rigidity, texture, and mass. As it turns out, this "mist" is the eternal foundation of nature, credited with everything from keeping the atoms of my desk intact to Creation itself.

Recall that, according to the current models of cosmogenesis, a freakish fluctuation of the quantum potential produced the entire contents of the universe, instantly. So, in an extreme example of getting something from nothing, the quantum potential is the source of all being.

What's more, the quantum potential is the end of all

things too. As some theories suggest, gravitational attraction will eventually overcome cosmic expansion until the whole universe is squashed back down to a quantum nugget of pure potential--an Alpha and Omega, if you will.

Let's see: immaterial, omnipresent, omnipotent, the ground of all being, some of the very same qualities of One who spoke from a burning bush ages ago.

A new kind of fundamentalism

Over 2500 years ago, the Greek philosopher Anaximander posited an eternal, ubiquitous substance he called the "apeiron." Like the quantum potential, Anaximander's apeiron was thought to be the fountain of all reality.

Yet, in the intervening time, we have come no closer to a fundamental understanding of this mysterious substance. Now, as was then, questions remain as to where it came from, what fuels it, and why its creative ability is limitless? Is the quantum potential even a "something" in the materialistic sense?

Those under the spell of materialism, will answer, yes. For them, any hole in our understanding of nature must be plugged up with physical mortar.

But since this mortar is neither matter nor energy, it is not physical. And because of its numinous nature, it can neither be observed. Rather, it must be inferred from its influence on what *is* observable.

If you think that sounds a lot like the "God of the Gaps," you're right. Except this "God" neither communicates nor obligates and, yet, as we will see, engenders a religious fervor rivaling that of the Desert Fathers.

"Truth must be stranger than fiction, because we have made fiction to suit ourselves." --G.K. Chesterton

Gimme that Spacetime Religion

Scientific achievement over the last one hundred years has been nothing short of breathtaking. In a mere wisp of human history, technology has advanced from wagon trains to space shuttles, blood-letting to antibiotics, horse power to nuclear power, and smoke signals to the internet.

Because of this unprecedented success, even cynics, who sneer at the very mention of truth, approach science with a deference that, in a bygone time, was reserved for heavenly beings and their avatars.

Take science popularizer, Gary Zukav. In his best-selling book, *The Dancing Wu Li Masters* (1979), Zukav marvels: "We need not take a pilgrimage to India or Tibet. There is much to learn there, but here at home, in the most inconceivable of places, amidst the particle accelerators and computers, our own Path without Form is emerging."[43]

The late Carl Sagan insisted that modern science could engender the same awe and wonder as religious faith. He went on to predict the popular acceptance of science-based religion. Years earlier, Sir Julian Huxley similarly envisioned a day when science would be the foundation for any viable religion.

The greatest story ever told
Today, judging by the number of television specials and news articles on string theory, climate change, black

holes, and the latest fossil finds it is clear that media and public, alike, are enraptured with the Delphic postulations of scientists. Even the oracles themselves have fallen under the spell of their own imaginings.

For instance, remarking on the theory that neutrinos—wraith-like, subatomic particles--were the first products of the Big Bang, one scientist fancied, "We're descended from neutrinos!" adding reverentially, "They're our parents." Another researcher rhapsodized, "Neutrinos may tell us why we exist."[44]

But no one expresses the religious dimension of science more fervently than Carolyn Porco, research scientist for the Cassini project.

Dr. Porco acknowledges that religion is an inextricable part of human culture; a part that science can equally, if not better, fulfill:

> "From energy to matter, from fundamental particles to DNA, from microbes to Homo sapiens, from the singularity of the Big Bang to the immensity of the universe…ours is the greatest story ever told."

I don't know about the greatest story ever told, but her venerated materialism is certainly the tallest tale ever spun. Dr. Porco continues,

> " We find gods in the nucleus of every atom, in the structure of space/time, in the counter-intuitive mechanisms of electromagnetism. What richness! What consummate beauty!"[45] Whatever.

Victims of presuppositions
Welcome to scientism, a belief system founded on the conviction that everything from neutrinos to supernovae to conscious beings who marvel at such things, are reducible to material processes explicable through

science. It is a conviction based on neither observed fact nor experimental evidence, but on dogmatic faith (funny how the "F" word keeps coming up) in naturalistic science. In scientism, Nature is God, science is Revelation, and scientists the new exegetes.

Echoing Dr. Porco, biologist Stuart Kauffman urges us to "reinvent the sacred" by embracing the universe "as a reinvention of 'God'."

Kauffman has unflagging trust in Nature, all the while acknowledging that Her laws, including Darwinian evolution, cannot account for the world as we know it. Kauffman cedes "beyond natural law...is ceaseless creativity." But just when you think he's opening the door to the Divine, the biologist adds: "with no supernatural creator."[46]

Stuart Kauffman is a victim of his own presuppositions. In a world where God has been dismissed, there is no escape from the absurdity that the universe is its own cause and effect. While creation *ex nihilo* is awe-inspiring, creation *per nihilo* is, to put it as delicately as possible, feeble-minded.

Others have attempted to avoid that pitfall with theories that could have been lifted from *The X-Files*.

In the documentary, *Expelled—No Intelligence Allowed* (2008), Darwinian pitchmen P.Z. Myers and Richard Dawkins were asked how life "went live." Both admitted they didn't know but, when pressed, P.Z. mumbled something about life's recipe riding through space on the backs of crystals. Dawkins offered haltingly that life originated from an extraterrestrial civilization. But if there hasn't been enough time for life to sprout up on earth, given the probabilistic resources of the entire universe, there's been even less time for it to sprout up elsewhere before travelling here. Surely Dr. Dawkins knows that. Surely.

Yet for someone who believes that everything is product of Darwinian natural selection," there are few options left.

To the less dogmatically inclined, theories upheld by crystals and alien intelligence smack more of Scientology than science. Indeed, the blinkered faith of scientism has led to a "spacetime" religion that would have done L. Ron Hubbard proud. It even has its own ecclesial model.

A "Church" of Latter Day Scientists

Dr. Porco envisions a "Church of Latter Day Scientists" with a full complement of ceremonies, rituals, missionaries, and apostles. She dreams of particle accelerators and observatories as sacred sites; with museums, planetaria and lecture halls serving as worship centers; while evangelists spread the "word" by praising the genius of Darwin. Her religion would even include church services:

> "Imagine congregations raising their voices in tribute to gravity, the force that binds us all to the Earth, and the Earth to the Sun, and the Sun to the Milky Way...can't you just hear the hymns sung to the antiquity of the universe...?... 'Hallelujah!' they will sing. 'May the force be with you!'?"

While Carolyn Porco doxologizes the *Star Wars* tagline, Rev. Michael Dowd goes from pulpit to pulpit preaching the gospel—not the good news of salvation through Jesus Christ, but of liberation and empowerment through Charles Darwin.

As Dowd explains, "[Darwin gives us] a far more empirical way of talking about human nature than through stories like the original sin." For instance,

"[Evolution] explains our frailties, our addictions, our infidelities and other moral deficiencies as byproducts of adaptation over billions of years. And that, he says, has a potentially liberating effect: never mind guilt; once we understand our sinful ways, we can get past them..." [47]

Putting that in a "more empirical" twist to a popular church hymn:

> *What can wash away my sin?*
> *Nothing but the pen of Darwin.*
> *What can make me whole again?*
> *Nothing but the pen of Darwin.*

If that doesn't ease your burden and get you right, you might try an Evolution Sunday service. Evolution Sunday is a church event celebrating Charles Darwin and his theory of evolution.

One pastor who led an event had this to say to friend, Denyse O'Leary: "[E]ach person in the congregation had a 65 million year old cephalopod fossil to hold while I spoke...They are tired of seeing God only through the size of their own imaginations... In Jesus, I have discovered a Savior on the front edge of biological, social, and spiritual change. He showed us his own evolved ways of thinking in Matthew 6: 'You have heard it said...but I say...'"

A Savior whose thinking (and perhaps, essence!) is subject to evolution? That might be a Savior that even Richard Dawkins could worship.

I can imagine, years from now, dogged followers of a faith that never quite took hold, looking wistfully back to a more hopeful time, raising their voices in exaltation:

> *It was good enough for Sagan,*
> *It was good enough for Porco*

It was good enough for Dawkins,
It's good enough for me.

Outside of the faithful remnant, trust in their "good enough" news had long collapsed for reasons we shall see.

"[T]he Darwinian brand of evolution is becoming increasingly vulnerable as the progress of science reveals its weaknesses."[48] – Historian, Paul Johnson

Darwinism: A Theory in Trouble

Prior to 1859, the humanistic ideals of the Enlightenment were insufficient to jettison God from the universe. The most that could be done was shove Him into a remote outpost of the cosmos to amuse himself with heavenly delights, while mankind goes about the business of perfecting society through science and technology.

But that all changed with the publication of *The Origin of Species*. When Charles Darwin penned his theory of evolution, he enabled "enlightened" thinkers to eject the Clockmaker completely – to become intellectually fulfilled atheists, as Richard Dawkins once put it.

Darwin's theory quickly became the cornerstone of a new world paradigm that needed no Creator, Savior, or heaven. With Marx's theory of social progress and Freud's theory of human nature, evolution completed the materialistic worldview in which everything, from finch beak size to human emotions, could be explained in terms of natural processes. It is of little surprise, that philosophical materialists, like Daniel Dennett, rank Darwin's "breakthrough" more important than any in history, including those of Newton and Einstein.

Over the past century, Darwinian evolution has grown into an 800-pound gorilla – a settled fact that must be accepted, rather than a scientific theory subject to critical analysis.

The strength of evolution, say its proponents, is the force of its scientific evidence - things like the fossil record, embryology, pesticide resistant insects, anti-biotic-immune bacteria, "junk" DNA, and species variation – evidence based on the very premise it is intended to prove -- and in some cases, outright fraud.

Fossil gaps and fakery
Take the fossil record for example. Ian Tattersall, Curator of the American Museum of Natural History, confesses, "The patterns we perceive are as likely to result from our unconscious mindsets as from the evidence itself."[49] Richard Leakey admitted as much when he disclosed the tendency of his father (paleontologist Louis Leakey) to arrange fossils and alter their criteria to fit into a line of human descent.

Compounding the problem is the lack of transitional forms that the late evolutionist, Stephen Jay Gould, acknowledged as "the trade secret of paleontology." (It is a secret that persists despite the "discoveries" of Java man, Nebraska man, Piltdown man, and Peking man, not to mention China's thriving fake fossil business reported in the February 2003 issue of *Discover*.[50])

Gould recognized that if all life forms today descended from simpler ones, as Darwin proposed, the fossil record should be replete with intermediate forms. In fact, considering the vast number of morphological differences between original and final forms, it would be expected that there should be just as many (if not more!) intermediate as final forms.

Instead, as Dr. Stephen Meyer notes in his book, *Darwin's Doubt*, geologists "have found no such myriad of transitional forms" but, rather, "the abrupt appearance of the earliest animals."[51]

For example, in the Cambrian Period the fossils of 20

phyla (out of 27 total in the fossil record) were laid down in a blink of geological time – roughly 5 to 6 million years. Not only is this their first appearance in the fossil record, their complexity represents a quantum leap over pre-Cambrian fossils with no traceable line of descent.[52]

In fact, the whole "bottom-up" pattern predicted by Darwin – that is, small, gradual changes over time leading to large-scale differences – is completely overturned in the Cambrian stratum where the sudden appearance of complex organisms, is followed by small-scale variation. But it's worse than that, if you're a Darwin acolyte.

The "top-down" pattern in the Cambrian fossil record is not the exception, but the rule. Even back in Darwin's day, Adam Sedgwick observed that the Ordovician, Devonian, and Triassic strata also exhibited the abrupt arrival of novel life forms without any trace of precursors.[53]

A case in point is the Ediacaran stratum where, Meyer writes, "the only living forms documented in the fossil record for over 3 billion years were single-celled organisms." Then, within the brief geological span of 15 million years, sponges showed up -- something akin, as Meyer puts it, to "transforming a spinning top into a bicycle."[54]

What's the response from the evolutionist camp to these inconvenient and well-known facts? "Ah, but those intermediate organisms were just too small or too soft to be preserved in the fossil record." The facts aren't kind to such excuses.

Fossils of single-celled organisms (including algae and blue-green bacteria), which are both soft and small, have been found in strata predating the Cambrian. What's more, that is not news. Louis Agassiz, premier

144

paleontologist in the late nineteenth century, remarked "the most exquisitely delicate structures, as well as embryonic phases of growth of the most perishable nature, have been preserved from very early deposits."[55]

More recently, researchers exploring a geological formation outside of Chengjiang, China in 1984 discovered "many excellent examples of well-preserved animals...including soft-bodied members of phyla," like corals, jellyfish, comb jellies, and segmented worms. Then in 1998, a researcher at that same formation found sponge embryos and, what appeared to be, "cells undergoing cell division." Upon closer examination with an electron microscope he was able to identify fossilized cell membranes and, within some specimens, cell nuclei (!).[56]

These discoveries flatly refute the "feeble artifact" theory, leaving Darwinian hard-liners with a thorny dilemma: the complex and highly-differentiated organisms found in the early fossil record could not possibly be the common ancestor of all organisms, and the simple, undifferentiated fossils found there leave no trace of gradualism.

Meyer goes on to explain *why* the evidence of gradualism is not there.

First, there is the limitation imposed on adaptive change by integrated complexity. Every biological system depends on myriad components that must be present and working in concert to perform its purpose. Claiming that the reproductive system, say, could be functional as it is being built by gradualism, is like claiming that you could fly an airplane as you're building it.

Second, the genetic mutations needed for body plan changes must: 1) occur early in embryonic development, 2) be viable, and 3) be transmitted to offspring.

However, those types of mutations have "never been tolerated in any animals that developmental biologists have studied."[57] for example, after nearly a century of inducing genetic mutations in fruit flies, only three things have been observed: unchanged flies, deformed flies, and dead flies.

Third, and most importantly, the immense quantity of functional information resident in the biological hierarchical structure of proteins, cells, cell clusters, cell regulatory networks, tissues, organs, and body plans vastly exceed the creative powers of undirected processes.

Ersatz embryo drawings

Evolutionists also tout the similarity of embryos among fish, amphibians, birds, and mammals to support the claim of common descent. But there's just one problem. The embryos of these groups are significantly different from each other. Their purported resemblances are based on the 19th century drawings of Darwin admirer, Ernst Haeckel, who later admitted to their fabrication.

Yet, even if the drawings were accurate, they could just as easily be rallied in support of a common Designer. The same is true for the structural similarities cited for things like the fish fin, the bird wing, and the human hand. Again, the neo-Darwinist interprets the evidence based on the presuppositions he brings to the laboratory table, which disallow, on the outset, any supernatural process or agent. That's why school books in print today contain the Haeckel drawings, even though the scientific community has known about the fakery for over a century. The same is true of the well-publicized study of Britain's peppered moths.

Dead moths and glue

In the much cited peppered-moth study, researchers claimed that light-colored moths underwent natural

146

selection, turning dark, after the pollution buildup on tree trunks made light moths more visible to predators. It was later learned that peppered moths do not normally rest on tree trunks and that the photos of them were staged by gluing dead moths to trees. Nonetheless, the shoddy moth study is still held up as a classic example of Darwinism in school textbooks.

For example, Patrick Chisholm of the Christian Science Monitor referenced the peppered moth phenomenon to emphasize that "Evolution is fact." Miffed at the wrongheadedness of school administrators aimed at putting evolution back in its rightful place, Chisholm writes "saying evolution is a theory is like saying the earth revolving around the sun is a theory." [58]

Chisholm also cites drug-resistant viruses and chemical resistant insects to bolster his point. Like other evolution advocates, Chisholm takes the speculative leap from micro-evolution: the generally accepted process of adaptation through genetic variation and inheritance, to the neither observed nor demonstrated phenomenon of macro-evolution: the emergence of new and improved species by those same accepted processes.

A theory in crisis
The Darwinism is a theory of human origins based on unguided, random variability through genetic mutation and natural selection. As a materialistic explanation of biological life, it is a theory that far overreaches – and, in some cases, ignores-- what has been demonstrated.

For example, Charles Darwin observed that the size of finch beaks increased on the Galapagos Islands after a drought. Since the drought reduced the number of small seeds in comparison to those of the large variety, only those finches with larger, stronger beaks had sufficient food to survive Darwin theorized. In a follow-up on Darwin's study, a Princeton research team estimated that if a drought occurred once every ten years, a new species of finch would evolve in only 200 years. [59]

What the research team failed to note was that the beak size of Darwin's finches returned to normal within a few years after the drought, resulting in no continued directional change of the species. Yet, even had a directional change occurred, it would not have demonstrated how a finch could one day become a falcon, any more than it would show how a primordial soup of chemicals could become a finch.

That is not to suggest that genetic alterations have not occurred after exposure to environmental stresses. Indeed they have. Radiation experimentation on the much-studied fruit fly is a case in point. Nevertheless, after countless fruit fly generations, nothing other than malformed flies have ever been produced. As has been said, Darwin's theory may explain the survival of species but not the arrival of species. That's because biological life is much more complex than can be accounted for by materialistic processes alone. And nowhere is this clearer than in the cell.

Little factories of life
In Darwin's day, the cell was viewed as a globule of protoplasm consisting of carbon dioxide, oxygen, and nitrogen. But after Francis Crick and James Watson unraveled the information-rich structure of DNA, the cell could no longer be thought of as a simple collection of chemicals reacting under the right environmental conditions; it was a microcosmic "factory," a manufacturing center consisting of complex hardware and highly specified software programmed in a chemical "language" communicating the instructions necessary for cellular operations.

It was such evidence that led the life-long atheist, Anthony Flew, to conclude that the origin of life on

148

earth by chemical evolution was untenable, even allowing the process 15 billion years to "get it right."

Before his death in 2010, Flew described his move from atheism to deism, "I have followed the argument where it has led me. And it has led to accept the existence of a self-existent, immutable, immaterial, omnipotent, and omniscient Being." [60]

For those who are more dogmatically entrenched, the response to the mounting counterevidence is re-messaging and re-packaging.

"Nothing in biology makes sense except in light of evolution." Theodosius Dobzhansky

Selling Evolution

On the floor of the Darwinian exchange, traders bark, "Evolution is fact, Fact, FACT!" But it's a fact that has proven to be a hard sell.

After 150 years of scientific "evidence," decades of inculcation in public education, and a raft of books, like *The Dragons of Eden, The Selfish Gene,* and *The Blind Watchmaker,* only 16 percent of Americans believe that humans developed from an unsupervised process of variation and natural selection. Belief that God had some part in the process has held steady over the last 30 years at around 80 percent. [61]

But what is becoming particularly bothersome to evolution brokers is the recognition that resistance to Darwin's Dangerous Idea is not limited to a scientifically-challenged public. In a book review on Darwinism, evolution popularist, Daniel Dennett lamented:

> "I was disconcerted to overhear some medical students talking in a bar recently. One exclaimed: 'How could anybody believe in evolution after learning about the intricacies of the DNA replication machinery?'"[62]

The students obviously missed class the day the prime axiom of Darwinism -- "nothing in biology makes sense except in light of evolution"[63] – was covered.

When a scientific theory is rejected by scientifically

trained individuals, that's bad, and Dennett knows it. I'll bet he had another drink (or two) before leaving the bar that night.

From denial to admission
Afterward, a sobering Dennett reasoned: "To the extent that well-meaning evolutionists had inadvertently convinced them that Darwinians are eager to gloss over or deny these facts [about complexity and design], this is evidence that the political tactic of denying teleology root and branch is apt to be self-defeating."

Inadvertently? Francis Crick's warning to biologists to "constantly keep in mind that what they see was not designed, but rather evolved" strikes this observer as neither inadvertent, hesitant, nor especially well-meaning.

Dennett realizes that to gain market share, the Darwinian community must admit what is plain to specialists and non-specialists alike: there is design in nature. To be clear, he is not pushing *actual* design, mind you, but *apparent* design – that is, design that happens through natural mechanisms and *happens* to be useful.

But that is what Richard Dawkins, Kenneth Miller, and the gaggle of Darwinists have been doing for decades. Each has spent a career expounding upon the talking points of Julian Huxley: "Organisms are built as if purposely designed...But as the genius of Darwin showed, the purpose is only an apparent one." And for decades, the unconvinced have remained unconvinced.

Death anxiety
The prevalence of ADD (Abiding Darwinian Doubt) has long vexed evolutionists. But recently, researchers at the University of British Columbia and Union College believe they have it figured out. It has to do with "death anxiety."

After conducting five related studies, the researchers found that evolution doesn't offer a satisfying answer to the existential questions of life when people are faced with mortality. And we would expect that it could?

Yes, says the lead investigator -- *if*, as their research suggests, individuals are "explicitly taught that taking a naturalistic approach to understanding life can be highly meaningful." And that, she is eager to add, "Indicate[s] a possible means of encouraging students to accept evolution and reject intelligent design."[64]

Get it? Since evolution can't go toe-to-toe with its competitor on technical merit, promoters should focus on style. Shift the pitch from evolution to *evolutionism*. Turn the biology lab into a philosophy salon, and science professors into pipe-puffing peripatetics. Explain to students what's in it for them and those nagging problems about "the intricacies of the DNA replication machinery" will seem less problematic. Indoctrination with metaphysical hand-wavering, that's the formula.

It would appear that the real "death anxiety" is that afflicting Darwinists whose scientifically threadbare theory is succumbing to exposure. Nevertheless, this research team is not alone in thinking that there is no objection to Darwinism that a soothing answer to our existential angst can't overcome.

What's in your worldview?
In a fluff piece on Darwinism for PBS, Alan Alda asks Daniel Dennett why he thinks Darwin's idea is dangerous.[65] Dennett's response:

"Because a lot of people believe, and not foolishly, that if that's true then somehow life has no meaning. They're afraid that their own lives won't mean anything, that morality will evaporate, that the whole pageant of human existence somehow depends on not giving up this sort of top down idea."

Refreshingly candid, his "and not foolishly." Dennett is keenly aware of *what's in his worldview*, and where it naturally leads. Alda, also aware, presses the point,

> "Do you suppose some people feel that there's a lack of purpose to life if life is only the way Darwin describes it?"

Dennett comes back, acknowledging our inclination to look "on high" for answers. But it is an inclination that we need to get over, because there is no "on high." Answers to life's meaning are not found by looking up, but by looking around. "If you want to be happy," Dennett coaxes, "find something more important than you are and work for it."

As I recall, a man of ancient history spent his life at that and found it to be pretty thin gruel.

In a bracing self-disclosure, King Solomon recounted his quest for meaning in "something more." With unrivalled success he completed grand projects, amassed fortunes, and enjoyed mountain-top experiences; each, failing to quell his heart's deepest pangs. His life lesson: lasting significance is not found in something, but in Someone.

The problem for evolutionists is that our thirst for transcendence is as universal as our thirst for water. The psalmist expressed it well, "As the deer pants for streams of water, so my soul pants for you, O God."[66]

But rather than consider whether our thirst points to a thirst-quenching Source, evolutionists explain it as an artifact of selfish genes; then, like a huckster offering a glass of brine to a thirsty man, suggest that it can be slaked by a thirst-inducing substitute.

C.S. Lewis once observed that since all of our desires (like for food, drink, love, and sex) can be fulfilled in things that actually exist, the most reasonable conclusion is that our desire for transcendence can also be fulfilled in something that exists; namely, God.

Dennett's invitation to "find something more important" frequently finds its way into commencement speeches and motivational talks, but it runs completely counter to the spin of the *iWorld*. For as long as I can remember, I have been told,

> *You* are special.
> *You* deserve a break today.
> Have it *your* way.
> Because *you're* worth it.
> We do it all for *you*.
> It's everywhere *you* want to be.

The *iWorld* message is loud and clear: I am the axis upon which the earth turns. Try as hard as I may, I look around, but find nothing more important than *me*. How could I in a world under the grip of Darwinian competition and survival?

By contrast, the message of our collective experiences agrees with that found in Scripture: anything less than God is too small to fill us and too impotent to change us. How could it be otherwise in a world held in the palm of His hand?

Daniel Dennett should brace himself for more disconcerting bar stool conversations, as I suspect that evolution will continue to be a hard sell. For it is not only in the origin and complexity of life that the creative power of unguided materialism fails.

"It's not enough to just fake being a cooperator and a good person." – Michael Shermer

An Unsolved Mystery

A man dives into an ice-cold lake to save a stranger, and drowns; a woman donates blood for someone she will never know; a volunteer takes a week off work to help the victims of a hurricane; many of us write checks to the community kitchen, the shelter for battered spouses, or the children's burn clinic. The question is, why? Why do we do sacrifice our self-interests and well-being for total strangers?

Are these actions merely mechanistic phenomena to be studied in the lab and expressed in an equation with error bar analyses for the purpose of constructing society according to the lights of some benevolent architect? According to a nineteenth century philosopher and sociologist, yes they are.

Altruism coined
Born in 1798, Auguste Comte became the founder of sociology. Comte was a positivist who believed that all phenomena (even human behavior) are governed by physical principles discernible through the scientific method. Interestingly, Comte also believed in moral responsibility toward others, a moral duty he coined as "altruism."

Interesting, because moral responsibility implies a duty transcending human convention and, as such, is incompatible with a materialistic worldview. Nevertheless, Comte argued that morality was what is determined, scientifically, to be effective in solving our social ills.

An evolutionary artifact

As a materialist, Comte considered altruism a direct and necessary consequence of our evolutionary heritage. His argument went something like this: In the beginning, small clans of *homo-sapiens* competed for scarce resources in a hostile, untamed world. Those groups that learned to cooperate and sacrifice for the clan became more "fit" than those who didn't. By putting aside self-interest for the common good, these altruistic ancestors were able to out-populate the rival clans that succumbed to self-interest and infighting.   After countless generations, the altruist impulse became embedded in the human consciousness as an evolutionary artifact.

That has a certain intellectual charm. But it doesn't quite explain why we should sacrifice our convenience, much less well-being, for someone outside of our clan. For example, how is evolutionary fitness enhanced for a German sheltering Jews from the Holocaust; a fireman rushing into the World Trade Center; or a volunteer at the AIDS hospice?

Even within one's clan, how does evolutionary fitness explain, much less justify, the caring for an aging parent or dying child? The ever imaginative Michael Shermer has a ready answer.

The real, real thing

On a PBS special, Michael Shermer mused why he felt good about being polite to strangers he would never meet again. Shermer, editor of *Skeptic* magazine and self-professed atheist, concluded to a diverse panel discussing the origin of morality,

> "It's not enough to just fake being a cooperator and a good person because it's hard to do...You actually have to be a good person. And you're more likely to believe it yourself if you actually do it...And I think,

over the long eons of our evolutionary history, we evolved a moral sense, an empathy, or a feeling of warmth about doing the right thing, not as a fake thing, but as a real thing."[67]

Note that this is not a statement of fact; it is a statement of faith. It is Michael Shermer's personal belief in a theory offered without evidence or proof. And this from someone who prizes the empirical method as supreme. But what else can Shermer do to keep his materialistic worldview intact?

That aside, Shermer's fanciful explanation is unconvincing for a number of reasons. First of all, Shermer's reasoning reduces humans to genetic robots, and altruism to a programmed response. Can such empathy be, as Shermer puts it, the "real thing"?

Hardly. It is contrary to everything we believe and experience in our humanity, including our universal longing for *unconditional* love: the real, "real" thing. I wonder when Shermer leaves his offices at *Skeptic* at the end of the day, whether he is warmed by the thought that the kisses and hugs of his loved ones are conditioned actions of automata. I guess we'll never know.

Then there's the Shermerian call to be a "good person" and do "the right thing?" By what standard? The degree to which my actions enhance the survival of the species? If so, wouldn't the "right thing" include exterminating or, at least, sterilizing individuals with congenital defects like diabetes, autism, or heart disease? Wouldn't it also include cutting off "useless eaters," like quadriplegics, Down's children and AIDS victims. Wouldn't the species be better served by taking the resources needed to maintain these individuals, and using them for curable diseases? Why shouldn't the hopeless few be sacrificed for the well-being of the many?

True altruism, the "caring for the least of these," makes little sense in a fully materialistic world. Not only is Shermer's explanation unhelpful here, Shermer himself is left with a much bigger question: Why, in a universe cobbled together by the unguided process of evolution, is the survival of the species necessarily a good thing? Since matter and energy have no teleology, "no end in mind," whatever is, is. There's no good or bad to it.

The Tao

All the same, Shermer like Comte acknowledges a code of conduct that continually presses upon us, influencing us to behave in certain ways; as if some behaviors were superior to others; like honesty over deceit, fairness over injustice, generosity over selfishness, and responsibility toward others irrespective of merit, status, or reciprocity. It is a notion derived for the presumption of human dignity.

But human dignity and its source are not features of the universe discoverable through observation and scientific analysis. They are things that are *revealed*.

Martin Luther King Jr. pointed to the eternal law of God; Immanuel Kant, the moral law within; and C.S. Lewis, the *Tao*. For these and other thinkers, the moral code is revealed through God's Word. With personal duty at its core -- first to God and, then, to fellow man – the moral code is not a description of what *is*, it is a prescription for what *ought* to be.

The yawning gap between *ought* and *is* attests that we are not evolved as genetic automatons but, rather, we are created as free-willed agents. We have the capacity to behave in ways that defy cause-and-effect explanation. The unreliability of torture in extracting confessions or information is a case in point. The intractability of the human spirit indicates that altruism is not some epiphenomenon of the material world that can be

158

packaged in a, yet to be discovered, physical law.

Equally flawed is the notion that even if love were reducible by science, educating the masses would lead to global brotherhood. For example, there have been more diet and exercise books purchased over the last twenty years than at any time in history and, yet, obesity is at epidemic levels.

There is little doubt that altruism will forever remain an "unsolved paradox" for those trying to unravel it through the rubric of science. Over 100 years ago, the materialist Sigmund Freud spent his life trying and failed. In a letter to a colleague, Freud confessed,

> *"When I ask myself why I have always behaved honorably, ready to spare others and to be kind wherever possible…I have no answer…Why I -- and incidentally my six adult children also – have to be thoroughly decent human beings is quite incomprehensible to me."[68]*

Freud's confession points to a wider problem for materialism.

"We have no government armed with the power capable of contending with human passions unbridled by morality and religion." John Adams

Upon Ethical Quicksand

Ever since the Enlightenment, men have imagined a secular society liberated from religion and founded upon certain knowledge -- that is, facts gleaned from the sensible world through science and human reason.

Yet, despite the urge to be unbound to transcendence, every noble foundation of the secular state is parasitic, feeding off the intellectual and moral capital of Christianity. It's a point that philosopher Stanley Fish makes, if unwittingly, noting that the secularist "prohibition against stealing in the Ten Commandments is all right because there is a secular version of the prohibition rooted in the law of property rights rather than in a biblical command."[69]

But where did the presumption of private property and rightful ownership originate, except in the eighth and tenth commandments of the Decalogue?[70] Indeed, the moral bedrock of our nation, as James Madison explained, is built "upon the capacity of each and all of us to govern ourselves, to control ourselves, to sustain ourselves according to the Ten Commandments of God."

Golden Rule ethics
Secularists will yawp, claiming that such sectarian codes are merely offshoots of *The Golden Rule* which, in their thinking, is the primal, self-evident standard of all moral conduct. Indeed, treating our neighbor as we would want to be treated has been recognized as a universal good in

nearly every civilization since the beginning of recorded history. However, *The Golden Rule* has a problem: the concept of one's "neighbor."

Are my neighbors those in my family, tribe, ethnic group, community, church, country or the entire global village? Do they include the disabled, the unborn, the feeble-minded, and the dying? The *Rule* is mute. While the principle of fairness and reciprocity in *The Golden Rule* is universally agreed upon, the concept of "neighbor" is not--it varies from the members of one's household to all of humankind. Consequently, despite its general esteem, the *Rule* has done little to keep individuals and civilizations from devouring each other.

Indeed, divergent beliefs about who does and who does not deserve neighborly consideration have been behind every conflict from Cain and Abel to modern day Jihadists. Without universal descriptions, definitions, and doctrines the *Golden Rule* is powerless to produce a just society.

Other secularists believe that morality can be established empirically. Take neuroscientist Sam Harris, who takes a his cue from Comte.

Science-based morality
Harris is a trenchant atheist (although he avers the label) and thorough-going rationalist who is confident that the shared moral values of society can, and should, be grounded in science.

His argument goes something like this: the natural world operates according to material laws discoverable through science; morality is a part of the natural world; therefore, morality follows material laws discoverable through science.[71]

The problem with Harris' argument is that everything in

the natural world does not behave in a law-like, cause and effect, manner; especially things pertaining to human behavior. True, morality has the feature of law, in that it predicts certain outcomes from certain actions (for example, people who are sexually promiscuous will have higher incidences of pregnancy and sexually transmitted disease).

But unlike the law of gravity which tells us what two heavenly bodies will do when one body enters the other's orbit, morality does not tell us what two people will do when one comes into the personal space of the other; rather, it tells us what they *ought* to do. As such, morality is not discernable, scientifically or otherwise, from what humans actually do. If it was, we should shudder, for it would suggest that we are little more than automata slavishly following the program of some moral gene.

Harris would be quick to say that morality specifies actions that enhance human flourishing, and we know, scientifically, what many of those are: proper medical care, education, sanitation, clean water.

Unarguably, applied science is credited with doubling human life expectancy over the last 150 years, and for cleaner air and water on the planet than at any time since the Industrial Revolution. Yet, tragically, the 20th century programs of eugenics, forced sterilization, and selective breeding were morally justified on scientific grounds, as are today the arguments for human cloning and embryo-destructive research.

If we cannot reason our way to morality from our study of human behavior, what about our study of nature? Consider the liberal ideals of freedom and equality.

From whence oughts
Using only nature as his guide, Charles Darwin became convinced that natural selection was as fundamental as

the laws of thermodynamics. His theories inspired a generation of social architects who imagined that they could manipulate the selection process and direct it toward their utopian ends. What nature taught Darwin and his disciples was that some people are taller, bigger, stronger, smarter, healthier, and more fit than others; what it didn't, was that they were in any way, "equal."

Oughts do not issue from the cosmos waiting to be discovered by researchers like light spectra from supernovae; they come from presuppositions about man's nature and dignity. As to the ideals of freedom and equality, they derive from Judeo-Christian presuppositions.

Belief in the intrinsic dignity of man was the inspiration behind the famous words of Thomas Jefferson (a co-opted saint of secularism): "that all men are created equal: that they are endowed *by their Creator* with certain unalienable rights; that among these are life, liberty and the pursuit of happiness." (Emphasis added.)

In his "Notes on the State of Virginia" Jefferson asked rhetorically, "can the liberties of a nation be thought secure when we have removed their only firm basis, a conviction in the minds of the people that these liberties are a gift of God?"

Our Founding Fathers realized that rights and freedoms depend on citizens whose darker angels are restrained by a received moral code. John Adams put it this way: "We have no government armed with the power capable of contending with human passions unbridled by morality and religion."

For the Founders, moral truth was not a matter of empirical observation, personal opinion, or popular consensus but, rather, it was the product of an external source of knowledge: the divine mind of God.

Without a transcendent origin, moral codes become matters of power and politics. Rights and freedoms, and those who have claim to them, are neither inalienable nor durable, but subject to the caprice of the tyrant or the tyranny of the crowd.

During the last century, the atrocities committed by the regimes of Stalin, Hitler, Mao, and Mussolini are sufficient to disabuse all but the most glassy-eyed dreamers of their enchantments with the secular state bereft of religious voice.

Effect of modernity
An unquestioned maxim among secularists is that the more technologically advanced a society becomes, the less religious and more secular it becomes. Problem is, the facts do not support the claim.

In the past century, technology experienced unprecedented exponential growth. From 1900 to the present, technological wizardry took us from gas lights to lasers, telegraphs to Twitter, ground travel to space travel, and horse power to nuclear power. According to the secularist creed, religious adherence should have plummeted in a commensurate fashion.

Instead, as reported by the *Economist*, "The proportion of people attached to the world's four biggest religions— Christianity, Islam, Buddhism and Hinduism—rose from 67% in 1900 to 73% in 2005." [72] What's more, as reported by the Pew Research Center, between 2010 and 2050, "Atheists, agnostics and other people who do not affiliate with any religion...will make up a declining share of the world's total population," from 16.4% to 13.2%.[73]

If book sales are any indication, that prediction could be on the low side. Consider that *The Purpose Driven Life* by Rick Warren has sold over 30 million copies worldwide compared to 2 million copies of *The God Delusion*, the book its author had hoped would turn religious believers into atheists.

Self-defeating

But secularism has a more fundamental problem: its commitment to materialistic science as the fount of all knowledge. That devotion is nothing less than an act of faith: faith that nature is a mechanism that can be explained by physical laws, faith that those laws are universal and unchanging, faith that our senses reliably perceive the world as it really is, faith that our minds accurately interpret those perceptions, and faith that the origin, diversity and complexity of nature is the unguided product of chance and necessity. From the outset, the secular project of establishing a kinder, gentler society on certain (that is, faith-free) knowledge is defeated.

And that's not all. Although science can help us collect, organize, and analyze data, it can't tell us *how* that data *should* be used for the flourishing of humankind. Quoting law professor Steven Smith, Stanley Fish writes, "going from observation to evaluation and judgment, proves difficult, indeed impossible... to yield any definite answer to a difficult issue — abortion, say, or same sex marriage, or the permissibility of torture."

Fish's remarks are not to be taken as support for transcendence. Fish himself is a secularist, just of a different stripe than those he criticizes. He is what is known as an "anti-foundationalist," a person who believes that metaphysical reality--that is, what is *really*, real--is ultimately unknowable, making all judgments situational and provisional. Anti-foundationalists swim in the same philosophical waters as postmodernists, relativists, pragmaticists, and deconstructionists.

For Fish, the dogmatism of secularists is as wrong-headed as that of religious believers. (Fish is an equal opportunity agitator and he is proud of it.) Because knowledge is uncertain, the guiding principles of society must remain elastic, ready to conform to the changing contours of culture. Of that, Fish and his fellow anti-foundationalists are quite certain.

Whether founded upon scientific materialism or anti-foundationalism, secularism self-destructs. Scientists cannot establish science as the wellspring of knowledge without exempting it from the criteria that they apply to the things they study. Neither can anti-foundationalists know that knowledge is uncertain without claiming to know (with certainty) something about knowledge. Either way, secularism collapses.

The best explanation
While secularists fancy that their worldview is objective, freed from commitment to ideological biases, it is anything but. Fish candidly remarks that there "are no neutral principles," including, I might add, those he favors.

Every ethical principle, every moral standard, and every ideal of truth, beauty, and goodness depends on a particular worldview; that is, a set of preconceived notions about how the world works. Although worldviews are neither neutral nor provable in an absolute sense, there is one that best explains the world as it really is.

The fact that, time and again, people irrepressibly smuggle Christianity into their ideological systems under the moral labels of "liberty", "freedom", "equality", "humanism", "tolerance", "social justice", "global brotherhood," is evidence of its singular explanatory power.

Not-So Good News

In post-WWII France, Sartre spoke to the anguish of his countrymen who were reeling in despair from the German occupation. Promoting the gospel of personal responsibility and choice, Sartre helped turn the mood of a nation from fatalism to optimism. But while autonomy and free choice can be liberating, it can also be paralyzing--as one young man realized after seeking Sartre's advice.

During the war a French student, agonizing over whether to join the resistance movement or stay home with his mother who was totally dependent on him, asked Sartre what he should do. Sartre's answer: "You're free, choose!"

I can imagine a choked "Huh?" from the young man as those pearls of wisdom rolled off the tongue of the famed philosopher—and his head-down, hands-in-pockets amble back home, as he strained for some moral scale to weigh his choices.

Thanks to Sartre and his sophistic forbears, classifications of "right" and "wrong" have been blurred if not obliterated, leaving us, like that French student, to wonder what it means to be moral.

Cookie-cutter morality?

A while back, Bob, an atheist, told me that there was no need for God to determine what's "good" and "bad"; human reason is fully sufficient to establish common concepts on ethical conduct. He characterized Christian morality as easy, a "follow-these-rules-to-be-good" excuse to avoid thinking deeply about real world ethical questions. He went on to ask whether I thought that biblical morality was moral only because God deemed it so.

My response went something like this.

Bob, you suggested that unlike Christians who have a cookie-cutter approach to morality, you struggle with "being a good, ethical person." Notice, that you are committing the naturalistic fallacy: a world in which nature is all there is, there is no good or bad -- only desirable or undesirable, fortunate or unfortunate, profitable or unprofitable.

You also said that morality is based on human concepts of justice, peace and harmony. But that really doesn't help, does it? If law derives from nothing higher than what has evolved in our collective psyche, then law is law, not because it's right, but because it's law—a contrivance of the ruling class. Some cultures care for widows, while others place them on the husband's funeral pyre. Without a standard that transcends such "human concepts," who's to say which should be legal or illegal, not to mention moral or immoral?

You also asked, "Is the only reason that it is wrong to steal, murder or rape because God *said* it was wrong?"

Sadly, I suspect, that if you took a poll of professed Christians, some would answer, "Yes." Yet, Christian morality does not originate from God's commands; it derives from his ontology (his nature, who he is).

In accordance with his ontology, God created a world of order, intelligibility and beauty governed by laws that include physical and moral dimensions. Simply stated, morality is aligning ourselves with those principles so that we can experience all the goodness for which we were created. In essence, morality is a purpose-driven set of operating instructions necessary for human flourishing.

It is the same for any engineering product, like a car. Cars are precision-made to provide owners the benefits of efficient and reliable transportation. But to enjoy those benefits, an owner must operate his vehicle within the bounds of its design, and maintain it according to the manufacturer's specifications. Failure to do so, guarantees poor performance and shortened life. It is no less true for us.

Take sexual morality. While God has said that sex outside of marriage is wrong, it is not wrong because he said so; it is wrong because it conflicts with our design. Witness, forty years after the Sexual Revolution the burgeoning rates of divorce, out-of-wedlock births, single parent homes, abortions, and sexually transmitted diseases with all of the concomitant problems of abuse, poverty, and emotional trauma. By disregarding our design, Freudianism defaulted on its promise of self-fulfillment through free sexual expression, despite more social acceptance and education than at any time in history.

Still, the Christian must ask himself, "*Why* be good?" If all he cares about is avoiding negative consequences, he might just as well adopt the hedonistic aim of "maximizing pleasure and minimizing pain" or the utilitarian "greatest good for the greatest number." However, neither conforms to the Christian ethic.

Allow me a little more bandwidth to explain, starting

with your suggestion that Christian morality is "an excuse not to think more deeply about ethics"—an easy way out, as it were. No one who has actually read Jesus could seriously think that.

A cursory read of his *Sermon on the Mount* will dispel any misgivings that Christianity is easy. In a series of "You have heard it said…but I tell you," Jesus raises the bar of morality to breathtaking heights. Even the *Golden Rule* of "love neighbor as self" fades to a penumbra with the dizzying directive: "Love your enemies and pray for those who persecute you." He concludes his discourse with the Herculean challenge, "Be perfect as your heavenly Father is perfect"—a standard that even Mother Theresa would not have claimed. All of that is bad news for those who take Jesus at his word. It forces us to ask what that "looks like" and whether there's any good news in his message.

Jesus answers the first part of that question in the Gospel of John: "As I have loved you, so you must love one another."

To a non-Christian, that may sound like nothing more than doing good things for each other. But for the Christian, who believes that Jesus answered the second part of that question with the Cross, the duty is nothing short of staggering. Out of gratitude for what Christ did for us, we should be willing to do likewise for all, including the "least and the last."

Little wonder that G.K. Chesterton once quipped, "Christianity has not been tried and found wanting; it has been found difficult and left untried."

We *do* good not because the bible says so, or out of fear of consequence, or for a utilitarian end—though, sadly, some Christians (maybe many) are motivated by those very reasons; we do good out of love for God who not only created all persons in his image, but humbled himself so that all could have community with him. For Christians, the Word made Flesh is the Standard of ethics and morality that informs our Western concepts of right action, justice, equality and human dignity.

■■

I went on to explain that deep inside we know this. Despite the fashionable heroism of embracing the absurdity of our existence, we have an irrepressible sense that there *are* objective standards of right and wrong, that justice *should* prevail, and that our choices *matter* for something supremely significant. It's a truth that even Jean Paul Sartre, who shaped the thought of a generation with his God-denying philosophy, could not hold down.

Shortly before his death, in the spring of 1980, Sartre made a startling disclosure: "I do not feel that I am the product of chance, a speck of dust in the universe, but someone who was expected, prepared, prefigured. In short, a being whom only a Creator could put here: and this idea of a creating hand refers to God."[74]

It appears that the dying philosopher had an illuminating encounter with *"the true Light which gives light to every man coming into the world."*

It may be that that Light has also broken through the defenses of a living skeptic.

"I just witnessed an event so mysterious that it shook my skepticism." -- Michael Shermer

Skeptical of His Skepticism

On the PBS special mentioned earlier, Michael Shermer pressed a Christian physician for how (how!) God raised Jesus from the dead. By presuming that the Resurrection *must* have occurred through a clever medical manipulation to be credible, Shermer's question was designed to ensure that naturalism wins.

It was also designed to make his Christian opponent appear badly misinformed, intellectually challenged, or worse. For, in our enlightened scientific age, smart people everywhere know "there is no such thing as the supernatural or the paranormal," Shermer reminds us, "there is just the natural, the normal, and mysteries we have yet to explain by natural causes." [75]

Such unswerving confidence in naturalism seals the imagination from any consideration of supernatural causation, even for things currently inexplicable by science (e.g., dark energy, quantum behavior, abiogenesis, consciousness, the big bang, etc.). However, when life collides with our worldview it can create cracks in our ideological foundation and shake our confidence. In June 2014, Michael Shermer experienced just such a collision.[76]

A fissure-forming event
It occurred on the day of his wedding in his California home. As Shermer tells it, his German wife-to-be, Jennifer, who shares his skepticism was feeling lonely, all her family and friends thousands of miles away. She was particularly saddened that her late grandfather, the

only father figure she had known, couldn't attend to give her away.

Months earlier, Jennifer's belongings had been delivered to Michael's home, among them a precious keepsake: a nearly forty year old transistor radio owned by her grandfather. Describing his efforts to revive it, Shermer writes,

"I put in new batteries and opened it up to see if there were any loose connections to solder. I even tried 'percussive maintenance,' said to work on such devices -- smacking it sharply against a hard surface. Silence. We gave up and put it at the back of a desk drawer in our bedroom."

Just as the wedding was about to proceed, the couple retreated for a few moments to a back area where,

"We could hear music playing in the bedroom. We don't have a music system there, so we searched for laptops and iPhones and even opened the back door to check if the neighbors were playing music. We followed the sound to the printer on the desk, wondering – absurdly -- if this combined printer/scanner/fax machine also included a radio. Nope.

"At that moment Jennifer shot me a look I haven't seen since the supernatural thriller *The Exorcist* startled audiences. 'That can't be what I think it is, can it?' she said. She opened the desk drawer and pulled out her grandfather's transistor radio, out of which a romantic love song wafted. We sat in stunned silence for minutes. 'My grandfather is here with us,' Jennifer said, tearfully. 'I'm not alone.'"

In that silence, a fissure formed in Shermer's worldview.

Later his daughter told him that right before the ceremony she heard music coming from the bedroom, even though he and Jennifer were there minutes earlier getting ready, hearing no music. Another crack. Another still, when, after playing classical music throughout the night, the radio went silent and didn't revive the next day, or since.

Shermer admits that had this been another person's story, he would have chalked it up to a random probabilistic occurrence. "With billions of people having billions of experiences every day, there's bound to be a handful of extremely unlikely events that stand out in their timing and meaning."

I should mention that Shermer's discovery of statistics was pivotal in his move from a born-again evangelical Christian pursuing theology to a premier atheist pushing skepticism. Which makes his admission all the more interesting.

In "Why I am an Atheist," Shermer explains, "In science, I discovered that by establishing parameters to determine whether a hypothesis is probably right (like rejecting the null hypothesis at the 0.01 level of significance) or definitely wrong (not statistically significant), it is possible to approach problems in another way. Instead of the rhetoric and disputation of theology, there was the logic and probabilities of science. What a difference this difference in thinking makes."[77]

But, as Shermer found out on that fatefu... uh, providential day, personal experience can trump all that to make a difference, a profound difference, in thinking.

Having had a mysterious experience he is at a loss to explain scientifically, Shermer now suggests an openness to the existence of the supernatural. And while he stops just short of endorsement -- "such anecdotes do not constitute scientific evidence that the dead survive or that they can communicate with us via electronic equipment" – he confesses that he has been rocked back on his heels, his skepticism shaken.

What was it?
So, was this a rare, probabilistic phenomenon of nature or a message from beyond?

Shermer dismisses the first possibility and remains agnostic on the second; but he says whatever causal mechanism may be attributed to it, these kinds of occurrences gain their significance from their emotional impact which, for his wife, was the heart-warming sense "that her grandfather was there and that the music was his gift of approval."

The word, "gift," suggests that Michael Shermer could be on to something -- a mystery that, hitherto, has eluded him: the grace of God.

In a piece on the compatibility of science and religion, Shermer asks how we can know that a God, outside of time and space, exists unless he steps "into our spacetime to make himself known in some manner -- say through prayer, providence, or miracles?"[78]

Well, he has and he does, by those means, and others as we will see later in Chapter 7.

Chapter 6

An Intelligent Proposition

"The object in life is not to be on the side of the majority, but to escape finding oneself in the ranks of the insane."-
-Marcus Aurelius

A Dangerous Idea

The revelation of the mind-numbing complexity of DNA produced skepticism in some scientific circles about the explanatory power of chance and necessity. And with that came a willingness to consider intelligent agency. As a result "intelligent design" has been creeping into the lingua franca for the last couple of decades.

But what is intelligent design? To some, it is fringe science. To others, it is not science at all, but religion in a lab smock, a stealth tactic of right-wing conservatives to sneak God back into the classroom. To its critics, intelligent design is a threat to the whole scientific enterprise which will hurl civilization back into the Dark Ages of religion and superstition.

But according to the Discovery Institute, a secular think-tank supporting science education, intelligent design is neither of these. Rather, ID theory "is simply an effort to empirically detect whether the 'apparent design' in nature acknowledged by virtually all biologists is genuine design (the product of an intelligent cause)."

Intelligent design, say its proponents, is not opposed to science, but to the philosophy undergirding it -- namely, that the universe is the product of a blind, undirected process of natural selection. ID theory challenges the ground rules, rather than the method, of science—a challenge that a Pennsylvania judge determined is against the cards.

In 2005 Judge John Jones ruled against a Dover school district policy requiring that students be made aware of ID theory. His basis? Since the 17th century, "science has been limited to the search for natural causes to explain natural phenomena...While supernatural explanations may be important and have merit, they are not part of science. It is therefore readily apparent to the Court that ID fails to meet the essential ground rules that limit science to testable, natural explanations..."[1]

Vying for hearts and minds
While many consider Dover a cause for celebration, philosopher and zoologist Michael Ruse understands the fragile pedestal upon which the ruling rests.

An ardent Darwinist, Ruse is troubled that court victories from Scopes to Dover and 80 years of Darwinian inculcation, have failed to win public confidence. In a nation where nearly 80% of the folks believe in some form of intelligent causation,[2] the biggest challenge for Darwin is not in a court of law, but in the court of popular opinion. It's a tough venue, where neither judicial rulings nor scientific proclamations have been able to move the dial. And Ruse knows it.

In an exchange with fellow evolutionist Daniel Dennett, Ruse fretted that the battle will be lost unless there is a serious effort to understand Christians and "make allies in the fight." Ruse scolded Dennett, along with Richard Dawkins, for flaunting their atheistic worldview and alienating people of faith. [3]

What the folks seem to get and what judges and scientists do not, is that constraining science to naturalistic phenomena is an arbitrary, philosophical decision, not one dictated by logic, reason, or the evidence itself. For example, when confronted by the large gaps in the fossil record, the Darwinian mantra is: "Absence of evidence is not evidence of absence." Interestingly, it is the same mantra they use when referring to ID theory--only with the "not" removed! Unfortunately their ideology blinds them to the obvious contradiction.

Perhaps more problematic, is the pillar of their ideology: Science as the sole revelator of knowledge. As the presupposition from which inquiry begins, that pillar is not testable by science and, therefore, not scientific. Which brings up the question, "What is science?"

A working definition
The word "science" comes from the Latin word, *scientia*, meaning to know or have knowledge. While there is no universal agreement as to what constitutes science, a working definition from standard dictionary sources could be paraphrased as: a structured method of empirical investigation and observation to seek the truth about how the world operates.

Going with that definition, science is not constrained from considering any and all effects and causes. Unlike the methodological naturalist, who is limited from considering design and a Designer, the ID theorist is not driven or constrained by ideology. He is free to follow the evidence wherever it leads, using critical thinking to evaluate *all* the alternatives, and accepting the one that best corresponds to the real world.

Of course, the mere mention of intelligence is enough to make the Darwinian establishment shriek, "God of the Gaps! It explains nothing. It's a science-stopper."

Science-stopper? The "God hypothesis" is nothing of the sort.

For instance, recall that according to the laws of electromagnetism the atom should collapse shortly after its creation. Why doesn't it? Well, no one knows for sure. So researchers came up with a tag. For some, it was "quantum potential," for others, "confinement energy."

Really, anything would have worked as long as it had a scientific jingle giving the impression that they had explained something, when all they'd done was report an observation and given it a lofty label. Lofty labels notwithstanding, that's "materialism of the gaps," a "scientific" fig leaf to cover ignorance.

On the other hand, an omnipresent Agent working in an interstitial dimension of the cosmos would equally describe, as well as explain, this phenomenon. And since physicists, from Heisenberg to Hawking, acknowledge that what *really* goes on beneath the sub-atomic veil is ontologically unknowable, the God hypothesis would not impede the further development of nuclear technology.

Consider the human genome. The discovery that a very large portion of human DNA (some argue, 99%) is identical to that of the chimpanzee did not depend on an *a priori* assumption of Darwinian evolution. To the contrary, the genomic similarities are there for anyone to discover. Actually, design theory not only explains but anticipates such similarities, much like one anticipates finding common features in different car models designed by the same manufacturer.

Equally independent of descent or design, is our ability to harness nature. Imagine discovering a box filled strange, tool-like items. Whether the box is of terrestrial, extraterrestrial, or supernatural origin is irrelevant to figuring out how its contents could be used for a task at hand.

Also, because design suggests intent and purpose, ID theorists are less likely than their Darwinian counterparts to settle for dead-ends.

The real science stopper
In the area of medical science, ID researcher Casey Luskin points out that "evolutionary science has wrongly assumed that many organs are 'vestigial' and thus unnecessary or unimportant. Those organs include the appendix, tonsils, coccyx, and thyroid" -- organs later found to have important biological functions. But worse, Luskin goes on, "By presuming nonfunctionality or reduced functionality in these organs, evolutionary science did great medical damage to many patients."[4]

The science-stopping effect of materialism became evident to me in a discussion I had with Joe a while back.

Joe is a retired microbiologist who was brought up in a Christian home and even attended Christian college. But in college, Joe learned about Darwin's theory of common descent and became intrigued; so much so that, by graduation, Joe had become a staunch atheist.

One day Joe's brother invited me along on an afternoon hike with Joe and some friends.

I found Joe to be quiet and introverted. His whole

demeanor seemed like that of a pursued prey. That made sense later when his brother told me about his frequent bouts with depression and withdrawal.

My first opportunity to talk seriously to Joe came when we returned home for coffee and cake. I asked him about his work as a microbiologist. He started talking about things like microbial immunology and viral pathogenesis. I was in deep water. But before I sank, Joe mercifully got up for a re-fill, allowing me to tread to a shallower reach.

"Joe, your work must have been truly fascinating. I mean, day-after-day being involved with the intricacies and wonders inside the cell...that must have been awe-inspiring."

"Why do you say that?"

"Well, I just read the other day where some geeks at Microsoft referred to the DNA molecule as a piece of highly advanced software.

"Well, I can see why they might say that. In reality though, the real wonder is why the thing works as well as it does, being cobbled together as it is."

"Huh."

"Yeah. A lot of DNA is just junk sequences that have no function or purpose."

"Really? How's that?"

"It's all part of our evolutionary heritage. Because of random variation, genes change and mutate over time. Some of those will result in an inheritable function, and others will be rendered neutral carryovers for the next generation: junk, it's an inevitable part of us all!"

The phone rang in the kitchen putting an abrupt end to our conversation.

Getting dangerous

A pivotal point in the life of C.S. Lewis came after he read the works of G. K. Chesterton. It was then that Lewis made the turn from atheism toward theism. Lewis remarked:" A young man who wishes to remain a sound Atheist cannot be too careful of his reading." To paraphrase Lewis, there are some dangerous ideas out there if you're an atheist.

Thinking back on my conversation with Joe, I recall how content he was with the notion that "Junk happens"— both on a cosmic and genetic level. It fit so well with the nihilism of his materialistic worldview. In a world ruled by chance and fate, purpose is not something we discover, it is something we create. There's enough intellectual satisfaction there to dull our spiritual pangs, at least for a while.

Since I talked with Joe, researchers have discovered that Joe's so-called "junk" has more significance than previously thought. As I mentioned in Chapter 1, the Human Genome Project found that only 2 percent of the human genome has a biological function. That was in 2003. Less than ten years later, the ENCODE Project put that number at 80 percent. Now, that's starting to get dangerous.

But for those who trust in the omnipotence of Nature and the omniscience of science, more danger awaits.

The Signature in the Cell

Intelligent design (ID) is the proposition that certain features in nature are best explained, scientifically, as products of intelligence. To date, its most comprehensive and compelling evidence is in Dr. Stephen Meyer's book, *The Signature in the Cell.*[5]

An important contribution to the debate is Meyer's clarification on what it is that scientists do.

The work of science
It is regularly charged that Intelligent Design is not "science" because its proponents don't conduct experiments, have laboratories, or publish in peer-reviewed journals. None of that is true, Meyer writes, but even if it were "it doesn't follow that we [aren't] 'doing science.'"

Meyer, whose doctorate is in the philosophy of science, notes that many of science's greatest breakthroughs were made not by experimental researchers but by theoreticians "who taught us how to think differently about what we already knew."

For example, Albert Einstein developed General Relativity, one of the twin pillars of modern science (the other being quantum mechanics), not by conducting a battery of experiments on a laboratory test bench, but by looking at the world anew, asking unasked questions, and thinking beyond the current paradigm.

Watson and Crick didn't crack the DNA mystery by their own experimental research but, as Meyer points out, "by explaining an array of preexisting evidence in a new and more coherent way."

Even Darwin's theory of evolution, as presented in his *On the Origin of Species,* "contains neither a single mathematical equation nor any report of original experimental research." Like Watson and Crick, Darwin sought to explain "disparate lines of observational evidence" with a "novel interpretation of that evidence." And the same goes much of the ground-breaking discoveries of Copernicus, Kepler, Newton, and other pioneers of the Scientific Revolution.[6]

All about information
Making the case for ID, Meyer builds upon the seminal work of other ID researchers, particularly mathematician William Dembski. In *The Design Inference*, Dembski presented a way to distinguish the effects of intelligent agents from those of chance and law.[7]

In a nutshell, products of law (planetary orbits, salt crystals, etc.) exhibit order, regularity, and predictability; products of chance, like the debris field of a tornado, exhibit complexity without order. But products of intelligence exhibit "specified complexity" -- that is, arrangements that do not follow any predictable or ordered pattern and yet have information content, whether in the carvings at Mount Rushmore or the letters on this page.

Consider the digital information stored in living cells.

The nucleotide sequences in DNA make up genes that "spell out" instructions for the manufacturing of proteins. The sequences are highly complex and not compressible to a simple expression or algorithm. Furthermore, since, chemically, the bases can attach anywhere along the DNA "backbone," their precise arrangement is not determined by chemical laws.

In Chapter 4, I showed (using some very generous assumptions) that the universe is neither old enough nor large enough for the chance production of a simple one-cell organism. That's because the instructional content in DNA is just one tier of biological information in a hierarchal structure.

Meyer points out, "In the same way that words are ordered into sentences and sentences into paragraphs, nucleotide bases are ordered into genes and genes are ordered into specifically arranged gene clusters." Gene clusters are further arranged into gene "folders" that are "themselves nonrandomly grouped along chromosomes to form higher-order folders."

And if that weren't enough, those "superfolders" are arranged by cell type according to specific organs and body plans. The multi-layered architecture of biological information, Meyer explains, "would seem to require considerable forethought, precisely what natural selection by definition cannot provide." *Would seem?* A considerable understatement.

The best explanation
Nested levels of instructions and information are characteristic of computer programs. Characteristics that even Richard Dawkins recognizes: "The machine code of the genes is uncannily computer-like."[8] And yet the unaccommodating reality for Dawkins is that the only thing known capable of producing a computer program are intelligent beings.

True, neo-Darwinian processes can lead to small, limited changes in the genome. But those changes are overwhelmingly detrimental, and in the few instances where a benefit is conferred (e.g., anti-biotic immunity, pesticide resistance) they are the result of information loss or suppression (i.e., of the genes controlling the digestion of the drug or pesticide), not information gain.

From probabilistic considerations *and* empirical evidence, the best explanation for the code-of-life is intelligent causation. Of course the Darwinist fold is ever ready with a machination that gives *chance* and *necessity* a "helping hand." Currently, the favored narrative turns on the "RNA World."

The RNA World was devised, specifically, to solve the conundrum of "which came first?", DNA or proteins. Proteins are built from DNA, but DNA needs proteins to process its information. Once it was recognized that certain RNA molecules had protein-like properties, an origin-of-life theory was cooked up, whereby, a fortuitous cocktail of primordial chemicals formed RNA molecules that self-replicated and synthesized proteins that produced DNA that, through the omnipotent wonders of natural selection, eventually led to the first biological cell.

Setting aside the probabilistic obstacles against the undirected creation of essential cellular systems, the production of biological information from RNA shares many of the same problems as it does from DNA – difficulty of synthesization, chemical fragility in a hostile pre-biotic environment – not to speak of the extreme rarity of RNA molecules that can self-replicate. Consequently, evolutionary biologist, Eugene Koonin, admits "neither the RNA world nor any other materialistic chemical evolutionary hypothesis can account for the origin of life, given the probabilistic resources of the entire universe."[9]

Answering the critics
Shop-worn criticisms of ID include: it invokes an unobservable entity, it is not falsifiable, and it makes no predictions. And Meyer handily rebuts them all.[10]

Reigning scientific theories are rife with entities and

processes that are not observable. In physics, researchers infer unseen gluons, gravitons, inflatons, and a host of fundamental particles from observational data. Meyer makes specific mention of the Higgs boson, an imaginary particle thought to produce the material properties of matter. On top of that, there is a whole category of "virtual" (as opposed to "actual") particles that theorists have concocted to explain otherwise inexplicable phenomena.

The same goes for Darwin's theory of evolution. Not only does Darwinism depend on mutational events and transitional forms that have never been observed, the evolutionary process itself "occur[s] at rates too slow to observe in the present and too fast to have been recorded in the fossil record."

The disciplines of cryptography, archaeology, and criminal forensics also infer unseen (and intelligent!) causes from their material effects: A detective knows that a body with six bullet holes in the back is evidence of murder, not an accidental shooting; an archaeologist who finds "All Cretans are liars" etched in stone can attribute it to another human being, without a moment's reflection about animal scratchings or weathering and erosion; similarly, a computer program, whether written in a series of "1's" and "0's" on a sheet of paper, or in a functional chemical sequence along the DNA spine, is evidence of a programmer.

Falsifying ID is simply a matter of successfully demonstrating that "large amounts of functionally specified information," corresponding to that of the most complex computer codes produced by man, "*do* arise from purely chemical and physical" causes. If that were done, Meyer cedes, ID would be reduced from the "best explanation" to a possible explanation for the origin of life.

Meyer goes on to predict twelve research results should ID theory be true, including: no unintelligent process will demonstrate the ability to create complex specified information; so-called "bad designs", "broken" genes, and "junk" DNA will be shown to have a hidden function or to have been corrupted from their original state; research will further demonstrate the RNA World scenario as implausible; the fossil record will give evidence of large, episodic infusions of information; and "successful" computer simulations of evolution will be shown to be the result of information supplied by programmers.[11]

For the "intellectually fulfilled atheist," Meyer's work comes as bad news, very bad news.

The Bad News of Intelligent Design

Darwinian evolution is the creation story of atheism. It is the tale of *nothing* becoming *everything* through an incremental, unguided process of random change and adaptation. Yet despite its many logical and technical difficulties, not the least of which is explaining how nothing became a "something" to get the whole process started, the narrative has captured the imaginations of a wide spectrum of individuals, religious and non-religious alike.

Today nearly any article or television program, covering any aspect of the natural world, from the eating habits of chimpanzees to the dreams of humans is sure to make mention of "our evolutionary heritage." What's more, phenomena as counterproductive to Darwinian fitness as homosexuality and altruism are increasingly being traced to some evolutionary advantage. It is as if to be taken seriously as a researcher, writer or thinker, one must pay homage to Darwin, no matter how tenuous the connection to the subject matter, or fatuous.

The charm of the tale comes not only in what it has to say about history, but in what it has to say about the future: the eternal struggle for survival will lead to change, change will lead to progress, and progress to perfection.

As the story gained currency, faith in a caring Superintendent began to be displaced by hope in an indifferent, impersonal mechanism of change – "Change we can believe in"; change we *must* believe in, if we reject the antediluvian myth and its Author.

It is no wonder that few phrases in recent memory have provoked as much comment, criticism and derision as "intelligent design."

The fear

Since its introduction into modern lexicons, intelligent design has been called everything from "creationism in a cheap tuxedo" to a "Trojan horse" to a "sham." And those are just some of the printable put-downs.

And ID opprobrium has not been restricted to the fever swamps of atheism. Educators, judges, politicians, scientists, journalists and even Christians have logged withering comments about the science of design. But why the invectives over a non-sectarian enterprise that makes no claims about the identity of the Designer?

Although the proposition of intelligent design is modest -- that certain features of the universe are best explained as the products of intelligence – there is fear that ID and science are mortally locked into a zero-sum game: for ID to win, science must fail. The fear is not unfounded.

Science, properly understood, is a systematic method of empirical investigation, philosophically open, for the acquisition of knowledge. It is the science, modern science, mid-wifed by individuals – Bacon, Ockham, Galileo, Kepler, and Newton – whose openness to an external Source of order, beauty and harmony made possible the game-changing discoveries that led to the Scientific Revolution.

Science, as it has become today, is an investigative enterprise ideologically confined to naturalism, which maintains the world as a material brute fact fully explicable in terms of matter and motion, without appeal to external causes.

For *that* science, ID is bad news.

Bad news for science

Like the pioneers of modern science, the ID investigator is not committed to rules of play and conventions of "good form" aimed at protecting the consensus view. He is free to follow the phenomena wherever they point, whether to chance, law, or intelligence, whether *of* the material world or beyond it.

Unfettered by the groupthink of the scientific establishment, he represents a threat to those for whom Oxford cardiovascular physiologist, Denis Noble, writes "[materialistic science] functions as a security blanket." The security of their paradigm, Noble continues, is that "It avoids the need to ask too many questions, to stare into the abyss of fundamental uncertainty."[12] Yet, sooner or later, that abyss will be encountered.

Over the last several decades, discoveries of the functional elegance and integrated complexity of the universe have made the materialistic underpinning of science increasingly untenable, leaving those so-committed to cede it all to luck or to some, yet to be discovered, final Law which, if found, would itself beg an explanation.

For instance, should an ultimate law be unearthed down that ever-receding shaft of exploration, it would not account for immaterial phenomena like thought, free will, creativity, and aspirations, except as illusions created by the chemical firings of neurons. Likewise, a meta-Law of the universe would neither provide, nor explain, the moral "oughtness" pressing upon the conscience of man.

If it could, humans could no more choose to violate it than they could choose to change their height or blood type. Yet not only do we violate it, we have *feelings* of guilt when we do, suggesting something behind Law, a teleology, a concern about humans and their social dealings... an intelligence. And that is bad news for another group.

Bad news for social engineers

Products of intelligence are engineered to satisfy the functional requirements of the designer. And like any engineered product, they provide optimum benefits when used according to their design and minimum benefits, to detrimental effects, if twisted and pressed into the service of personal desires or popular fashions.

Consider sexuality. According to the theories popularized by Freud, Kinsey and Hefner, sex exists for the fulfillment of personal happiness through the satisfaction of sensual desire, with pregnancy as a byproduct. Even a cursory consideration of design shows that this popular conception has it exactly backwards: Since sexual satisfaction could be realized on a mono-sex planet and only on a heterosexual one could civilization survive past the first generation, it is evident, even through the prism of Darwinism, that reproduction is the purpose of sex, with sensual satisfaction as a byproduct.

Design suggests that the "machine" is not infinitely malleable as Darwinian theories would have it, but fixed with an in-built limit of "flex." And that is bad news for social engineers who view humanity as an intermediary life form in the march to our utopian, transhuman future.

Bad news for the culture of death

Although the outward, visible features of design can tell us important things about an object's purpose, they are not always the whole story.

Imagine a native of a primitive culture happening upon a DVD, loaded with *Microsoft Office*. The thin, flexible, perfectly circular disc of foreign construction would lead the native to conclude it was of unnatural, maybe supernatural origin. Yet nothing about the appearance of the DVD would reveal its rich information content, much less the purpose for which the information was intended.

The same is true of human beings. Although outward appearances may tell us a lot about human nature, there is much more than meets the eye.

Giving consideration only to the material dimension, humans share a genetic code that, while variable from person to person, is distinct from all other living creatures, both in its internal structure and in its external, visible expression. It is the recognition of human exceptionality that inclines most people to acknowledge the superior worth of a person over everything else; even another product of design, like a priceless work of art.

Yet many folks who would never think of discarding an irreparably damaged Monet, have few qualms "discarding" a person who is unborn and unwanted or who has been irreparably damaged through injury or impaired through the onset of age.

The design inference suggests that all persons -- even the least-developed and most-infirmed among us -- have intrinsic value, worthy of vigorous protections against forces that would threaten their lives and welfare. And that is bad news for the culture of death.

For those who have built careers, labs, and reputations on the shoulders of Darwin; for those whose investigative quest is driven by an ideological commitment; for those who want to make peace with "science" and appear reasonable to their peers; for those who are more concerned about protecting orthodoxy than in the pursuit of truth; for those whose hopes for the planet lie in evolution's inexorable march of progress; for those who would litter the road to Utopia with carcasses of the unwanted, the disabled, the aged, and infirmed; and for those who seek escape from the deeper implications of human existence, intelligent design is bad news, very bad news.

For behind every design is a Designer.

Chapter 7

The Designer behind the Design

"He has not left himself without testimony." --St. Luke

"It is easy, it is intuitive, it is natural. It fits our default assumptions about things."
--Psychologist Justin Barrett, concerning belief in God

God: An Invention or Discovery

Belief in God. Sigmund Freud called it a childish fantasy. Bertrand Russell compared it with believing that a celestial teapot was orbiting the earth. Richard Dawkins is fond to say that there are many things he disbelieves: woodland fairies, fire-breathing dragons, and Flying Spaghetti Monsters. God is just one more imaginary being he adds to the list.

Instead of tackling time-tested theological arguments for God, atheist popularizers dismiss him to the realm of elves, trolls, and the Easter Bunny. It's an evasive maneuver that plays well to those inclined to disbelief.

Russell's teapot and Santa's elves are on the long list of things that lack objective evidence, but cannot be emphatically disproved (to do so would require the omniscient perspective under assault). Nevertheless, no clear-headed person accepts them as real. So, the argument goes, the same should hold for God: even though his non-existence cannot be proved, the absence of physical data demands that rational folk place Him alongside other childish myths and imaginary figures.

It's a clever argument, but flawed from the outset.

The orbiting teapot and the Flying Spaghetti Monster are admitted inventions which, like fairies, elves, and Santa Claus, are not necessary beings. That is to say the universe, life, and the fulfillment of man's transcendent yearnings are not contingent upon the existence of such beings. So, while simple and great thinkers alike have been entertained by the exploits of Odysseus and Peter Pan, they have been transformed by the story of God.

But could God also be an invention borne out of human need and fear? Sociologist Rodney Stark presents evidence to the contrary.

The Axial Age
In his book, *Discovering God,* [1] Stark identifies a "big bang" that occurred in the sixth century BC. No, it wasn't the cosmic explosion of a supernova; it was a spiritual explosion that led to a constellation of religious movements. In the mere span of one hundred years, civilization witnessed the rise of Zoroastrianism, Orphism, Jainism, Buddhism, Taoism, Confucianism, the "new" Hinduism, and post-exilic Judaism.

Added to the sudden appearance of these faiths was the introduction of new and shared theological concepts. Doctrines of transcendent morality, sin, the afterlife, and salvation, hitherto unknown, were common among the new religions. Why the explosion and commonality?

Stark attributes it to "survival of the fittest." Writes Stark, "Humans will tend to adopt and retain those elements of culture that appear to produce 'better' results, while those that appear less rewarding will be discarded." That applies equally to concepts of God which, observes Stark, incline toward deities who are rational, loving and limitless in scope and power.

Even in the earliest cultures--amid animism, naturism and totemism--there was belief in high Gods: eternal, all-knowing and all-powerful creator-deities who established a moral order and kept an eye on the affairs of mortals. Contrary to the notion that primitives embraced a hodgepodge of superstitions, many had a more advanced concept of God than those who came later.

The devolving of religion
With the rise of civilization, people began moving away from high Gods toward polytheism. It reflected their desire for gods that were more approachable. The Greeks, Sumerians, Egyptians, Mayans and Aztecs had a rich assortment of deities with limited, specialized powers. Not only were these new gods more human-like, they were less morally demanding than the gods of yore.

In fact, the gods of the pantheon lacked any concern for moral behavior, as evidenced by their petulance and penchant for puerile pranks. Their only interest in human matters was the worship and devotion owed them. Hence, with the rise of polytheism, the moral dimension of religion was eclipsed by elaborate systems of ritual and sacrifice.

Because famine, flood, plague, and other disasters were taken as judgments for neglecting the gods, religion became a matter of national security and welfare. To ensure that divine appeasement was properly attended, despot rulers built temples and installed professional priests, creating "state" religions where public involvement was not only unnecessary but discouraged, being reserved for members of the noblesse. Also discouraged, was competition from outside religions.

But temple faiths had little to offer commoners other than the distinct "privilege" of financially supporting the religious activities of the elites. Consequently, in contrast to religions in an open spiritual marketplace, these theocratic religions tended to receive low levels of public commitment. That's because, as Stark observes, "pluralism is the natural state of any religious economy." Nowhere was pluralism more evident than in the Roman Empire

Plural Rome
Early Rome played host to a plethora of religions, none of which received any appreciable state subsidies. Greek and Roman polytheism, Judaism, Zoroastrianism and smatterings of new religious movements comprised a brisk religious economy. In this pluralistic, non-subsidized economy, rival faiths were forced to compete for market share.

Hence, unlike its earlier versions, polytheistic faiths in Rome invited public involvement and depended on public support. At the same time, they were burdened by the same shortcomings: gods who were limited in power and, despite being more human-like, were generally unconcerned with the plights of men, providing no principles by way of rule or example for human dignity, moral behavior, or spiritual fulfillment.

This was a time when popular interest in existential questions had piqued, where up to half of the populace were slaves and women had few legal rights. This created a perfect storm for more humanistic and salvific faiths. The tempest had been building for several centuries.

Prepping the soil

After a long hiatus, monotheism began its comeback. In the sixth century BC, belief in an uncreated eternal, omnipotent and beneficent God, was introduced to the Persian Empire through the combined influence of Jewish exiles and the teachings of Zoroaster. Common in these two religious streams were the concepts of one true God who is both creator and sustainer, the existence of good and evil, individual moral responsibility, an afterlife, and the eternal consequences of personal choices.

Further east, doctrines of good and evil and the importance of right moral actions (karma) were introduced by several concurrent movements: Taoism, Confucianism, Jainism, Buddhism and a revamped Hinduism. In contrast to the moral muteness of traditional polytheism, each of these religions addressed man's irrepressible need to know "How now shall we live?", with the latter three advancing doctrines of a meritable afterlife.

Moral codes, sin, salvation and life-after-death were revolutionary discoveries that prepped the soil for Christianity.

The rise of the Christian faith

The early appeal of Christianity came from a message that was attractive and accessible to all people regardless of state or status. Novel teachings about human dignity, social responsibility, and love of fellowman created followers whose lifestyles were fetchingly distinct from their pagan counterparts.

In a culture endemically indifferent to the disadvantaged, "Christians," writes Stark, "created a miniature welfare state in an empire which for the most part lacked social services." Their care for the poor, widows, orphans and sick extended beyond their own to the wider community. This was particularly evident in the second and third centuries when plagues ravaged the empire. To hearts that had been yearning for a caring God, the lives of Christians became a convincing argument that such a God exists.

New York Times columnist, David Brooks, points to the revolution in morals brought about by the Gospels – namely, a "shift from a desire for power to a desire for sacrificial love. Even speaking as a historian of ideas, culture, and behavior," Brooks notes, "that was a radical revolution that created a radical counter culture."[2]

Little wonder that, by the fourth century, the Christian population grew to become the majority in Rome and other principle cities of the Aegean world.

Invention or revelation?
Secular historians are fond to point out the many similarities of Christianity with pagan religions: ritual cannibalism (associated with the Eucharist), Olympian deities impregnating human women to sire half-gods, and dying and rising Corn-Kings. The commonality, they argue, is proof of human invention. Rodney Stark offers another interpretation.

Assuming that God reveals himself, these early undeveloped myths would be expected from a principle of "divine accommodation," by which God-talk is limited to what humans in their present capacity can grasp. C.S. Lewis saw it the same way.

To Lewis, myth at its best is a penumbra of divine light that inspires the human imagination about the true nature of things—much of which is stamped onto the design of nature.

Myths about the Corn-King abound because of the natural pattern of life, death and new life which presages the "*real* Corn-King who will die once and rise once at Jerusalem." Lewis writes, "We pass from a Balder or an Osiris, dying nobody knows when or where, to a historical person...*under Pontius Pilate.*" He concludes, "We must not be nervous about 'parallels' and 'pagan Christs': they *ought* to be there—it would be a stumbling block if they weren't."[3]

Faced with a multitude of disparate religious doctrines, how does one distinguish human fabrication from divine revelation? Stark gives two criteria.

The first is *consistency*. Faiths whose doctrines deviate from a consistent core "can be relegated to human origin." Stark sees little compatibility among most religions. Some believe the universe was created; others insist it is uncreated. Although most religions acknowledge the existence of God, there are widely varied doctrines about the number Gods, their nature, and the duty owed them. There is little agreement on the afterlife. For some, it's a conscious state of bliss, for others it's an impersonal state of non-existence.

The other criterion is *increased complexity*. According to the principle of divine accommodation, revelation should become increasingly sophisticated, telling us more, not less, about God over time.

By those measures, the monotheistic religions stand out. The exception is Islam. Its doctrine of Allah as capricious and unknowable makes Islam theologically regressive. But it is also morally regressive. With an evangelistic mission to spread the faith "by the sword," Islam is a throwback to the ancient theocratic religions.

Judaism, Zoroastrianism and Christianity, on the other

hand, share fundamental beliefs about the nature of man, God, and creation. And, in contrast to Islam, they involve a progression from divine "baby talk" to the revelation of Christianity's comprehensive belief system with the *complexities* of the Trinity, substitutionary atonement, and other-centered love, embedded in a historical context corroborated by multiple means.

The Word in Multimedia

Contrary to the things of fantasy and fancy, God is not silent. From creation onward, he has spoken, broadcasting his message in six ways.

The apostle Paul wrote that "faith comes from hearing the message." To a first century audience, to hear meant more than audile reception; it meant to *understand.* Paul went on to explain that hearing was accomplished "through the word of Christ."[4]

In Christian circles the "Word" is generally associated with the 66 books of the bible. But as used in Scripture, it more generally refers to the revelation of God -- whether directly by him or indirectly through some aspect of his creation. What's more, as attested in scripture, the Word encompasses more "teaching, rebuking, correcting and training."[5]

The psalmist says that by God's word "were the heavens made."[6] The author of Hebrews writes that the word of God judges, discerns, and sustains all things. Jesus says His word is life-giving. When the apostle John refers the "Word," he uses a Greek concept (*logos*) for the ultimate source of rational order and knowledge. These attributes suggest something that cannot be fully communicated within the limitations of human language. In *A Footnote to All Prayers,* C.S. Lewis wrote that all prayers blaspheme because they are symbols for things that are inexpressible.[7]

Indeed, while God's word is contained in scripture, it is not bounded by the material properties of ink and paper or fully comprehensible through human linguistic conventions. Paul's testimony that "the Spirit himself intercedes for us with groans that words cannot express," reveals that pure divine thought transcends physical expression.[8]

That is why Scripture attests to six aspects of God's word, accessed through the physical, rational, social, and spiritual domains of the human experience. They are like the threads of a tapestry that come together to tell a story that engages the heart, soul, mind, and body of our humanness. Below is a brief summary that will be expanded in the following sections.

The Created Word

"The heavens declare the glory of God; the skies proclaim the work of his hands. Day after day they pour forth speech; night after night they display knowledge."[9]

The Psalmist speaks of the "Created Word"--the four-dimensional fabric of the sensible world breathed into existence by the utterance of God. From the infinitesimal to the infinite, God's "voice" reverberates throughout his creation. Its design, in integrated and functional complexity, bears evidence of the Designer. Its grandeur and expanse give testimony to his eternality and omnipotence. Its rational order and exquisite beauty attest to his omniscience and benevolence. Creation is a tangible witness to God accessible to all people.

The Imprinted Word

"Let us make man in our image."[10]

The book of Genesis reveals that mankind carries a marker's-mark--the *Imago Dei*, God's image. Part of that "mark" is the transcendent yearning Solomon referred to when he wrote that God has "set eternity in the hearts of men."[6] C.S. Lewis called it our "God-shaped hole." Another part is our rational and moral agency, as suggested in the words of St. John: *"[He is] the true light that gives light to every man was coming into the world.*"[11]

The "Imprinted Word", stamped on every person, includes the irrepressible drive to fill a longing that can only be filled by God, the light of reason that enables us to apprehend the universe and our place in it, and the light of conscience—our internal sense of oughtness that alternately defends and accuses us. The universality of the Imprinted Word across time and culture is evidence of its transcendent origin.

The Written Word
"All Scripture is God-breathed and is useful for teaching, rebuking, correcting and training in righteousness." [12]

God's activity in and beyond time is recorded in the "Written Word" of scripture. In 66 books penned by 44 authors over sixteen hundred years, the Written Word is a narrative told in two parts. The first part deals with a nation and God's relationship with it; the second part centers on a Person and the church he established. In preview and review, the "Written Word" tells of God's redemption of the human race through Jesus Christ. In so doing, it lays a belief system that is logically coherent, corresponds to reality, and has proven capable of filling our "God-shaped hole."

The Incarnate Word
"The Word became flesh and made his dwelling among us… □No one has ever seen God, but God the One and Only, who is at the Father's side, has made him known."[13]

Jesus Christ is the fullest revelation of God through his words and works. As opposed to the remote, indifferent deities of paganism, the "Incarnate Word" is a personal God who takes great interest in his creation. So much so, that He entered the world in human form to walk in our shoes and experience temptation, hunger, and rejection before suffering the penalty for our guilt. He is an Advocate who, because he took on human flesh, empathizes with our failings and sufferings. The "Incarnate Word" is the most compelling evidence of God's limitless love.

The Indwelling Word

"But the Counselor, the Holy Spirit, whom the Father will send in my name, will teach you all things and will remind you of everything I have said to you." [14]

There is perhaps no Christian doctrine less understood than the Holy Spirit. And yet, as Paul tells us, it is exclusively by him that a person comes to confess "Jesus is Lord." At that point, the Spirit takes up residence in the heart and mind of the believer. The "Indwelling Word" is the ever-present Comforter and Counselor who launches a life-long process of transformation in the citizens of the Kingdom. The otherworldly change in the lives of Christians has caused even their critics to wonder, "Look how they love one another."

The Corporate Word

"His intent was that now, through the church, the manifold wisdom of God should be made known to the rulers and authorities in the heavenly realms." [15]

The invisible body of individuals across space and time who profess Jesus as Lord is the Church. As the incarnation of Christ between the cross and second coming, the "Corporate Word" advances God's kingdom by shaping culture and leading people to saving faith and holy living. The transformational impact of Christ's image-bearers on society, and their care for the "least" and the "last," is a testimony to the world-changing message of God.

A Divine Tapestry

Contrary to popular criticism, God has given ample evidence of his existence. The Created Word, Imprinted Word, Written Word, Incarnate Word, Indwelling Word, and Corporate Word are interwoven threads of a divine tapestry that reveals the nature of Nature and what can be known about Nature's God.

"For since the creation of the world God's invisible qualities--his eternal power and divine nature --have been clearly seen, being understood from what has been made, so that men are without excuse"[16]

The Word of Creation: *the physical world*

Among religious critics, God is a myth whose origin is traced to the irrational fears and superstitions of man. Beyond the imaginings of weak and gullible people, His existence is nil. For the believer, God is as real as maternal love.

A mother's love is not a material object subject to scientific analysis, yet it is communicated in material ways establishing a rational basis for belief. The same is true for God. Although the Creator is not a part of the physical world, he has nonetheless revealed himself through it. Like the artisan whose choices of media, colors and brush stokes are his signature, God has created a masterpiece writing his name in every corner of the canvas.

God's masterpiece is "The Created Word"— the corporeal fabric of spacetime through which the Divine will is expressed. Of the various ways that God communicates, the Created Word is one, of two, that speaks to every person, directly.

In combination with the "Imprinted Word"--man's inborn spiritual, rational and moral faculties--the Created Word comprises "general revelation." It is general because it is *universally* accessible. Furthermore, it is *directly* accessible. In contrast to sacred texts, teachings, and traditions that come through human agents, the Created Word issues directly from God for every ear to hear and eye to see.

A challenge

I was once challenged to defend this claim by a religious skeptic who asked me to provide an example in the physical world that is explained by Christianity.

Without hesitation, I cited the internal workings of the atom. I explained that because leading scientists, past and present, acknowledge that nature's innermost region is fundamentally unknowable, the "guiding hand of God" is as reasonable an explanation as any. I added that the stability of the atom, matter, and the material world, are strongly attested to in scripture (e.g., Hebrews 1:3 and Colossians 1:17).

My example didn't go unchallenged. The interlocutor granted that "God" could be conjectured, but how is He the *best* explanation for quantum phenomena. Moreover, how could a particle physicist distinguish the work of the Christian God from a pagan deity?

The *best* explanation

I responded that according to field theory, the quantum potential is thought to be the fabric of spacetime, an invisible gossamer web of unimaginable energy that fills and fuels the cosmic expanse, giving birth to exotic particles that continuously emerge and disappear within the folds of the cosmic fabric.

These characteristics suggest a cause that is not only omnipresent and omnipotent, but transcendent. I brought the admission of quantum physicist Henry Stapp, "Everything we know about Nature is in accord with the fundamental process of Nature that lies outside of space-time,"[17] adding that even multiverse theories depend on transcendent causes as they involve processes and events that occur beyond the borders of our universe.

I went on to explain that the "gods" of pantheism, although omnipresent, are not transcendent or omnipotent; those of bare monotheistic traditions, like Islam, are transcendent and omnipotent, but not immanent; and those of ancient polytheism, are none of those, being nothing more than Olympian heroes who exhibited the same flaws and foibles as their earthly counterparts. Only the Christian God is all three, the One who is "over all, through all and in all"[18] and by whom "all things were made."[19]

At this point the skeptic objected that if a supernatural agency was at work, it ought to be scientifically verifiable. It's a common, and logically flawed, charge.

If the supernatural could be explained by naturalistic science, it wouldn't be supernatural. It is right to expect that a world created by supernatural Benevolence is governed by laws that make life predictable. But since those laws are fashioned by Supernature and not the other way around, Supernature can never be reduced to the orderly patterns observed.

While Supernature interlocks *with* nature and, at times, manifests itself *in* nature to give us a sudden, unexpected glimpse, it has no obligation to conform to the laws *of* nature. Thus, if we are honest, we would expect a barrier to our investigative pursuit—a point beyond which we could probe no further. And that is exactly what we find.

Although our analytical journey ends in opacity and mystery, we have discovered laws that enable us to build skyscrapers, launch satellites, and surf the internet. And, in the process, we've noticed some very peculiar things about our cosmic home.

With us in mind

Imagine driving cross-country and stopping in a town you've never been. Gritty, tired and hungry, you look for a motel, and then,

"There's one! Just beyond that stop light." The sign reads, "VACANCY."

You pull up, check in, and take the key card.

"Room 1028. That's my birthday, October 28th. Now that's weird!"

Upon opening the door, your jaw goes slack.

A copy of your favorite painting, Van Gogh's "Avenue of the Poplars in Autumn," is hanging on the wall; your favorite aria, "Mio Babbino Cara," is playing on the radio; there's a basket stuffed with all of your favorite snacks; the complimentary toiletries are the exclusive brands that you buy; and spread out on the coffee table are the latest editions of *Golf Digest*, *Numismatist News* and *Skeptic*—periodicals that you had been waiting anxiously to read back home.

The set of coincidences is so unlikely that any reasonable person would assume that the motel staff knew you were coming. And yet the coincidences in our cosmic home are far greater in number and in precision. In fact, researchers have identified dozens of features that have to be just the way they are for life to exist.

For example, the formation of stars depends on a narrow range of values for the gravitational and nuclear forces; and without stars, there would be no habitable planets. The formation of atoms hinges on the strength of electromagnetism and the masses of the electron, proton and neutron. If these were varied by more than a small amount, chemistry and biological life would not be possible. Astronomer Hugh Ross has cataloged nearly 60 fined-tuned conditions necessary for life, including many involving our solar system such as,

- The size, temperature, and brightness of our sun
- The size, chemical composition, and orbit of the Earth
- The fact that we have one moon and not more or less
- The distance of the Earth from the sun
- The Earth's axial tilt and rotational period
- The time it takes the Earth to orbit the sun

The odds that all 60 could come together by chance is 1 in 10^{60}(that's 1 followed by 60 zeros!), about the same chance as landing heads on 200 consecutive coin flips.[20]

On top of that, our position in the universe—not too close to the center of the Milky Way and not too far out, and nestled between two of its spiral arms—is the ideal location for making astronomical observations and discoveries. Some have dared called Earth, the "privileged planet."

We are left with one of two conclusions: our *Goldilocks* home is a happenstance of mind-numbing improbability, or it is a creation meticulously crafted by Someone who had us in mind.

> *He who created the heavens,*
>   *he is God;*
>   *he who fashioned and made the earth,*
>   *he founded it;*
>   *he did not create it to be empty,*
>   *but formed it to be inhabited*
> *He says,*
>   *"I am the Lord*
>   *And there is no other."* [21]

Next, we will examine the evidence from biology.

"Biologists must constantly keep in mind that what they see was not designed, but rather evolved." Francis Crick

The Word of Creation: the living world

Life is the most awe-inspiring feature of the universe. Living things have the unique abilities to metabolize, grow, reproduce, and respond and adapt to their environment. Discovering how the universe "went live" is the sacred grail of origin-of-life studies.

Nearly 150 years ago, Charles Darwin put forward a theory of life involving innumerable, small changes accumulated over geologic periods of time. Through the holy trinity of random variation, adaptation and natural selection, the tree of life sprouted and grew with ever-increasing diversity and complexity. Today's life forms are branches that won out over their neighboring limbs in the fierce competition for sun and sap.

While Darwin explained the *survival* of species, what many people don't realize, he never explained the *arrival* of species. His theory assumed the existence of a common ancestor from which all living organisms descended. Darwin wrote his celebrated, *On the Origin of Species*, at a time when the biological cell was thought to have the complexity of grandma's homemade jelly. But that notion would change.

A cellular factory
Over the next century, advances in electron microscopy and x-ray diffraction revealed a structure beyond anything Darwin could have imagined.

As it turned out "grandma's jelly" is packed with data storage media, information processors, molecular machines, transcription devices, and error correction systems. Inside a bubble of microscopic dimensions a genetic code directs the assembly and repair of cellular components. Even more amazing, each cell is encoded with addresses, routing directions, and instructions for assembling into one of 200 cells types.

In essence, the living cell is a tiny, self-sustaining biological factory.

Imagine discovering an unmanned space station that 1) manufacturers the equipment it needs to probe deep space, 2) monitors damage done to it by asteroids, 3) repairs the damage, 4) constructs its own spare parts, 4) makes copies of itself and 5) directs those copies in an intergalactic network to optimize exploration. Would any straight-thinking person reason it to be the product of an unguided, haphazard process? Hardly.

And yet the engineering of the biological cell is equally astonishing—down to its most fundamental component, DNA.

Complex Specified Information
As we saw in the previous chapters, DNA is the famous double-helix structure that contains the instructions for life. Functioning like the hard disk on your computer, DNA stores the software that controls the construction and maintenance of biological systems.

Cell instructions are written using a chemical "alphabet" of four base molecules--adenine (A), cytosine (C), guanine (G) and thymine (T)--segmented according to functional units called, genes. The complete code consists of hundreds to tens of thousands of genes which, in turn, consist of thousands to hundreds of thousands of letters. Even the smallest organism requires nearly one million molecules to "spell out" all of the necessary instructions.

Each molecule attaches to the strand in identical fashion, which means that the DNA sequence, like letters in a sentence, is not determined by its chemistry.

As Lincoln's *Gettysburg Address* is not reducible to the chemical reactions between ink and paper, neither is the "complex specified information" (CSI) of DNA a product of chemical laws. That leaves two options: blind chance or design.

However, as shown in Chapter 4, even considering the age of our universe there hasn't been enough time to allow for the formation of the most elemental cell.

So if CSI is inexplicable by natural laws or chance, it must be a product of design. In fact, the evidence for design is so overwhelming that atheist and DNA co-discoverer, Francis Crick warned: "Biologists must constantly keep in mind that what they see was not designed, but rather evolved." [22] Somewhere George Orwell can be heard clearing his throat.

Irreducible Complexity
From genes to organisms, life also exhibits "irreducible complexity" (IC). A system is irreducibly complex if it has multiple interacting components which are essential for the system to function.

At the genetic level, DNA depends on amino acids and proteins which, themselves, are manufactured by DNA. At the cellular level, cell survival depends on a membrane, DNA, RNA, and assorted cellular machinery. At its most fundamental level, life exhibits an interdependency that cannot be explained by gradualism.

Moving up to organs--the eye, blood clotting and the

bacterium flagellum are examples of IC. Each depends on a host of integrated parts which, if any is missing, render the system non-functional.

For instance, the flagellum is a motorized propulsion system made up of 40 different proteins enabling a bacterium to navigate in its aquatic environment. Its onboard components include a stator, rotor, bushings, U-joint, and a propeller that can turn over 1000 rpm and reverse directions in one-quarter revolution. The flagellum is, as Harvard biologist Howard Berg describes it, "the most efficient machine in the universe."[23] Let that sink in for a moment.

For the Darwinian faithful the flagellum is a big problem. Any organism whose fitness depends on 40 integrated, co-existent parts spells trouble for gradualism. However, after years scrambling to keep this pillar of faith from crumbling, evolutionary scientists made a discovery.

They found that the needle-like structure of *Salmonella* used to infect healthy cells was made up of seven proteins identical to those in the flagellum. The similarity was taken as evidence that the two systems evolved from a common ancestor, and that a partial flagellum *could* have had a viable function during its evolutionary development.

My mountain bike shares many similarities with my *Ford Escape*: both have wheels, brakes, and gears and are made of a metal frame. Yet, who would dare suggest that given enough time, the creative effects of quantum jitters, cosmic rays, and wind erosion could combine to morph my bike into an SUV? And an SUV comes nowhere close to being "the most efficient machine in the universe."

Combined Specified Complexity

Living organisms also depend on numerous functional systems—each, irreducibly complex--for survival. Because of "combined specified complexity" (CSC), a dog can enjoy a long dog life without its tail, but it won't survive a moment without a central nervous system, heart, lungs or brain.

According to Darwin, land creatures began their evolutionary journey in the sea. To survive in water, they needed gills, but to move to land they needed lungs. A fish with lungs would drown, but a mammal with gills would suffocate. And that's only one of over 50,000 morphological changes needed for the transition.

Because of the glacial pace of evolution, Darwin's theory is difficult-to-impossible to verify. In fact, the only changes that have ever been observed are small-scale variations due to genetic inheritance and adaptation; otherwise known as *micro-evolution*. But one place where large-scale changes (*macro-evolution*) should be demonstrable is in the microbiology lab. There researchers have access to billions of organisms whose rapid replication allows follow-up for many thousands of generations. One such organism is *Plasmodium falciparum,* the single-celled parasite responsible for malaria.

For several decades, researchers have studied *plasmodium falciparum*, applying various environmental pressures to see how it responds. Yet after trillions upon trillions of replications—many more than occurred in the putative evolution of fish to mammals— the bacterium never evolved into a multi-celled organism. It remained what it had always been: a single-celled parasite which, in some cases, developed a resistance to anti-biotic drugs.

Similar results have been obtained with other microbes and drosophila. While none of these studies disprove Darwinism, they are strongly contraindicative of its macro-evolutionary claims.

Richard Dawkins once wrote, "Biology is the study of complicated things that give the appearance of having been designed for a purpose."[24] Maybe that's because, to the unbiased seeker of truth, they have been designed for a purpose. Indeed, even Francis Crick was forced to admit, "An honest man, armed with all the knowledge available to us now, could only state that in some sense, the origin of life appears at the moment to be a miracle." [25]

That was over thirty years ago, and all the knowledge we have accumulated hence, has only made those "appearances" look all the more actual.

The Word of Creation -- Information and Language

It is said that if you really want to know an artist, don't read his biography, study his art. Whether it is a painting, drawing, or sculpture artwork says something not only about its subject, but its creator as well.

One evening I was watching an episode of the *Antiques Roadshow*, when a furniture expert was presented a rather unexceptional-looking table. I'm no carpenter, much less an accomplished woodworker, but the table struck me as something I could put together in an afternoon in my garage. The piece was unimpressively simple with no decorative embellishments and no maker's mark; yet the expert identified it, on the spot, as the work of George Nakashima, an innovative furniture maker of the last century. Cradled in that unadorned, unmarked piece of wood was information sufficient to identify the craftsman with the certainty of a DNA analysis. I was duly impressed.

The universe is also a crafted work and, as scientists have plumbed its depths and probed its expanse, they have marveled at its information-richness.

From the eerie behavior of subatomic particles, communicating instantly over galactic distances, to the biological software of cellular machinery, to the host of delicately-balanced parameters that govern the cosmos, information, as scientists are coming to learn, is the fundamental ingredient of the universe. Physicist John Archibald Wheeler once put it this way, "Every physical quantity derives its ultimate significance from bits, binary yes-or-no indications."[26] In computer-ese, that's information.

Paradoxically, the fundamental ingredient of the material world *is not* material. While its transmission depends on material means – sound waves, electromagnetic signals, ink and paper, photographic images, and the like – information itself neither consists, nor is a product of matter.

Consider the cells of our body. During the course of a normal life span, every cell in the body, including the brain, is replaced many times over. The molecules that make up our bodies are undergoing constant change and, yet, those changes have no commensurate effect on the instructions that govern cell activity, or our personal library of knowledge, memories, beliefs, and aspirations.

The existence of information is evidence that reality is more than matter moving under the influence of physical forces: at the root of nature is order, an order we neither invented nor imposed. So where did it come from?

In the beginning
When the apostle John wrote "In the beginning was the Word," he was revealing something elementary about the Creator and his creation: God is a communicator whose handiwork, like the Nakashima table, contains no artist stamp, but teems with information made intelligible, , through *words*.

We think in terms of words. We process our feelings with words. Words are information carriers which, when vocabularized and governed by rules of grammar, form language, the organizing structure of information. Words and language are in-built into creation itself. As the Psalmist writes,

"The heavens *declare* the glory of God; the skies

proclaim the work of his hand. Day after day they pour forth *speech*; night after night they display knowledge. There is no *speech or language* where their voice is not heard. Their *voice* goes out into all of the earth, their *words* to the ends of the world."[27]

The information built *into* creation is communicated *by* creation through words and language. The logocentric creation reflects its logocentric Creator who, with three words, "Let there be," filled the void and turned chaos into cosmos, giving form and order to what was formless, making it intelligible. He is no detached deity who begets and forgets as he moves on to other divine amusements. Instead, with three more words, "Let us make," he fashions a pair of intelligent beings to tend his creation and enjoy fellowship with him.

Unlike the rest of creation, the proto-couple come factory-equipped with language. No sooner are they formed from the dust of the earth, than Adam and Eve are given instructions and, from the get-go, understand how they relate to their earthly home and their moral duties. They recognize and make sense of relationships. More on that in a moment.

Adam promptly puts his language skills to use in naming the flora and fauna; Eve uses hers in the epic *tete-a-tete* with the Serpent. All this, mind you, without ever having had to diagram a sentence, memorize a vocab list, or endure a course in earth science.

The story of Genesis opens with the Creator creating an intelligible world with intelligent beings endowed with a tool – language -- enabling them to apprehend, communicate and use information.

Relationships galore
Language presupposes *relationships*: true and knowable correlations between objects and subjects, causes and

effects, sensory inputs and human perceptions, man and his environment, matter and energy, forces and the objects they affect. The arresting successes of science and the practical utility of mathematics confirm that there *is* congruence between what is, and what can be known. Real and cognizable relationships make our universe comprehensible.

That realization has provoked comments from the palace guard of scientism that would set off any "baloney detector" within shouting distance. Consider this from Princeton physicist and Nobel laureate, Steven Weinberg: "The more the universe seems comprehensible, the more it also seems pointless." [28]

Comprehensibility suggests point-*less*-ness? To the contrary; comprehensibility is evidence of point-*ed*-ness – purpose, goals, ends. For example, gravitational phenomena *point to* the purpose of objects to follow the contours of spacetime, quantum behaviors *point to* the purpose of matter stability, and DNA coding instructions *point to* the purpose of cell function and assembly. Teleology forms the warp and woof of the universe.

Dr. Weinberg is flummoxed to explain how all this teleology came about from a non-intelligent process -- so it is "pointless." This is an uneasy Article of Faith that he *has* to accept if he's to keep divine fingers off the machine.

A divine gift
The pre-eminent relationship presupposed by language is that between creation and Creator. As intelligent design theorist, William Dembski writes, "Human language is a divine gift for helping us to understand the world and by understanding the world to understand God himself." [29]

Language enables intelligent beings to say intelligent things about the intelligible world they inhabit; it points

224

to an immaterial reality, and a Source of intelligence who desires to be known. Human knowledge is not confined to the Kantian sensible world; humans can know and say meaningful things about the super-sensible world, as well. In this unified schema of reality, the knowledge-building power of language is immense, as was evident at the dawn of civilization.

From language to tongues

Within a few generations of the Flood, a universal language enabled the descendents of Noah to build the World Trade Center of Babylonia. Aiming to "make a name" for themselves, they laid the foundations of a megalopolis in the plain of Shinar. The enterprise was a double affront to God. Not only were they shirking God's command to "fill the earth," their monolithic tower was a bid to achieve divine-like status through human effort.

The divine response was quick and effective. The language God had given Adam and Eve was atomized into a multitude of "tongues," thwarting communication and putting an end to the ambitious urban project. Thus began a deepening of the alienation man had experienced with the Fall.

With no common language, mankind was forced into tongue-centered enclaves. Enclaves became cultures which, over time, became increasingly isolated from each other with their own set of social customs, conventions, and values. Within each culture, language, which had created culture, was being changed *by* culture: Still under the conviction that truth existed and could be apprehended through language, new words, and new meanings to old words, were introduced reflecting changes in cultural needs, attitudes and beliefs.

But the malleability of language and the relativization of truth gradually led to the denial of language as a carrier of meaning. According to the late deconstructionist, Jacques Derrida, a linguistic expression is nothing more than a string of characters with no fixed truth content or relevance. Ironically, Derrida, and his fellow deconstructionists, spent decades writing libraries of books and essays, filled with, uh, language, to educate the logocentric masses with the "truth content " of their philosophy.

From Eden to the philosophy wing of modern universities, language is a gift that ever points to the Giver. The Lord of Hosts is also the Lord of language, whose gift is given that we may have fellowship with him and, in fellowship, know him.

The Imprinted Word

Social scientists have long recognized that man's thirst for God is as universal as his thirst for drink. Although the particular God he believes in, like the brand of drink he prefers, is influenced by cultural factors (nurture), the spiritual impulse is intrinsic to his nature.

Which brings up the question beneath the question: "What is the *nature* of man's nature?" As the Psalmist asked -- and philosophers, mystics, and reflective thinkers of every age have pondered -- "What is man that you are mindful of him?" [30]

Is man a stimulus-response organism that won-out over his knuckle-dragging neighbors on the exit from the savannah; is he a robotic machine blindly programmed by "selfish genes"; or is he a free-willed being created by God?

In the biblical account, God infuses a clump of clay with "the breath of life" to create beings in His image. That suggests something immaterial about our humanness. The scriptures associate the incorporeal faculties of heart, mind, and conscience with our "spirit." For it is there that our religious yearning (heart), rational ability (mind), and moral compass (conscience) dwell -- each a part of our divine imprint.

Heart

When Solomon wrote "He has also set eternity in the hearts of men; yet they cannot fathom what God has done from beginning to end," he was revealing something fundamental about our humanness: We have an intrinsic longing for Transcendence.[6] For centuries hence, many thinkers have agreed.

Augustine, in the classic work *Confessions*, wrote "Thou hast made us for thyself, and our hearts are restless till they rest in thee." Others, like Pascal and C.S. Lewis, have written about a spiritual desire that is pressing and inborn. The desire is so universal that evolutionary scientists scramble to explain it.

Take Dean Hamer, for instance. Hamer is a microbiologist for the *National Cancer Institute* who characterizes humans as "a bunch of chemical reactions running around in a bag." In his book, *The God Gene: How Faith is Hardwired into Our Genes*, Hamer writes about a study indicating that religious beliefs are pre-dispositioned based on what chemicals are present in the brain -- chemicals that derive from certain molecular sequences in our DNA some have called, the "God gene."[31] If Hamer is right, I'm sure that other genes account for his belief about "a bunch of chemical reactions running around in a bag."

The not-so subtle implication is that man's spiritual leanings are not rooted in objective reality, but in an arrangement of molecules produced by a blind, unguided process of nature. Or, to put it another way, "eternity" is set in man's genes by evolution, rather than in his heart by God.

C.S. Lewis saw it differently.

Lewis observed that all of man's desires (for food, drink, love, sex, and so on) are rooted in things that actually exist; therefore, the most logical conclusion is that man's desire for transcendence also derives from something that exists: God.

Whether the object of our longings is carnal gratification or eternal significance, our desires are ever-prodding us

228

for fulfillment. To determine how and under what circumstances to satisfy them, we use another faculty of our spirit: the mind.

Mind

While the heart is the seat of our yearnings, affections and emotions, the mind is the center for thought, reflection, and imagination. Through its cognitive abilities, the mind sifts sensory input, analyzes problems, devises solutions, foresees outcomes, and imagines what could be. It enables us to unravel mysteries in the universe that make life in this world livable, while allowing us to dream about a better world, another world.

In the book of Job, Elihu states, "It is the spirit in man, the breath of the Almighty that gives him understanding."[32]That reveals another fundamental truth about our nature: Our mental functions take place in an immaterial "substance" (mind) imparted to us by God.

Yet, to scientific materialists like Dean Hamer, mind and brain are one in the same—a hunk of thinking matter cobbled together by evolution. And human thought? Just atoms and molecules bumping around our cerebral cortex according to the laws of physics and chemistry.

With thoughts reducible to physical laws and chemicals, free will and independent action are illusions. On the down side, man is but a slavish machine of nature. On the up side, all of his thoughts (and even dreams) are open to investigation. Imagine a spectrographic analysis on Einstein's brain revealing his unpublished thoughts on unified field theory, or a crime solved with brain scans of the victim and suspects, or, better yet, a crime solved *before* it happens.

That's the thread of 2004 film, *Minority Report*. The story takes place in a not-to-distant future when technology has yielded a nearly fool-proof method of eliminating crime: the ability to analyze neurochemistry to preemptively prosecute those who *would have* committed a crime.

The idea that we are automatons whose destinies are fatalistically determined by embedded laws, chafes against everything we "can't not know" about ourselves: We are free-willed beings who bear personal responsibility for our choices—which are neither pre-determined nor illusionary, but real.

The passions of our *heart* are processed by the intellect of our *mind*, but our choices and actions are weighed in the balance of *conscience*. Even Freud acknowledged this tripartite relationship in his theory of human nature: The *id* (man's animal instinct), is controlled by the *ego* (man's rational intellect) which comes under the influence of the *superego* (cultural mores).

Whether it's called "conscience" or "superego", study after study confirms what all of us inherently know: There is an "oughtness" that continually presses upon us.

Conscience
Evolutionary scientist James Q. Wilson identified common motifs of oughtness: sympathy, fairness, self-control, and duty. Psychologist Martin Seligman cited a 70-nation study concluding that wisdom, courage, love, temperance, spirituality, and transcendence span human culture from Greenland to the Masai.[33] C.S. Lewis wrote about a law, he called the *Tao*, which was core of the Jewish Decalogue and embedded in all cultures throughout time.

We co-habit a globe with over seven billion neighbors embracing thousands of religions and scores of governmental styles. We are at odds over which of these social systems is best, yet we are in unanimous agreement on a code which, contrary to the tenets of

Darwinism, requires both self-restraint and self-sacrifice.

"Darwin's Bulldog," Thomas Huxley, once noted, "The practice of that which is ethically best--what we call goodness or virtue...is opposed to that which leads to success in the cosmic struggle for existence." [34] Exactly! So how did we get it? If the *Tao* is a merely an artifact of culture or evolution, it is certainly the only one enjoying such universal acceptance.

Lewis argued that the code is not about what we do; it is about what we feel we *ought* to do, and feel guilty when we don't. Because it does not describe what men *actually* do, it cannot be ascribed to deterministic mechanisms like instinct or selfish genes. If it were, men would have no control to resist it. And since it is not revealed by direct observation, an extraterrestrial observer could not detect it from man's actual behavior.

What this adds up to is that we have been programmed; not to slavishly obey our cranial chemicals or to preserve our selfish genes, but to discern certain actions as right and others wrong. And, as we know from experience, wherever there is a program, there is a programmer.

Heart, mind and conscience are stamped into human nature like a maker's mark. Through their collective faculties, we are able to apprehend truth, discern right from wrong, and sense purpose and meaning to our existence. As a self-revealing expression of God, it teaches us *that* God is and *what* He is—a Creator-God who has endowed beings with every resource to know him and experience the life abundant.

"Above all, you must understand that no prophecy of Scripture came about by the prophet's own interpretation. For prophecy never had its origin in the will of man, but men spoke from God as they were carried along by the Holy Spirit." [35]

The Written Word

Two generations of postmodern thought has led to growing cynicism about truth claims, institutional authorities, and even history. Among revisionists, the historical record is a product of oppression and coercion written by the ruling class. At best, history is unreliable; at worst, it is propaganda—a story written by the winners in the perpetual struggle for power. That goes for the biblical record as well, which many dismiss as myth or legend.

A person who was eminently qualified to answer that charge was C.S. Lewis. As a literary historian and scholar in ancient literature, Lewis wrote, "I am perfectly convinced that whatever else the Gospels are they are not legends. I have read a great deal of legend (myth) and I am quite clear that they are not the same sort of thing."

Lewis went on to explain why he came to that conclusion: "They are not artistic enough...Most of the life of Jesus is totally unknown to us...and no people building up a legend would allow that to be so." In other words, they lack the drama, the colorful detail and rich imagination of the ancient story-tellers.[36]

In not legend or myth, what?

History?

In four separate historical records, Jesus is described as a first-century Jew who traveled throughout Palestine preaching, teaching, and healing; was charged with blasphemy, executed on the order of Pontius Pilate, and laid in a tomb for three days before rising from the dead.

Of the sayings attributed to him, "Anyone who has seen me has seen the Father" and "I and the Father are one," are arguably the most bracing and immodest. So much so that, to riff off of C.S. Lewis, anyone who said these kinds of things and did the things that Jesus did (like forgiving sins), would have to be a quack, madman, or God himself. However, even among non-Christians, the first two options are not seriously entertained, given the high moral character of Jesus' life and teachings.

Thus, if true, these records are evidence for the one, true God; if false, Jesus and his Father warrant no more deference than is due Chronos and his son Poseidon. Determining which they are involves considering the "three W's" of investigative inquiry: when, where, and by whom they were written.

The criteria
Events recorded far-removed from the time and place they occurred have low reliability. That's because the "once upon a time, in a land far away" feature makes such events unavailable for critique by contemporaries to them.

Also suspect are accounts authenticated by a sole author (the Qur'an and Book of Mormon come to mind), or by persons benefiting from them -- like Muhammad whose Qur'an-inspired campaigns gained him lands, subjects, and political capital.

By contrast, accounts written in spatial and temporal proximity to the events described, and corroborated from multiple points of view by eyewitnesses, have a high measure of historical reliability.

How they stack up

Paleography is the study of the script and letter style of written records. A competent paleographer can pin the date of an ancient text within a decade of when written and even identify the school of scribes where the author was trained. For many New Testament manuscripts, paleographic analysis supports a first century authorship.

There's also the fact that the scriptures make no mention of the fall of Jerusalem in 70 AD. Jesus predicted that calamity forty years earlier. Since fulfillment of that prophecy would have bolstered Jesus' messianic claims, its omission in the NT suggests authorship before 70 AD.

Thus, it is generally agreed by competent scholarship that the synoptic gospels of Matthew, Mark, and Luke were written in Palestine between 50 and 70 AD – that is, in the very region that Jesus lived and worked, and within the lifespan of people who would have had memory of him.

Indeed, the apostle Paul recounted the historical facts of Jesus' death, burial, and resurrection in a 56 AD letter, reminding his readers of hundreds of surviving eyewitnesses to those facts.[37] And, what is unparalleled in any other literary work, dozens of predictions concerning those events were recorded in the Septuagint, written three centuries earlier. In short, Paul's readers had access to living witnesses who could challenge the gospel record, including any attempt to manipulate it to match prophesy.

Of the synoptic authors, only Matthew was a personal associate of Jesus; Mark was the ministry partner and spiritual son of Peter, one of Jesus' closest disciples; and Luke was a ministry companion of Paul who sourced his material from "those who were first eyewitnesses."[38] The non-synoptic author John was also a personal disciple of Jesus, recording his gospel account around 90 AD.

Each of the authors wrote from a unique perspective for a specific audience: Matthew for Jews, Mark for Romans, Luke for Greeks, and John for Christians. Thus, there are differences in voice, emphasis, length, chronology, material included, events described, and details reported between the four narratives.

However, in no case is any doctrine of faith affected. To the contrary – not only do these features contraindicate collusion, their unique viewpoints and emphases combine, much like a four-color printing process, to give a richer, more complete image of the work and Person of Jesus Christ than any one record in isolation. In very real sense, the Apostles' account is more than the sum of its parts.

Considering spatial-temporal proximity and multiple attestation, the gospel record enjoys high historical reliability.

The early church canon also included apostolic testimony. Peter acknowledges Paul's writings as holy writ when he stated, "His letters contain some things that are hard to understand, which ignorant and unstable people distort, as they do *the other Scriptures…*" [39]

In 160 AD, Justin Martyr wrote that reading "the memoirs of the apostles" was a weekly custom for the assembly of believers. Theologian, Ben Witherington, cites the work of Martin Hengel and Harry Gamble showing that the four gospels and Paul's writings were circulated together in codex (book) form in the early second century--further evidence that apostolic writings were accepted as Scripture by the early church.[40]

Like all works of antiquity, there are no original

autographs of the NT documents. That said, the NT enjoys manuscript support (copies of the autographs) far in excess of any other ancient literary work.

Consider that there are about 5000 Greek manuscripts of the NT and 24,000 copies of portions, thereof, in existence. Not only is that level of support unparalleled for ancient works, but the time span between the originals and the first manuscripts is exceptionally short; within one hundred years versus many centuries to millennia.

Also, the textual variation among the existing copies is extremely small. For all the hoopla over bible contradictions, errors and inconsistencies, only about one-half of one percent of the bible is under competent dispute--none of which affects any "material question of historic fact or of Christian faith and doctrine," according to biblical scholar, F.F. Bruce.[27]

Compare that with Homer's *Iliad* which has the next best manuscript support among ancient literature. For people of antiquity, Homer "was held in the highest esteem and quoted in defense of arguments pertaining to heaven, earth, and Hades," writes Bruce Metzger. Like the bible, Homer was memorized, served as school primers, and was allegorized and enhanced.[28]

Yet there are only about 650 surviving copies of the *Iliad,* written over a thousand years after the original. Among those copies, there are over 100 times as many textual differences as the bible. Matched up against the writing of the ancients, the transmission of the biblical narrative is in class of its own.

Added to that, the extra-biblical quotations of the early church fathers (second and third century) are so extensive, they could be used to reconstruct the entire NT.

The upshot is that there is high confidence that the bible we have is what the authors wrote; but is what they wrote, the word of God? Let's see.

A unique word

As already mentioned, there are hundreds of biblical prophecies written well in advance of the events they describe. One that is shocking in precision was told to King Nebuchadnezzar by the prophet Daniel. It concerned the coming of the Messiah:

> "Know and understand this: From the issuing of the decree to restore and rebuild Jerusalem until the Anointed One, the ruler, comes, there will be seven 'sevens,' and sixty-two 'sevens.' It will be rebuilt with streets and a trench, but in times of trouble. After the sixty-two 'sevens,' the Anointed One will be cut off and will have nothing."[41]

Time "zero" for this prediction is the decree to rebuild Jerusalem, issued by King Artaxerses in 445 BC. Given the Jewish idiom of "seven" as a week of years, or seven years, the prediction is that the Messiah will come as ruler in 69 (7 plus 62) "weeks" or 483 years.

Correcting the Jewish year (which was based on 360 days) for a 365.25 day year, the period between the decree to rebuild Jerusalem and the arrival of the Messiah becomes 476 years.

The gospel of Luke states that, in the 15th year of Tiberius, Jesus began his public ministry. Tiberius became emperor when Augustus Caesar died in 14 AD. Including the year he was enthroned, the 15th year of his reign occurred in 28 AD.

Three years later, in 31 AD, Jesus was received as king and ruler on his triumphal entry into Jerusalem. Note that the interval between 445 BC (the decree to rebuild Jerusalem) and 31 AD (the Messiah's coming as king) is 476 years—the precise period predicted by Daniel some 300 years earlier!

Recall that since the gospel record of the fulfillment was written within the lifetime of eyewitnesses, any fabrication on the part of authors to fudge the facts would have been readily contested by any number of hostile contemporaries.

A veritable word

After weighing all of the evidence, the late paleographer and classical scholar, Sir Frederick Kenyon, concluded, "We have in our hands, in substantial integrity, the veritable word of God."[42] He was in good company.

For over two thousand years, paupers to princes have acknowledged the Divine authorship and transformational power of the written word. One of the earliest was Justin Martyr who challenged early second century unbelievers to "...come and partake of incomparable wisdom, and be instructed by the Divine Word, and acquaint yourselves with the King immortal... The Word exercises an influence which does not make poets: it does not equip philosophers who are skilled orators, but by its instruction it makes mortals immortal...Come, be taught; become as I am, for I, too, was as ye are..." --Justin Martyr, *Discourse to the Greeks*

"The mystery of God, namely, Christ, in whom are hidden all the treasures of wisdom and knowledge."[43]

The Incarnate Word

Over two thousand years ago, Jesus challenged his disciples with, "Who do you say that I am?" It was a haunting question because the possible answers were few. His contemporaries accused him of being a deluded babbler, knowing fraud or demon-possessed lackey. Some accepted him as a great moral teacher, and a few, the Lord he claimed to be. Today, the expanse of intervening time has led some to another conclusion.

In an open online exchange, I used a version of C.S. Lewis' *Liar, Lunatic, Lord* trilemma[44] to establish the divinity of Jesus. One participant countered: "That's well and fine, but for the fact that there is no reliable record that Jesus actually lived."

"Come again?"

"Jesus goes completely under the radar of the Roman records, the Palestinian historians--everyone!"

He was referring to the "Jesus myth"—a claim that the Jesus of the bible never existed. Although it has circulated among skeptics since it was originally trotted out in the 19th century, today no reputable scholar supports the Jesus Myth, for several reasons:

First, there are the extra-biblical references to Jesus by Josephus, Tacitus, Pliny and Suetonius--men who weren't particularly inclined toward this messianic figure or his fringe following.

Next, there is the emergence of a Christian community within the living memory of Jesus' contemporaries. Modern naysayers would have us accept that this community endured persecution for a fictitious character whose existence could have been checked out from any number of surviving eyewitnesses.

Finally, there is the historical record of the bible itself: Namely, that Jesus was a Jew who lived in first-century Palestine; he was executed on the order of Pontius Pilate; and after his death his disciples began saying he had risen from the dead.

Consequently, even some not-so-sympathetic authorities dismiss the myth theory. For instance, atheist and historian Michael Grant cedes, "Modern critical methods fail to support the Christ-myth theory...It has again and again been answered and annihilated by first-rank scholars." [45]

Considering the remaining options, the one that best fit the facts is the one reached by the apostle Thomas: "My Lord and my God!"

Then there's Saul of Tarsus, a Jewish zealot and Christian persecutor, whose turn from Saul to Paul was as inconceivable to first century Christians as it would today if Richard Dawkins were to become the successor to Billy Graham. It was on a dusty trail to Damascus that he came to the same conclusion as Thomas, eventually describing Jesus as "the image of the invisible God," in whom "all the fullness of the Godhead resides in bodily form." [46]

The earthly invasion of God was an event that all of history had built up to.

240

In the period prior to the Incarnation, mankind was aware of three things: a spiritual realm that was pure and unchanging; a material world that was corrupt and fleeting; and the infinite gulf between them. Therein, lay a problem.

For pre-Christian people, God was a distant and impersonal deity whose true identity and desires were largely unknowable. Anxious about relying on personal guesswork to forge the divine divide, people looked to enlightened go-betweens. The proliferation of temples, priests and priestesses over the ages was a response to man's felt need for mediation.

When the Incarnate Word broke into history, he was unlike all the mediators that had gone before. They were human; he was human *and* divine. He was the perfect bridge over the gaping chasm between the earthly and the heavenly--a priest who not only intercedes *for* man, but who reveals God *to* man. As the apostle John wrote, "No one has ever seen God, but God the One and Only, who is at the Father's side, has made him known." [47]

Of all places, it was in a cave that the "One and Only" was revealed.

Cut into a hillside
Caves were shelters for animals, lepers and refugees. Darkness, and the threats of disease and physical danger, made them undesirable habitats for all but those on the margins.

The cave was Plato's metaphor for the material world--the impermanent, corrupted "shadow" of reality, a thing to be despised. If man was to learn the true nature of things, he must turn his attention from the cave to the heavens—the pure and unchanging realm of Being.

In time, a Persian coterie left the cave and followed the

heavens until they landed on the outskirts of Bethlehem. There, G. K. Chesterton notes, they came upon a cave cut into the side of a hill, where a young mother was caring for her newborn.

Never could they have imagined what they would find at their journey's end: A refuge for outcasts, a cave where an impoverished couple was attending a suckling infant, wrapped in strips of cloth and resting in a feeding trough.

Neither could they have processed the reality before their eyes: "A child who was a father and a mother who was a child." Yet, in some inexplicable way, they sensed that, in this humble scene, Truth was not outside the cave, as Plato would have it, but inside.[48] For those who had been studying the matter, the time for "God with us" had come and with that, a divine statement about the world had been made.

Although spoiled by the effects of sin, the material world is not a loathsome object corrupted beyond repair. It is a creation loved by its Creator who came, by way of a cave, in the flesh and form of a human infant to restore it and make himself known.

Out of the cave
Out of the cave and into the world, Jesus came, revealing God to people restless for transcendence. Teaching moments were reinforced by life example:

He, who taught the greatness of servanthood, left the head of the table to take up the towel and basin.

He, who taught his disciples to pray, withdrew to a mountainside, a garden, and quiet places to talk with the Father.

He, who taught his followers to take up their cross,

242

took up his on the Golgothan hill.

He, who on another hill, taught the crowd to love their enemies, pleaded for his, "Father, forgive them."

From the cave to the cross, Jesus modeled his command to love[49] through his healing touch, comforting words, and advocacy for the least, last and lost. Submitting himself to the full breadth of human experience, Jesus endured hunger, thirst, temptation, the loss of loved ones, and the rejection of family and friends, before laying down his life that we might enjoy eternal fellowship with him.

The Incarnate Word is evidence that God not only exists and loves us, but identifies with us, cave-dwellers.

From the cross, Jesus was laid into another cave that became the site of something so startling, it shook a group of seasoned soldiers to their core.

The other cave
After Jesus' body was removed from the cross, Joseph of Arimathea laid it in a tomb cut out of rock. As a newborn infant, Mary had swathed his wriggling body in strips of linen. Now, as an executed adult, Joseph wrapped his lifeless corpse in a cloth loaded with spices.

The next morning when the women visited the tomb, they found a highly-disciplined Roman detachment rattled to the point of paralysis. Maybe it was the earthquake, or the spectral figure that rolled back the stone sealing the entrance. Or maybe it was what Peter and John saw after they stooped to peer inside.

It has been oft-claimed that the resurrection of Jesus rests on the empty tomb; it does not. An empty tomb could be dismissed as the result of theft, or of returning to the wrong tomb. This tomb was not empty; it held something that established the resurrection beyond all rational argument.

On the slab were burial wrappings that no longer contained a body. The grave clothes were not littered about the tomb willy-nilly; they were altogether, in a piece, conformed in the shape of a human body, but collapsed, like a cocoon whose contents had vaporized and oozed out through its fibers.

To men who had not understood that their leader must die, much less rise from the dead, the sight of the crumpled "chrysalis" was a faith-galvanizing moment. It prompted reflection on all they had been taught, including the ultimate revelation of their Master, "Because I live, you also will live. On that day you will realize that I am in the Father, and you are in me, and I am in you."[50]

The resurrection of Jesus Christ is the linchpin of Christianity. As the apostle Paul himself asserts, "If Christ has not been raised, your faith is futile." [34] On the other hand, if Christ *is* raised, we are left with one and only one conclusion: that he is the Lord and Savior that he claimed to be. And that makes all the difference. So which is it?

A resurrection ruse?
The most credible arguments against the traditional account involve some sort of conspiracy theory or "Passover plot." Critics allege that after Christ's death, the disciples hatched a plan to steal his body and fabricate a "risen Savior" for political or financial gain.

Among the many implausible features about such theories is that they depend on men like Peter, who just hours before had denied his leader three times, to rise to a level of heroism unsurpassed by New York City firemen on 9/11. Not only did this cowering band of misfits have to sneak past a Roman guard and remove a one-ton stone; they had to psyche up enough courage to sneak past them again with a body that the guards were stationed to secure at penalty of death.

But even if such a conspiracy scheme was possible, it collapses under the weight of historical evidence, as acknowledged by some not-so sympathetic authorities. For instance, historian Michael Grant admits, "Their testimonies cannot prove them to have been right in supposing that Jesus had risen from the dead. However, these accounts do prove that certain people were utterly convinced that that is what he had done."

And then there is Duke professor E. P. Sanders who says, "That Jesus' followers (and later Paul) had resurrection experiences is, in my judgment, a fact. What the reality was that gave rise to the experiences, I do not know." [51]

Even for the impartial critic, nothing short of steadfast belief could explain how a band of cowards could be transformed into men of valor overnight. Despite the constant threat of torture, alienation, imprisonment, and death, the disciples held firm to their account of a resurrected Messiah. They surely had ample opportunity and motive for coming clean about the "cover-up;" or at least, for reconsidering their testimony. Yet, although ten of the eleven Apostles were martyred for their faith, there is no evidence that any one of them ever recanted.

The behavior of the disciples only makes sense once we accept that they actually believed that the incredible story they were telling was true.

Some have attempted to associate the Apostles' actions with the ever-ready martyr wish of religious fanaticism. But that only further invalidates the charge of conspiracy. Yes, men may suffer and die for what they believe to be true, but it goes against human nature to suffer and die for what they know to be false. Nobody knew that better than the late Charles W. Colson.

All the president's men
In his book, *Loving God*, Chuck Colson wrote about his involvement in the Watergate conspiracy.[7]

While Special Counsel to President Nixon, Colson was one of a small band of "hand-picked loyalists" who believed passionately in their leader and sacrificed careers, privacy, and family life for their cause -- and they were on the winning team, their leader just re-elected in a landslide victory.

They were influential men, enjoying the perks and prestige that comes from the highest office in the land. They were powerful men who, with a word, could mobilize the military, fire personnel, or order a private jet. They were men who had everything to gain from maintaining their story, and everything to lose from a failed cover-up. Yet, despite all that was at stake, Colson writes, they "could not hold a conspiracy together for more than two weeks."

Compared to Christ's disciples who could expect floggings and martyrdom, the Watergate conspirators faced, at most, personal embarrassment, public disgrace, and a prison term. Nevertheless, writes Colson, "the natural instinct for self-preservation was so overwhelming that the conspirators, one by one, deserted their leader, walked away from their cause, [and] turned their backs on the power, prestige, and privileges."

The disciples, by contrast, were powerless men who lacked social position and political clout. What's more, their unpopular leader had been killed and they had become guilty by association.

Yet, these fugitives boldly entered Jerusalem, circulating

a report that chafed against hearers who had every motive, means, and opportunity to refute it with the counterevidence: a corpse.

The absence of evidence

In the days, weeks and months after Jesus's death, the discovery of his corpse would have been certain. Both the Jewish leadership and the Roman authorities were not only highly motivated to quash any resurrection ruse, but had the political muscle and wherewithal to extract confessions and find the body, if indeed it existed. That no such evidence came forth is reflected in the late first century account by the Jewish historian, Josephus:

> *Now there was about this time Jesus… [the] Christ. And when Pilate, at the suggestion of the principal men amongst us, had condemned him to the cross, those that loved him at the first did not forsake him; for he appeared to them alive again the third day; as the divine prophets had foretold these and ten thousand other wonderful things concerning him. And the tribe of Christians, so named from him, are not extinct at this day.* (Antiquities 18.3.3)

There are several remarkable things about this passage. First, Josephus was a member of the community most offended by the Christian message. Second, there is no hint of criticism about the reports of Christ's post-resurrection appearances; to the contrary, Josephus seems to give credence to the apostolic account. Third, Josephus' indictment of his countrymen and his Roman rulers was sure to rile both groups, and stands as a testimony to his objectivity. And lastly, this first century account runs counter to the historical revisionists who propose that Christ's divinity was a concoction of a fourth century theocracy.

The disciples' case is so strong that Irwin H. Linton, a lawyer who has argued cases before the U.S. Supreme

Court, writes that the resurrection "is so supported that it is difficult to conceive of any method or line of proof that it lacks which would make [it] more certain."

Even for people disinclined to accept the Christian message, Linton goes on to say that they have been "unable to refute the irresistible force of the cumulative evidence upon which such faith rests." [52]

"On this rock I will build my church."[53]

The Corporate Word

Before Jesus ascended into heaven, he entrusted his disciples with the "keys of the kingdom." He commissioned them to make disciples, with authority to "bind" and "loose." In a very real sense, they were to be living witnesses to their Lord and his world-changing message. Collectively, they were the Church--the incarnation of Christ between the Cross and Second Coming.

As the visible extension of God in the here-and-now, the Church gives light to the lost, aid to the least, and comfort to the last. Jesus told his followers that by loving others as he had loved them, men would take notice— and notice they did.

In the second century Tertullian wrote, "It is our care of the helpless, our practice of loving kindness that brands us in the eyes of many of our opponents. 'Only look' they say, 'look how they love one another!'" But as one of the sharpest critics of the Church attested, Christian love extended beyond the "one anothers."[54]

In 362 the emperor Julian, frustrated over the decline of realm's pagan religions, grumbled "[Christianity] has been especially advanced through the loving service rendered to strangers...It is a scandal that there is not a single Jew who is beggar, and that the [Christians] care not only for their poor but for ours as well; while those who belong to us look in vain for the help that we should render them." [55]

Centuries earlier St. Peter had explained the cause-and-effect. To a scattered community of beleaguered believers, Peter urged: "Live such good lives among the pagans that, though they accuse you of doing wrong, they may see your good deeds and glorify God on the day he visits us."[56] Peter could have scarcely known just how much God would be glorified through the witness of the Church.

A different worldview

From its inception, the Church was distinguished for the care of widows, orphans and the needy. But it was their charity in times of plagues and epidemics that stunned the watching world.

In 165 AD, a smallpox epidemic raged throughout the empire causing the deaths of up to one-third of populace, according to the estimates of sociologist Rodney Stark. In 251, a second epidemic swept through the empire, claiming as many as 5,000 lives a day in the capital city alone.[57]

During the outbreaks pagan citizens, priests, and even medical practitioners left the cities in panic, abandoning the sick to die. Dead bodies were thrown to the roadsides or left to decay in the homes of victims. Christians, on the other hand, remained in the population centers, at huge risk to themselves, to care for the sick and bury the dead. Their different response was born out of their different worldview.

Christians believed in a personal God, a divine command for brotherly love, and an afterlife. The pagan culture knew nothing of these. Their gods were impersonal deities who made no moral demands on human behaviors and offered no salvation from mortality. Since charity was not a divine requirement, it was something that in the throes of an epidemic, only an extremely brave or foolish person would exercise.

250

The different worldview of Christians also led to a different outcome. By attending to the sick with the basic necessities of food and drink, Christians helped many victims survive who would have, otherwise, perished. Their ministry of love and compassion resulted in the deaths of many attending Christians, as reported by Dionysius during the second plague,

> "Most of our brother Christians showed unbounded love...Heedless of danger, they took charge of the sick, attending to every need...Many in nursing and curing others, transferred their death to themselves and died in their stead..."

And that resulted in a significant, unexpected impact on the growth of the early Church.

The rise of Christianity
Rodney Stark explains that caring for the sick not only improved the survival of plague victims, it bolstered the immunity of Christian care-givers against future outbreaks. Higher survival rates and greater immunity against disease caused Christians to become a larger proportion of the wider populace, putting pagans in closer and more frequent contact with Christians whose lifestyles reflected beliefs about this world and the next that were more compelling than those of their religions.

For the fledgling Church, that created the perfect storm; for between 150 AD (fifteen years before the first plague) and 300 AD (fifty years after the second), Stark estimates that the number of Christians grew over 150-fold—from around 40,000 to over 6 million!

Over the next seventeen hundred years, Christian ranks continued to swell, making Christianity the world's largest religion with around two billion adherents. That, alone, is an impressive validation of Jesus' cause-and-effect teaching. But when the culture-shaping influence of the Church is also considered, the validation is nothing short of phenomenal.

More than numbers
Civilization, and Western society, in particular, owes much to its Christian heritage.

Christians established the first hospitals, orphanages and universities. They were the vanguard of the Scientific Revolution. Men like Bacon, Ockham, Kepler, Galileo, Newton, Faraday, Kelvin and Pasteur—all believers— forged the way from medieval alchemy to modern science and medicine.

The Western rule of law, including personal liberties, consent of the governed, and the separation of powers, owes its existence to Christian thought. The same goes for the great social movements of history: abolition, child labor laws, suffrage, and civil rights. And Christians remain on the frontlines today, fighting against the human rights injustices of sex trafficking, prison rape and religious persecution.

When warlords ravage communities and natural disasters strike, it is not societies of "Brights", free thinkers and secular humanists that rush to far reaches on the globe to help victims; it's churches and faith-based organizations who are among the first to arrive and the last to leave. And that hasn't gone unnoticed.

In the aftermath of the Katrina disaster, *U.K. Guardian* columnist Roy Hattersley echoed the sentiments of Emperor Julian. After noting that all of the relief groups had a religious affiliation, Hattersley remarked "Notable by their absence are teams from rationalist societies, free thinkers' clubs and atheists' associations." He closed his article betraying, what was perhaps, a prick of conscience: "The only possible conclusion is that faith comes with a packet of moral imperatives that, while they do not condition the attitude of all believers, influence enough of them to make them morally superior to atheists like me." [58]

Today, as in the first century and throughout history, the lips and lives of *abiding* Christians are making the world take notice and ponder afresh Jesus' probing question: "Who do you say that I am?"

Now, if all of this doesn't strike you as strange, it should.

Screaming for explanation
The Macedonian Empire of Alexander the Great began splintering soon after his death. Within five centuries of the assassination of Julius Caesar (the "dictator in perpetuity"), his "Eternal City" was sacked, leading to the collapse of the Roman Empire. Scarcely one century after the death of Karl Marx, the Berlin Wall fell, the rest of the Iron Curtain came down, and the Eastern Bloc was dismantled.

Yet the kingdom inaugurated by a Galilean carpenter has not only endured for two millennia, it has grown numerically and influentially, despite being driven underground for the first 300 years of its existence, and being a target of persecution from its beginning to the present day.

Had Jesus been just another would-be world-changer, his following would have faded fast into obscurity. Instead, the Church he established has become the world's largest and most influential institution.

The implication was not lost upon one would-be world-changer, Napoleon Bonaparte. While exiled on the island of Saint Helena, the ex-Emperor of France told fellow émigré, Count Montholon,

"Alexander, Caesar, Charlemagne and I myself have founded great empires; but upon what did these creations of our genius depend? Upon force. Jesus alone founded His empire upon love, and to this very day millions will die for Him. . . . I think I understand something of human nature; and I tell you, all these were men, and I am a man; none else is like Him: Jesus Christ was more than a man. . . . I have inspired multitudes with such an enthusiastic devotion that they would have died for me . . . but to do this it was necessary that I should be visibly present with the electric influence of my looks, my words, of my voice… Christ alone has succeeded in so raising the mind of man toward the unseen, that it becomes insensible to the barriers of time and space… This it is which proves to me quite convincingly the Divinity of Jesus Christ."[59]

The phenomenon of the Church is a fact screaming for explanation. The one that best fits the facts is that the early Christians believed, *really* believed, that Jesus was more than a great moral teacher or charismatic leader; they believed that he was Lord and God. Their belief was based on the testimony of eleven men who claimed to have seen something that defied scientific explanation, reason, and common sense: the risen Lord.

Singular and unprecedented
When Jesus, three days dead, passed through the locked door of the upper room, the disciples became witnesses to a thing unprecedented in history.

Sure, there were cases of resuscitations by physicians and stories of "raisings" by metaphysicians. There were the biblical accounts of the Sidonian widow's son raised by Elijah and the Shunammite's son who was raised by Elisha, as well as Jesus' raisings of Jairus' daughter and Lazarus that the disciples were privileged to witness first hand. But never before had the disciples (or anyone else) known of a dead person rising *on their own power,* and in a *reconstituted body.* Only Jesus had done that.

Initially dazed and confused by what they had seen, the disciples soon realized that Jesus' mastery over death only made sense if he was the God he had claimed to be. The disciples became so convinced about the Resurrection (and what it meant), that barely one month after bailing on their crushed leader and withdrawing from the public eye, they re-entered the city and began broadcasting their news to the most unsympathetic audience on the planet.

The turnabout

The shift from jellyfish to ironman was exemplified in Peter. Shortly following his second imprisonment for preaching the resurrection, Peter was brought before the Sanhedrin for repeatedly defying their gag order. After the robed masters rail against his intransigence, Peter responds bluntly: "We must obey God rather than men!" Then, continuing in his obduracy, Peter reprises his unwelcome testimony:

> The God of our fathers raised Jesus from the dead—whom you had killed by hanging him on a tree. God exalted him to his own right hand as Prince and Savior that he might give repentance and forgiveness of sins to Israel. *We are witnesses of these things,* and so is the Holy Spirit, whom God has given to those who obey him. (My emphasis.)[60]

This from a man who just a few weeks prior cursed at the mere suggestion he knew Jesus. It is not a little ironic that after Peter's saucy response to the Sanhedrin, one of their number, Gamaliel, proposed a litmus to his colleagues:

> "Men of Israel, consider carefully what you intend to do to these men. Some time ago Theudas appeared,

claiming to be somebody, and about four hundred men rallied to him. He was killed, all his followers were dispersed, and it all came to nothing. After him, Judas the Galilean appeared in the days of the census and led a band of people in revolt. He too was killed, and all his followers were scattered. Therefore, in the present case I advise you: Leave these men alone! Let them go! For if their purpose or activity is of human origin, it will fail. But if it is from God, you will not be able to stop these men; you will only find yourselves fighting against God."

Gamaliel was right. If Jesus was just another dead messianic leader, his following would come to nothing. But it didn't; despite the suppressive forces of the cross, the stake, the coliseum, the gulag, and anti-religious legislation, law suits, speech codes, and political correctness, the kingdom has steadily advanced in hearts of men and in man's institutions.

Outside of the truth of the Resurrection, the phenomenon of the Church is inexplicable – a fact, which itself, is sufficient to establish that the "faith once given," was given by none other than God. By his own criterion Gamaliel would be compelled to agree, as would persons of any era who honestly consider the facts.

The Indwelling Word

Few doctrines of Christianity are as misunderstood as that of the Holy Spirit. I suspect this is partly due to his title. The word "spirit" conjures up a fuzzy, if not, spooky image -- a mysterious life-force, a formless immaterial being, a wraith – that inclines us to think of the Holy Spirit as "it" rather than "him."

There's also the matter of instruction. Although the Holy Spirit is given a nod in Christian slogans, mission statements, and church talk, he is largely ignored in Christian teaching, except as he relates to spiritual gifts and prayer life. In fact, in my 40 plus years as a Christian, I've heard only one sermon devoted to the comprehensive ministry of the Spirit.

He creates
For folks inclined to think of the Holy Spirit as a New Testament phenomenon, his mention throughout the Old Testament can come as a surprise. For instance, in the opening verses of Genesis, the Holy Spirit is described as "hovering over the waters" of the unformed earth, insinuating his role in creation.

Later, the creative partnership of Father, Son, and Holy Spirit is reinforced when God says, "Let *us* make man in *our* image." While counseling Job in his troubles, friend Elihu further confirms and clarifies the Spirit's creative role: "The Spirit of God has made me; the breath of the Almighty gives me life." [61]

The Spirit's impartation of "breath" -- the immaterial "something" that turns a lump of clay into a living, thinking being – is a witness to the immaterial God who is the source of life.

He empowers

From Creation to the Incarnation, the scriptures tell of the Spirit descending upon individuals who are tagged for some divine task: defeat a pagan foe, lead a rebellious nation, or speak a prophetic word. In contrast to the "indwelling" of believers in the Church Age, the Spirit's Old Testament "ondwelling" was temporary and selective.

But whether by "ondwelling" or "indwelling," the Holy Spirit empowers humans to accomplish things that are humanly impossible, thus giving witness to the God with whom "all things are possible."[62]

He inspires

The second letter of Peter is addressed to a church that was scattered, suffering, and swaying under the influence of heresies. To encourage the believers and help shore up their faith, Peter reminded them of the apostles' accounts of Jesus's life, death, and resurrection; eyewitness accounts detailing the fulfillment of Old Testament prophesies.

Peter went on to explain the Source of prophetic accuracy: "No prophesy of Scripture came about by the prophet's own interpretation. For prophecy never had its origin in the will of man, but men spoke from God as they were carried along by the Holy Spirit." [63]

Because of the Holy Spirit's inspiration, the biblical narrative contains dozens of prophesies fulfilled in precise detail centuries after they had been predicted and recorded, making the bible unique among all man-made literary works.

He gifts
In his first letter to the Corinthians, Paul introduces the concept of "spiritual gifts," writing "There are different kinds of gifts, but the same Spirit. There are different kinds of service, but the same Lord. There are different kinds of working, but the same God works all of them in all men."[64] Notice the Trinitarian partnership. Spiritual gifts come from the Holy Spirit, in service of the Son, according to the sovereign purposes of the Father.

Paul goes on to say, "Now to each one the manifestation of the Spirit is given for the common good." (Between this letter and Romans chapter 12, Paul lists 15 spiritual gifts including things, like wisdom, knowledge, serving, giving, prophesy, teaching, and mercy.) Also notice, that it's not a question of whether a believer has a gift. It's a question of what gift or gifts he has, and in what measure.

Although everyone has some capacity for each gift – with some, like mercy, giving, and serving, that every Christian needs to cultivate -- it is our primary gift that determines our spiritual role within the Church, whether as an ordained pastor or lay "helper."

The gifts imparted by the Spirit support the work for the God-sized task of kingdom-building.

He teaches and convicts
With the Cross looming before him, Jesus spent his last hours on earth preparing his disciples for his departure. He promised not to leave them as orphans; he would send the Spirit to teach them and remind them of all they had been taught.

The good news, though it didn't register at the time, was that unlike the pre-resurrected Lord whose company and wisdom they could enjoy only when he was physically present with them, the Spirit, unencumbered by the limitations of a material body, would reside *in* them, all of them, as an ever-present Teacher, Comforter and Equipper.

What's more, the Spirit's ministry would extend to non-believers, as well. "He will testify about me," Jesus told them, and "convict *the world* of guilt in regard to sin and righteousness and judgment." In fact, without the ministry of the Holy Spirit to the unbelieving world, belief "unto salvation" is not possible. As Paul explained, "No one can say, 'Jesus is Lord,' except by the Holy Spirit."[65]

He "ondwells", indwells, and fills

In the Old Testament, as already mentioned, the Holy Spirit came upon ordinary individuals to accomplish extraordinary things: Bezalel to craft the tabernacle, Samson to defeat the Philistines, Gideon to defeat the Midianites, and David to take over the kingship of Israel, just to name a few. In each case, the "ondwelling" was a transitory visitation upon a selected individual for specific assignment.

After Pentecost, the Holy Spirit began to indwell people -- collectively, the Church, and individually, the heart of every believer. Unlike ondwelling, the Spirit's indwelling is permanent and without regard to the spiritual condition of a specific assembly or its individual members. Consider the case of the early Corinthian church.

If ever a church was characterized by sinful strife and immorality, it was that of Corinth. Immoral behavior, and complacence towards it, had reached the point to where an open, incestuous relationship went unchallenged. Disputes between members were being aired in civil courts, rather than being resolved in the community of faith. The weekly assembly was becoming more of a bacchanalian banquet than a celebration of the Lord's Supper. On top of that, the church was tolerating – maybe, even accepting – some heretical teachings.

Yet, despite their woeful spiritual condition, Paul reminds the Corinthians that they are members of Christ's body; a body that is a temple of the Holy Spirit, who resides in them, and whom they have received from God.[66]

The lesson of Corinth is that while churches and their members are indwelt by the Spirit, they may not be *filled with* the Spirit. *Indwelling* is about the presence of the Spirit; *filling* is about his measure -- that is, his influence and control – in a believer's life.

Paul likens it to the control that alcohol has over an inebriated person: "Do not get drunk on wine, which leads to debauchery. Instead, be filled with the Spirit."[67] Thus, while indwelling is a one-time gift of salvation, filling is a recurring process leading to sanctification.

The process is illustrated in the Acts church. A short while after their initial filling at Pentecost, the believers were "re-filled" after a prayer meeting to seek boldness in proclaiming the gospel to adversarial audiences. Afterwards, boldly preaching they went!

In His manifold ministries of creating, empowering, inspiring, teaching, convicting, gifting, indwelling, and filling, the Holy Spirit is an ever-active, omni-present witness to the God "who is there." By His power, a tiny band of unlikely misfits, quailing after the execution of their leader, ignited a movement that, as we have seen, changed the world forever.

To the unblinkered critic, the combined witness of creation, scripture, the Imago Dei, the historicity of Jesus' life, death, and resurrection, the phenomenon of the Church, and the ministry of the Holy Spirit provides objective evidence of God's self-revelation in whom, "all the fullness of the Deity lives in bodily form"[68] – evidence beyond reasonable doubt that there almost certainly is a God.

Chapter 8

Some Objections

"I don't want anyone to suffer anymore. And if the suffering of little children is needed to complete the sum total of suffering required to pay for the truth, I don't want that truth, and I declare in advance that all the truth in the world is not worth the price!" – Ivan Karamazov in *The Brothers Karamazov*

A Hidden God

When asked what he would do if, at death, he discovers that God exists, Richard Dawkins replied that he would ask God why he didn't make himself more evident. Dawkins is not alone. Throughout the ages, others have been bewildered, if not maddened, by the hiddenness of God. But perhaps no one expressed that bewilderment more than God's servant, Job.

Job was a man of moral rectitude without peer. But suddenly, without warning, he becomes the object of supernatural attentions that claim his wealth, children and health. In the crushing aftermath, several friends attend him, but, in the end, their efforts to comfort fail to comfort and all their answers fall short. Overcome by his loss, Job directs his voice heavenward with the tortured question: "Why do you hide your face?"[1]

The same question issued off the lips of Habakkuk, David and the psalmists in their dark night of the soul. The absence of God in a hurting and unjust world can be outright exasperating, even among believers.

Whether it's the woman abandoned by her husband after a 20-year marriage, the man left jobless after corporate down-sizing, or the couple grieving the death of a child, the person caught in the grip of sudden loss raises voice-- and sometime fist—pleading: Where is the restraining hand of God? Where is the Advocate of righteousness? Where is the Father of all comfort? Viscerally, we sense this is not the way it's supposed to be. And it's not.

In the world as it was (and will be again), there was intimate union between man and God, man and fellowman, and man and creation. But in one act of rebellion, an impurity was introduced in the original state that began contaminating everything it touched. The infection weakened and degraded the whole created order, making it unable to withstand the full blaze of His presence.

Had God not withdrawn behind the gossamer veil of creation, all would have been consumed in the radiance of his glory as surely as dry grass in a blast furnace. Thus, divine hiddenness is an act of love and mercy that retards the process of death, allowing the plan of restoration to unfold.

How we deal with that in the crucible of life is the subject of C.S. Lewis's acclaimed novel, *Till We Have Faces.* [2]

Two sisters
The story is about two princesses: one beautiful, the other ugly; one whose love is selfless, the other whose

love is self-serving; one who lives by faith, the other by sight; one named Psyche, the other Orual—two sisters whose lives are punctuated by transformational moments.

Through her beauty and goodness, Psyche wins fevered devotion throughout the realm. But after a string of woes is visited upon the kingdom, public opinion turns. It is determined that Psyche has enraged a jealous goddess and, for her offense, must be abandoned to Grey Mountain as an appeasement offering.

Psyche faces her sentence with uncommon courage. Recalling her childhood dream of being married to a mountain king, Psyche wonders if it was a presage of her impending ordeal. Could it be that her whole life has been a run-up to this glorious event? Imagining the possibility, her expectation overcomes her doubts and concerns.

Orual, believing that the gods are "lies of poets," fears that her sister will be ripped apart by wild animals, ravaged by a deranged mountain man, or merely left to die from hunger.

Hoping to persuade Psyche to escape, Orual, in cunning sophistry, suggests that the gods are real, but are given over to evil things. Psyche shoots back that perhaps the gods are real, but those "evil" things "are not what they seem to be," adding, "How if I am indeed to wed a god?"

Wed a god she does.

Transformational moments
Psyche is led up the mountain, bound to a tree and left to the fates. But before she succumbs to the elements, the mountain god swoops down and whisks her off to his castle.

Days later Orual journeys out to find Psyche, or her remains. Instead of a corpse or emaciated figure, Orual finds her sister in good health and spirits. Psyche gushes as she tells Orual about her castle and her husband. Orual is dumbfounded—she sees no castle, no husband; only rocks, trees, and brush.

Psyche goes on to tell Orual that her husband visits her only in the dark of night, forbidding her to look upon his face. Orual bristles, what sort of god is this "that dares not show his face?"

Convinced that Psyche is out of her wits, Orual tries to coax her off the mountain. When Psyche declines, Orual becomes angry and jealous. Angry with those poetic immortals for stealing her beloved sister and jealous that Psyche would choose a phantom lover over her.

Desperate for her sister see the truth, Orual convinces her to bring a lamp into her husband's chamber. When she does and gazes upon him, Psyche screams in horror; not by what she sees, but by what she feels—overwhelming guilt for her betrayal. Psyche goes into exile, and an ineffable Visage flashes before Orual's eyes, renting open her heart.

In that transformational moment, Orual's conscience is quickened and her doubt dispelled. She now knows that the gods exist and that she bears blame before them; still there is anger.

Anger, as Richard Dawkins might argue, with Immortals who keep hidden. Had they made themselves, and their will, more plain, her offense and its consequences could have been avoided. Miffed by their detachment, Orual proceeds to write out her grievances against them.

Before she is finished, she has a jolting self-revelation. Peering deep into the mirror of her soul, Orual sees a devouring, life-quenching narcissist for whom people, even her sister, are means of personal gratification rather than as objects of unsparing love. The wretched image brings on the next revelation: Before she dies, she must *die*.

Orual realizes she can't accomplish that on her own; but frustrated that the AWOL gods will not assist her, the princess-now-queen completes penning her grievance.

Till we have faces
In a dream (a vision or near-death experience?) Orual is brought to "court" by an ethereal being and invited to read her accusation.

After reciting her litany of charges, she is asked, "Are you answered?" Without hesitation, Orual responds, "Yes." As the queen would explain shortly before her death, "The complaint was the answer. To have heard myself making it was to be answered."

Orual got it. In our present condition, questions and answers are but structured collections of words: human devices that are often inadequate in expressing our own thoughts and feelings, much less for understanding the thoughts of God.

Beyond vocabulary, we lack the faculties for pure dialog with God. Indeed, a divine utterance falling on human ears would be as unintelligible as tensor mathematics to a rhesus monkey. As Orual rightly concludes, "How can the gods meet us face to face till we have faces?"

To enjoy full communion with our Creator, we await for the day when we will become who we are created to be. What that is, we do not know, save for the inspiration of John: "But we know that when he appears, we shall be like him, for we shall see him as he is."[23] Sharing in his nature and his vocabulary, we will be equipped for intimate, unbroken fellowship with our Lord and Savior.

Until that day, our comprehension of heavenly things is as vaporous as a pet's comprehension of his master. While "now we see but a poor reflection as in a mirror," Paul writes, "then we shall see face to face." And though "now I know in part," he continues, "then I shall know fully, even as I am fully known." [3]

Job's conclusion

When Job is finished with all his "whys," God responds, not with answers, but with his own cannonade of questions, beginning with the scorching, "Who is this who darkens my counsel with words without knowledge?"

Singed by the blast of God's utterance, Job is reminded of who is Creator and who is creature, and of the yawning chasm between them. At this point, Job could have pressed his grievances or slumped and withered. Instead, he "mans up" and, in one of the most humble affirmations in scripture, submits to God's sovereignty, trusting that history will unfold according to his perfect will:

> *"I know that you can do all things; no plan of yours can be thwarted...Surely I spoke of things I did not understand, things too wonderful for me to know... My ears had heard of you but now my eyes have seen you."*[4]

The same choice is ours. We can pound the gates of heaven for answers to our anguished questions, or we can surrender to the process of "*dying* before we die," preparing for the communion for which we were created and have long-awaited.

Of that process, Paul writes, "We, who with unveiled faces all reflect the Lord's glory, are being transformed into his likeness with ever-increasing glory," and later, "you died, and your life is now hidden with Christ in God. When Christ, who is your life, appears, then you also will appear with him in glory."[5]

Then, we will have faces.

A Cosmic Tyrant

Megalomaniacal; bloodthirsty; homophobic; racist; genocidal—those are just a few of the offenses Richard Dawkins pins on God in *The God Delusion* which, as someone once quipped, would be more appropriately titled, *God in the Hands of an Angry Atheist,* in a hat tip to Jonathan Edwards.

Among less trenchant skeptics, God is a mythical authoritarian who, at times, behaves more like a capricious bully than a cosmic father-figure. Yet even among Christians, the Yahweh of the Old Testament seems incompatible with the Good Shepherd of the New. As a consequence, some believers avoid the Old Testament, venturing only to the comforting passages of the Psalms and Proverbs.

What do we make of the two faces of God? On one side, there is the God of swift justice who executes sentences with sword, plague, and flood; on the other, the God of long-suffering mercy who allows tares and wheat to co-exist. Somehow, the God who swept through Egypt destroying the firstborn seems at odds with Him who said "Suffer the little children."

God of judgment
There is probably no account of God's justice more chilling than that of Jericho's conquest. After circling the city seven times and flattening its wall with a trumpet blast, the Israelites put the sword to "every living thing...men, women, young and old, cattle, sheep, and donkeys." As offensive as that may be to our modern sensibilities, what followed is downright numbing.

Before the Israelites entered Jericho, God commanded that all of the city's precious metals were to be devoted to him. Despite the divine order, one of Joshua's men, Achan, was caught red-handed with a few items of contraband. For such an offense, it would seem that a moderate civil penalty would have sufficed. Yet in God's court of law, Achan was sentenced to be stoned and, there being no court of appeals, was promptly executed.[6]

The Old Testament contains a sizeable list of capital crimes ranging from cursing one's parents to child sacrifice, but the thought that Achan's offense warranted the same penalty as murder goes completely against our concept of a punishment befitting the crime. Even more troubling was that Achan's punishment extended beyond him to his entire family.

The collateral annihilation of "innocents" leaves us speechless. It's as if God lost control, clearing out a swath of judgment against all those caught in the crosshairs of a divine temper tantrum.

Is this the work of a loving God or of Dawkins' megalomaniac? Interestingly, the answer hinges not with how we view God, but how we view ourselves.

Our natural tendency is to think of ourselves as basically good. It's not that we deny the existence of evil or our own vices. What we resist is the thought that we are inherently evil, that we carry a moral virus inclining us toward wrong-doing and that, from the womb to the grave, we are under a sentence of death.

Notions of justice
When we take umbrage with the harshness of Yahweh and the capital offenses of the Old Testament, we forget that, ultimately, every transgression deserves the death penalty: "The soul who sins is the one who will die."[7] Thus, the Old Testament judgments represent a radical reduction in the capital punishments warranted.

In the Church era, while still "dead men walking," we view the notion of capital offense as a relic of a distant past. So, when the child dies of cancer, the earthquake kills thousands, the suicide bomber takes the lives of civilians, or when Achan's family is stoned, we question God's justice for executing it, or we question his love for allowing it.

It would help to remember several things here. First, is our tendency to consider loss and affliction in this world as meaningless, with no higher purpose in the "now" or the "not yet." To set the matter straight, the apostle Paul—no stranger to adversity—put it this way; "I consider that our present sufferings are not worth comparing with the glory that will be revealed in us."[8]

Next, although we may be innocent with regard to our fellow man, before God we stand guilty and rightly deserve death. And lastly, God's mercy is not obligatory. If it was, it wouldn't be a product of his grace; it would be a right, an entitlement, something to be earned.

For example, God was equally just to take the life of Pharaoh's son, while allowing Joseph Stalin to live to the age of 74. Likewise, God would be equally just in allowing me to be the victim of a drive-by shooting, as he would to let me live to the ripe age of 100. Although each case involves a different measure of God's mercy, each involves the same punishment: death.

We stumble here because we suppose that when God extends mercy to one person, he is bound to extend it to all in equal measure. It is the error of believing that God's mercy is infinite -- that in the end, all our differences will fade away and we will all unite in His loving embrace. As comforting as that notion is, it is diametrically opposed to the coming judgment revealed by Jesus: "There is a judge for the one who rejects me and does not accept my words; that very word which I spoke will condemn him at the last day."[9]

A day is coming when God's mercy toward evil and evil-doers will end. But in the long delay, we have become so used to God's mercy that his grace no longer amazes us. What amazes us, notes theologian R.C. Sproul, is justice. In *The Holiness of God*, Sproul recounts an experience that vividly illustrates the point.[10]

Dr. Sproul had given his class of 250 students an assignment with a warning that they would receive an "F" if not turned in on time. On the due date, 25 anxious students arrived without their papers and begged for an extension, which Dr. Sproul granted. The next month another assignment was given and, on the appointed date, 50 sheepish students came to class without their papers. After hearing their excuses and pleas for mercy, Sproul relented a second time, stipulating that it would be the last extension he would grant.

Nevertheless, by the third assignment, 100 students "strolled into the lecture hall utterly unconcerned" that they hadn't completed the work, telling the professor, "Don't worry, Prof, we're working on [our papers]. We'll have them for you in a couple of days, no sweat." When Dr. Sproul began recording F's in his gradebook, the students bellowed, "That's unfair!"

You think it's not fair?

Yes.

I see. It's justice you want. If you insist on justice, I'll not only give you an F for this assignment but for the others you turned in late as well.

After a period of stunned silence, the students apologized, gladly accepting the "F" for the late assignment. Sproul's story illustrates that what we really want from God is not justice, but mercy.

Indeed, God tempers his justice with mercy. But his mercy is neither limitless nor egalitarian. If it were, our choices would have no ultimate consequence, leaving our lives devoid of meaning--a condition more easily accomplished in a world of automatons. But thanks to the grace of God, we are not programmed robots, but free-willed beings able to make real choices—choices that count for eternity.

For the world is not a stage of marionettes which, when finished with their performance, are returned to the trap boxes of their owner; it is a richly designed macrocosm in which every person has eternal significance, either towards unending joy or everlasting removal.

In the confusing, tumultuous between-time, Paul reminds us that "our light and momentary troubles are achieving for us an eternal glory that far outweighs them all" and then coaches us to "fix our eyes not on what is seen, but on what is unseen. For what is seen is temporary, but what is unseen is eternal."[11]

And this from a man who knew all about troubles, having been struck blind, beaten, shipwrecked, imprisoned, stoned, and given a persistent "thorn."[12]

An Angry World

Three days after Easter Sunday 2011, 288 tornadoes churned through a section of the southeast, claiming the lives of over 340 people. By the numbers, it is the worst outbreak of twisters since 1936 when 148 tornadoes caused 304 deaths.

In Alabama whole communities were wiped off the map. One aerial photograph showed a mile-wide swathe of destruction stretching out as far as the eye could see. A marine with two tours of duty in the Mideast, called the devastation "worse than Iraq."

Survivors told of loved ones snatched violently from their clasp, swept up and disappearing into a black vortex of debris swirling in excess of 175 miles per hour. Within a few miles of my house in Tennessee, one family lost relatives from four generations. Across a six-state region, hundreds of people were left homeless.

And yet the human tragedy, so crushing, so heart-rending, and so close to home barely registers on the same scale with the 2011 tsunami in Japan, much less the 2004 Indonesian tsunami. Those disasters claimed in excess of 15,000 and 200,000 lives, respectively.

A recurrent question

Young, old, rich, poor, religious, unreligious; trailers, brick homes, shopping centers, churches. These disasters were no respecter of persons or property. For some people it is further evidence that we are alone in a hostile, unsupervised universe that is deaf to our cries and indifferent to our pain. For others, it raises again the question of "why."

The standard Christian answer, "it's the consequence of

sin and the fall," can come up short, especially for the victims of nature's fury. While it is easy to draw a cause-and-effect relationship between man's moral choices and much of human suffering -- diseases, plagues, poverty, and war -- man's culpability for tornadoes, earthquakes, and volcanoes is less than apparent.

So the question remains: Why in a world created by an all-powerful, all-good God, are natural disasters, which claim hundreds to hundreds of thousands of lives, permitted to exist? Is God a monster or merely a klutz?

A striking discovery
Over the last several decades, one of the most striking discoveries in science is the integrated complexity of the universe. The array of physical constants and relationships that give structure to the cosmos are so precise and interdependent that if any were varied but a smidgeon, life as we know it would not exist.

Theoretical physicist, Steven Weinberg, is a bristling atheist who admits that the host of delicately-balanced parameters is "far beyond what you could imagine just having to accept as a mere accident."[13] Stated differently, the scientific evidence points a created, rather than a chance cosmos. And that is an unsettling fact for Weinberg and the peddlers of scientism -- so unsettling that they have had to conjure up fictions of parallel worlds and multiverses to sustain their commitment to materialism.

By all accounts, our cosmic home appears to be a creation intentionally designed for us, except for those sporadic hostilities of nature. But maybe those hostilities were not part of the original creation.

Frustrations
In the biblical record, at each stage of creation God pronounced that what he had made was "good." The

divine utterance suggests that, in its original state, the world was a hospitable place for man and that nature was responsive to man's nurturing touch.

But after the fall, the world became less hospitable and nature less responsive. According to the account in Genesis, man's sin led not only to his removal from God's presence, but to an accursed ground. As the apostle Paul put it thousands of years later, "the creation was subjected to frustration."[14]

In a real sense, it was a matter of the cause and effect of sin. With the introduction of that moral virus, creation was subjected to a new limitation: the laws of thermodynamics, which British scientist C.P. Snow summarizes this way[15]:

> Law of conservation: You cannot win (that is, you cannot get something for nothing, because matter and energy are conserved).
>
> Law of entropy: You cannot break even (you cannot return to the same energy state, because there is always an increase in disorder; entropy always increases).
>
> Law of absolute zero: You cannot get out of the game (because absolute zero is unattainable).

The laws of thermodynamics make dysfunction, decay, and death a universal condition. Another outcome is that every system, no matter how well designed and engineered, involves trade-offs to achieve its intended function.

A balancing act
The design of high performance bicycle must balance the competing requirements for aerodynamics and light weight with the needs for structural integrity and rider

comfort. The features that make a racing bike fast also make it prone to flat tires, bent rims, broken spokes, and its rider more prone to saddle sores.

Likewise, the combined influences of the gravitational, geological, and meteorological conditions that are necessary for biological life make the earth more prone to floods, hurricanes, and earthquakes than a planet not suitable for life. Consider just one of the earth's features: its 24-hour rotational cycle.

Among other things, the earth's rotation 1) stabilizes the earth's temperature, 2) provides global coverage of solar radiation for photosynthesis, and 3) generates a magnetic field that shields the earth from the harmful effects of cosmic radiation. Each of those functions is essential for the fecundity and well-being of biological life.

But the earth's rotation is also what causes curving weather patterns that organize into the spinning air masses of tornadoes and cyclones. What's more, as the earth turns it causes friction in the viscous regions of the earth's core that generates subsurface heat that gives rise to volcanoes and earthquakes.

Birthing pains
Paul writes that we groan, longing for the "redemption of our bodies" so that mortality "may be swallowed up in life." The universal human desire to transcend the limitations of the present world is a sign that the present world is not what it once was or will one day be. Paul suggests that, like a woman in labor, the whole creation is in the throes of childbirth waiting for redemption.

Thus, tornadoes, hurricanes, tsunamis, volcanoes, and earthquakes are the wails of a world that longs to be "liberated from its bondage to decay" and "for the sons of God to be revealed." [16]

278

"In this meaningless life of mine I have seen both of these: a righteous man perishing in his righteousness, and a wicked man living long in his wickedness." [17]

An Unjust World

Early in my career, I spent two years in the Big Apple commuting daily on the city's transit system. The sights, sounds, and smells of a New York subway are enough to make even the most iron-clad stomach queasy. So when I heard Ken Boa tell the following anecdote, that experience came back, in Technicolor.

> One day a commuter boarded the "C" train with a stomach rumbling from an overindulgent lunch. After a few stops, the pressing bodies, squealing breaks and the stench of perspiration, bad breath, and urine became too much. When the train doors opened to let the woozy traveler off, all he could do was pitch his entire *carte du jour* onto the poor fellow waiting to board. As the doors closed, the bewildered man on the platform looked up blubbering, "Why Me?"

"Why Me?" is the great existential question of all time. When the "subway of life" dumps its refuse in our lap, we shake our head in wonder. After all, we reason, we haven't hit the wife, neglected the kids, lied to the boss, or kicked the dog--leastwise, not today.

Life's unfairness is troubling. When the church member slanders us, our job is "surplused," the diagnosis of cancer comes, or our neighbor is killed in a car accident, we are stupefied by the injustice of it all. Centuries ago, the wisest man in the world was likewise confounded, declaring it meaningless that the righteous get what the wicked deserve, and the wicked get what the righteous deserve.

Some, like Clarence Darrow, take such troubles as proof that life "is a ship that is tossed by every wave and by every wind; a ship headed to no port and no harbor, with no rudder, no compass, no pilot, simply floating for a time, then lost in the waves."[18] Indiscriminate misfortune, they argue, is the logical outcome of an unsupervised universe governed by chance.

Nevertheless, our initial reaction betrays the nagging sense that there *should be* a cosmic order at work; that life must be fair; that rewards can be earned; and, if one is successful, life will be good. Some even imagine a benevolent Bookkeeper who immunizes them from calamity if their ledgers are "in the black", while those "in the red" are left to suffer.

This "pay-for-performance" mentality conditions us to view tragedy as judgment, either from a nebulous principle of karma or from God himself. Reality, though, is another matter: the Indonesian tsunami claims the lives of righteous and unrighteous alike, Sudanese children are massacred while their totalitarian butchers run amok, Christian bookstores struggle while adult bookstores thrive. Such inequities not only disturb us as they did Solomon, they disturbed the people of Jesus' day as well.

A question of judgment
Pontius Pilate was a difficult and insensitive tyrant in Palestine. First, he incensed the Jews by erecting Roman ensigns with Caesar's image throughout the Holy City. Then, he demanded tax from the temple treasury. When the Jews objected, Pilate directed an armed force, disguised as ordinary citizens, to go into the temple crowd and slaughter the rebellious malcontents.

Like the Birmingham church bombing which took the lives of four young black girls in 1963, the killing of God's people at the hands of a pagan tyrant was unthinkable. It wasn't long before Jesus was forced to field the question which was on everyone's mind: Was this a divine judgment?

Jesus quickly countered the suggestion, replying, "Do you think that these Galileans were worse sinners than all the other Galileans because they suffered this way? I tell you, no! But unless you repent, you too will all perish." In plain language, Jesus said it is wrong to read God's intent into life's tragedies.

To drive the point home further, Jesus continued his discourse by recounting another incident involving a group who happened to be in the wrong place at the wrong time,: "[How about] those eighteen who died when the tower in Siloam fell on them -- do you think they were more guilty than all the others living in Jerusalem? I tell you, no! But unless you repent, you too will all perish." Notice, in both cases, how Jesus turns the focus from *why* some die to *how* one can live. [19]

Death, Solomon writes, is "the destiny of every man," and along with pain, loss, and suffering, is the natural consequence in a world tilted on its axis from sin. But while we can't choose whether we'll die in this world, we *can* choose whether we'll live in the next. Jesus explained, "whoever hears my word and believes him who sent me, has eternal life; he does not come into judgment, but has passed from death to life."[20]

All the same, we pine for the day when justice will reign and all things will be made right. In the shadow time, we struggle with a God who admits, "I will have mercy on whom I will have mercy, and I will have compassion on whom I will have compassion."[21] Does that mean God plays favorites, and if we could figure out what makes him tick, we get on the inside track of his good graces? Well, yes and no.

Playing favorites

Diversity in the kingdom Hall of Fame is legion. From Abraham, whose geriatric wife was far beyond childbearing age, to Mary, a young peasant girl without a husband, God's selections seem strange and ill-conceived to any modern day HR consultant. His most strategic assignments go not only to the least able and least qualified, but often to those who don't even want the job, like Moses, Jonah, and Paul.

Such is the nature of God's "favorites," chosen not according to personal wishes, merit, or achievement, but according to a different selection criterion: "It does not, therefore, depend on man's desire or effort, but on God's mercy."

If we think this unfair, we would do well to consider the fate of the Old Testament prophets or New Testament apostles before we insist on being the beneficiaries of God's favoritism.

Divine inequity

OK. Maybe God doesn't play favorites in the usual sense. But what about the inequity of his punishments? Consider Ananias and Sapphira who were struck dead after they lied to Peter about the proceeds of a land sale. Their sins were hardly any different from the person today who fails to tithe, and yet the disparity in consequence is incomprehensible. Granted, but the inequity there is only apparent. For in both cases, the punishment is death. The only difference is the timing: in one case, it is immediate; in the other, it could be 10, 20, or 70 years.

What's more, punishment in this world says nothing about destiny in the next. For example, when Paul addressed the church in Corinth about a man having an affair with his stepmother, he pressed them to turn the man "over to Satan, so that the sinful nature may be destroyed and his spirit saved on the day of the Lord."[19]

Thus, punishment in the "here and now" has no necessary bearing on destiny in the "yet to come." At the same time, an untimely death *does* cut short the opportunity to fulfill our earthly commission -- to restore culture and multiply God's kingdom -- affecting our rewards, rather than our membership, in the world to come.

Some are sure to view such punishment as brutally severe. However, in the case of the believer, as for the Corinthian adulterer, such discipline Paul writes, is intended so that we "will not be condemned with the world."[22] Discipline, up to and including death, is a merciful act of Him who keeps his sheep in the palm of his hand, allowing none to be snatched away.

God, to hold us secure in his kingdom without violating our free will, would not only be justified, but merciful in executing the sentence we rightfully deserve before we reach the point of apostasy. Thanks to him, Jude writes, "who is able to keep you from falling and to present you before his glorious presence without fault and with great joy."[23]

It is right for us to be upset over injustice in this world. At the same time we need to remember that the greatest injustice of all was suffered by Him who died so that death would not be the final word in a narrative filled with heartache, suffering, and pain. As C.S. Lewis writes,

> "Does God then forsake those who serve Him best? Well, He who served Him best of all said, near His tortured death, 'Why hast thou forsaken me?'...There is a mystery here which even if I had the power, I might not have the courage to explore. Meanwhile little people like you and me, if our prayers are sometimes granted... had better not draw hasty

conclusions to our own advantage. If we were stronger, we might be less tenderly treated. If we were braver, we might be sent to far more desperate posts in the great battle." -- *The World's Last Night*[24]

A Mean Ol' World

In *The Brothers Karamazov*, Ivan Karamazov levels a powerful charge against God. Ivan is an intellectual skeptic who sees a world full of suffering and injustice. Particularly offensive is the cruelty done to innocent children. What purpose can such evil possibly serve? Where is God in this mean old world? Ivan wants to know. After graphically recounting the horrors of a young girl mercilessly abused by her parents, Ivan concludes that whatever reason God may have had, the price is too high.

To human sensibilities the existence of cruelty and suffering is a scandalous indictment against Omnipotence. It is what drove Einstein to reject the God of the bible for "Spinoza's God"--the non-personal principle of reason, harmony, and cosmic order. Throughout the centuries, the "problem of evil" has led countless others to conclude that God is negligent, impotent, or non-existent.

Consider media mogul Ted Turner.

Until the age of 15, Ted was a self-described Christian who attended Christian school, studied the bible, prayed for one hour every day, and even planned on becoming a missionary. But that all changed after his younger sister succumbed to terminal lupus. Despite the prayers of family and friends for healing, Ted's sister died after a painful five-year struggle. Unable to reconcile his sister's death with his Christian faith, Turner turned his back on God. As one observer has noted, "It's not so much that Turner doesn't believe in God as he doesn't want to give God, who allowed his sister to be crushed by disease, the satisfaction of recognition."[25]

Ted Turner believes that if God exists he is a detached, impersonal Governor who is aloof about human suffering--an *un-God* who may be all-powerful, but not all-good; and for that reason undeserving recognition, much less human devotion.

Rabbi Harold Kushner, author of *When Bad Things Happen to Good People*, has a somewhat different view. Rabbi Kushner trusts in God's infinite goodness, but the pervasive existence of human misery and injustice is evidence that He has little-to-no power over these things; otherwise, they wouldn't be so rife and unmitigated.[26] Like Ted Turner, Rabbi Kushner came to his belief after his own personal tragedy: the agonizing death of his teenage son.

The classic response to these positions goes something like this: A perfect God created a perfect world which included, necessarily, free will and morally responsible agents. Thus, evil was not created by God, or the result of divine negligence or incompetence, but as a consequence of choices made by moral agents in the unfettered exercise of their will.

That argument offers us a certain intellectual satisfaction; still, there can be a lingering notion it is little more than a rhetorical sleight-of-hand to cover embarrassment for a God who, in our lowest moments, seems an indifferent deity. Yes, there are times we need more than clever logic.

"Jessie"
Several years ago some friends lost their 12-year old daughter to cancer. During her last five years, "Jessie"

had been in and out of hospitals receiving radiation treatments and chemotherapy for an inoperable brain tumor. Despite the impassioned prayers of family and friends, improvements in her condition were only temporary, necessitating frequent trips back to the hospital.

As her condition deteriorated, the doctors decided that Jessie should live out her remaining time at home. Her last days where far from peaceful. The pain from her cancer-ridden body was so intense that large doses of narcotics gave her little relief. Her parents became increasingly fervent in prayer, yet the pain was so intolerable that the only alternative for lasting relief was to sever her spinal nerve. Two weeks later Jessie died.

We're all familiar with those "name-it and claim-it" verses of the bible. But somehow the joy of those passages doesn't jump off the page in situations like Jessie's. Like the disciples who asked Jesus about the cause of the blind man's blindness, we want to know what went wrong. Did we fail to pray hard enough? Did we not believe strong enough? Are our sins too great? Or do we conclude, as Ted Turner and Rabbi Kushner, that God is not all he's cracked up to be.

Two months before her death, Jessie made a decision to be baptized. But what should have been an occasion for rejoicing, turned into turmoil for her family.

You see Jessie's church required baptism by immersion, no exceptions -- an impossible requirement considering Jessie's frail condition.
In frustration her parents approached another church across town that agreed to baptize her in a less traditional fashion. The resulting ceremony was a moving testimony to hundreds of witnesses of this young girl's courage and commitment to the Lord.

Looking for meaning

The apostle Paul's afflictions, primarily his imprisonments, provided the opportunity for writings that would become the *Magna Carta* of the Christian faith. But perhaps more significantly, his trials were evidence of his sincerity and love, evidence that was essential to gain the credibility and acceptance of those he had previously persecuted.

For Paul, it is clear how God used his adversity to advance the kingdom. But for Jessie, God's purpose is not as obvious. Perhaps he wanted to demonstrate the unshakeable quality of child-like faith to a world in desperate need of hope. Maybe he wanted to awaken a dying church out of its misplaced focus on legalism. Perhaps he sought to secure Jessie's place in his eternal family at an early age. Perhaps.

At this point we must admit we don't know. And even if we did, it would not attenuate our feelings of loss this side of eternity. So where do we go for comfort? How do we reconcile our lingering yearning for a world turned right-side-up.

The divine predicament

If Paul's hardships were necessary to win over beleaguered Christians skeptical of his motivations, what about God? What did He need to win the love of His created beings? Certainly he could have overwhelmed them with staggering displays of power. But he had already done that through the general revelation of creation. If that wasn't enough, the chosen nation of Israel experienced God's providence and protection, as well as some pretty spectacular miracles during its history.

Yet God's blessings, frequent manifestations, and dramatic wonders had no lasting effect on Israel's love for him. To the contrary, although God's marvelous favors produced awe and respect (and sometimes fear), they did little to engender enduring love. Clearly something else was needed.

Inexhaustible love

At the heart of love is other-centeredness. From small acts of kindness to the laying down of life for another, love is lived-out and authenticated through personal sacrifice. It is thus, in the Incarnation, we find the highest expression of divine love. For there we find a God who refused to exempt himself from the stinging injustice of a world gone wrong. For a brief moment in history God set aside his omnipotence to be the *Son of Man*, the Advocate who presents God to man and man to God.

Making himself as one of us, God invaded the world, not as sovereign king but as a helpless infant. Associating with the downcast and outcast and ministering to the least and the last, he was shunned by his brothers, rejected by his countrymen, convicted on phony charges, tried by an illegitimate assembly, sentenced to an unjust death; spat upon, beaten, cursed, and scourged; nailed to a tree and, crying out in anguish, died in infamy with common criminals as the hand of his Father was withheld. If anyone knows, from first-hand experience, about injustice it is him.

Because he walked in our shoes, he is the only deity who can understand our pain, sympathize with our suffering, and be patient with our questioning hearts. The Incarnation is the shocking and irrefutable display of inexhaustible Love.

We can join Ivan Karamazov in railing against God for this mean ol' world, or we can consider the injustice He endured and wonder why He subjected himself to it. Could He have taken a less costly course to set the world right?

The short answer is yes. But only in a sin-scarred world can the infinite dimensions of God's love be expressed through the nail-pierced hands of a risen Savior. Such is the love of Him who silently listens to all the charges Ivan makes against him; then, without a word, moves over to his accuser and kisses him.

Chapter 9

Between Two Messages

*"I went down to the crossroads, fell down on my knees.
Asked the lord above for mercy, 'Save me if you please.'"*
-- Robert Johnson, *Crossroads*

Why the Cross?

The Cross. No doctrine is more central to the Christian faith and, yet, more of an offense to our human sensibilities. For the unbeliever, it represents everything that is wrong with Christianity. A wrathful God who must be appeased by the brutal murder of his own son is deserving of contempt not worship; any religion he inspires can't help but promote violence and bloodshed. Remember the Crusades, Inquisition, and witch hunts.

Even people inclined to Jesus and his teachings, have difficulties with the Cross. In his book, *Death on a Friday Afternoon*, the late Richard John Neuhaus wrote of one person's halt, just short of the cross,

> "I have no doubts about God, and I completely agree
> with the Church's moral teachings… I am a little
> embarrassed to say it, but my problem is with the
> cross. Why Jesus had to die, this whole business of
> blood and sacrifice, I just don't get it. Since the cross

is the main symbol of Christianity…I suppose that's a pretty big problem, right?[1]

Yes, and it has been ever since Good Friday. As Paul put it, the Cross is both foolishness and a stumbling block: foolishness to our intellect and a stumbling block to our faith. The root of our difficulty is our failure to understand what actually happened on Golgotha 2000 years ago.

God and his nature

The bible tells us that God is love. That is no mawkish sentiment. It is an ontological statement about God that is unique to him. But love requires an object, at minimum, the fellowship of two. Of all the deities in all the religions throughout time, only the Christian God exists in a co-eternal fellowship of Father, Son, and Holy Spirit. Joined in a perfect union of intimacy and interdependence, the triune Godhead is the source of *shalom*, a Jewish concept for universal wholeness, peace, harmony, and flourishing.

Philosophy tells us that God is necessary. Not that the God of the bible is necessary, but that a pre-existent, non-contingent being is necessary to avoid the absurdity of infinite regression when peeling back the onion of where we came from.

Finally, *logic tells us* that if A equals B, and A equals C, then B equals C.

Putting these truths together in syllogism: if God is love, and God is necessary, then love is necessary. Give that a moment to sink in.

For creation to fulfill its created purpose as shalom-saturated, shalom-sustaining work, it must be infused with love. Yet, as is evident from the shalom-deficit in our sin-stained world, universal love is not a present reality. With the fall of Lucifer, and later Adam, the fellowship between creature and Creator was broken, disrupting the shalom of the pre-fall creation.

It is a cosmic-sized problem for which the creature, while culpable, is incapable of fixing, lacking the ability, resources, and even knowledge of what to do. The only one up to the task is he "who fills the cosmos." But how?

Restoring shalom

It would have been within God's power to extinguish his handiwork, once spoiled, but it would have been contrary to his nature. He is love, remember, and love is not sparing or exclusive; it is generous, ever expanding its circle of fellowship and intimacy. And because love is necessary, it could be argued, with some justification, that God has been doing just that -- creating for all eternity (not just the six days recorded in Genesis), the bible being the telling of *this* creation. But that is a discussion for another day.

Alternatively, God could have forgiven his creatures without penalty or consequence. On the surface, that would seem to have been the lovingly thing to do; in reality, it would have been anything but.

One of our deepest human longings is to know, that in the cosmic scheme of things, we matter. If, in the final analysis, our choices and actions are inconsequential beyond our fleeting existence, then, by any ultimate measure, we do not matter. On the other hand, if our lives have consequences that spill into eternity, we matter more than we know, immensely more.

For the world to make moral sense and for man to have the dignity of moral status, wrongs must have consequences, either by punishment or restitution. The first is strictly punitive, penalizing the offender for his offense; the second is reparative, restoring that which was lost.

In the case of the fall, God chose the reparative. Instead of punishing untold multitudes for their guilt, he took payment in what the liturgy of the Eucharistic calls, a "full, perfect and sufficient" sacrifice. Since nothing in creation, even in its entirety, could fill that bill, restitution had to be made by none other than God himself, in the second Person of the Trinity.

What had to be

This was not a decision made by the Father, executed by the Son, and with the Holy Spirit flitting idly about; it was a plan borne out of the perfect union of Father, Son, and Holy Spirit, working as One to restore shalom by reconciling man into right relationship with Creator and creation. Considering our human limitations, it could be no other way.

Earth-bound man could not ascend to heaven to work out the sin problem with God. Like Icarus on his ascent to the sun, he would have been consumed by the blaze of the Presence. Neither could man have known, much less have remedied the myriad consequences that his rebellion set in motion.

No, God had to take the initiative, descending to earth in the humble cloak of humanness to be one of us, experiencing our wants, fears, pains and temptations without sin and, eventually, to be crucified at our hands. For we were there.

When Jesus uttered, "It finished," all the transgressions of past, present and future were paid for in full. It is a deep mystery that has an important and intentional side effect.

Foundation of trust

On the battlefield, a soldier must trust his commanding

officer. But to trust him, really trust him, he must know that his commanding officer knows what it is like to be a soldier: to come under enemy fire, to be gripped with fear, to be combat weary; to march for days, who knows where, hungry, tired, and homesick; to have a buddy die in your arms. Only a commander who has walked in a soldier's boots can know those things. And only one who knows those things can earn a soldier's trust.

Because of the Incarnation, we know that our Commander knows those things. He is not a deity barking orders from an Olympian hilltop to subjects below cowering in terror. He is an involved God who spent over 30 years on planet earth, a loving Creator who desires fellowship with his creatures, a welcoming Master who opens his banquet hall for all to enjoy, an involved Father who calls his children near, an indwelling Spirit who teaches and comforts, a Savior and an elder Brother who leads and intercedes.

The Incarnation gives us reason to trust that God understands our predicament and is ready and able to help us through it. As the author of Hebrews writes,

> "For we do not have a high priest who is unable to sympathize with our weaknesses, but we have one who has been tempted in every way, just as we are-- yet was without sin. Let us then approach the throne of grace with confidence, so that we may receive mercy and find grace to help us in our time of need."[2]

The decision
At the foot of the Cross, we come face-to-face with a decision: Will we accept the payment that God has made on our behalf, or reject it?

We are like the prisoner who hears that a friend has offered to pay the fine for his release, and must decide whether to accept his friend's gift or insist upon earning his release with "good behavior." The difference is that while the prisoner *can* earn his freedom, we cannot earn our salvation.

Mercifully and graciously, the Offended has chosen payment over punishment: the sacrifice of One for all, once and for all. It is a gift, plain and simple. We have either to receive it with gratitude, or turn it down in pride.

For some, a gift for which personal merit has no merit is an unwelcome affront to self-esteem. For others, it is an awe-inspiring testament to the Word who has stamped them with the word signifying their worth: Mine.

"It has been the cross which has revealed to good men that their goodness has not been good enough."[3]

Standing at the Crossroad

Crossroads, the blues classic by Robert Johnson, is a song about a man seeking escape from his desperate existence. Will he find it in a road trip, a drinking binge, a flight from one destination to the next, or in God's grace? At the song's end, we are left to wonder.

A crossroads is a place where divergent paths meet, forcing us to make choices which can be at once exciting and scary. It can be a place of crisis, where the pain of the past butts up against our hopes for the future; or a place of opportunity, where the road ahead promises brighter prospects in the vast frontier beyond.

In either case, a crossroads is a call to change: from where we've been to where we're going; from what we're leaving behind to what we're striving for; from whom we are to who we're becoming.

As free-willed creatures, we are continually leaving one crossroads and entering another. Will we pick up the ball or the doll? Will we eat our food or play with it? Will we wear blue socks or black socks? Will we finish high school or work as a mechanic? Will we propose to Susan or play the field? And on it goes.

Like a string of beads forming a necklace, crossroads connect the past, present, and future of human experience in an unbroken thread of possibility. But the central crossroads, the one through which every life must pass, lies on a hill in Golgotha.

Standing in paralysis

"I am the gate; whoever enters through me will be saved. He will come in and go out, and find pasture."[4] That was the self-description of a first century mystic named Jesus Christ. Not only did this traveling teacher profess equality with God, he insisted that he and God were one and the same.

Was he serious? Or was this the babbling of some megalomaniac, simpleton, or quack? If it was, we are confronted by the absurdity of such characterizations against his life and teachings. What about his followers who backed up his extravagant claims? Were they deluded or deceitful, dying for what they knew to be false, or did they really believe what they testified to have seen and touched?

Yet, in the face of these outrageous claims is a moral philosophy held in universal esteem, even among his critics. We are left to attribute this to either a befuddled or dangerous individual or worse…take him at his word.

We stand at this crossroads paralyzed. On the one hand, we are forced to consider how a moral teaching, no matter how useful, could have any integrity when the message and the man don't match. On the other, we're completely undone by the staggering implications of God's physical visitation. Can we move forward? Will we?

Splitting the horizontal and vertical

The God of the Bible is intrinsically complete in the eternal community of Father, Son, and Holy Spirit. Thus, creation is a work not of God's loneliness or lack, but of his love. Love binds, love makes perfect, love completes. Love bridges the chasm of isolation bringing fellowship where there is separation, making true community a reality. And the wider the chasm, the greater measure of love needed to bring distant parties together.

Between God and man, the chasm is unfathomable; in fact, it's unbridgeable. Without divine intervention, communion with God is impossible. Yet between that divide stands the Cross. Jesus Christ, through his life, death, and resurrection reaches over the infinite expanse in an unequaled act of love.

In everything, the Cross is central.

Along the vertical
As the vertical penetration of God into spacetime, the Cross allows God to present himself to man and man to present himself to God.

At the head of the Cross, God's love flows earthward from a thorn-gashed brow. At the foot of the Cross, man's gaze moves heavenward to a pair of nail-pierced feet. In divine descent, the Son atones, the Father forgives, and the Spirit indwells. In response, man reaches up to receive and, then, marvels at the wonder of the divine gift. In this divine-human interchange, the Cross brings together the earthly and the heavenly, uniting what was separate and imparting life to what was life-less.

Across the horizontal
Across the horizontal, the Cross links all that has gone before with all that is yet to come. Standing at the interface of eternity past and eternity future, the Cross is the junction of both *historical* time and *historic* time. Although these two expressions of time appear synonymous, they reflect the differing aspects used in the New Testament: *chronos* and *kairos*.

Time as a quantity is *chronos:* a linear measurement of historical change. It's from *chronos* we get the term, *chrono*logical time: the continuous thread of time sewing the past, present and future into a seamless fabric.

Kairos time is qualitative of a moment or event metaphysically pregnant with meaning and importance. It is the time spoken of when Paul writes the Galatian church, "But when the time had fully come, God sent his Son, born of a woman, born under law, ⬚ to redeem those under law, that we might receive the full rights of sons." *Kairos* brings together the types, "shadows," and prophesies of the scriptures with their fulfillments in the spacetime continuum in which, the Cross is central. [5]

In *chronos*, the Cross splits historical time into BC and AD. In *kairos*, the Cross stands between the epochal phenomena of the Creation and the New Creation, the Fall and Redemption, Israel and the Church, the Old Covenant and the New, law and grace, and the pre-incarnate Word and the Word made flesh. In *Kairos,* the eternal transcends and fulfills the temporal.

Where they meet
Where the upright timber and crossbeam meet is a crown of thorns adorning Him whose utterance, "It is finished," announced to the universe the unimaginable: Everlasting communion with God is possible! At that momentous juncture, a pair of hands fastened to a rough hewn log reaches out to a broken and hurting world.

In a posture of divine openness, God invites us to move out from the crossroads toward the Cross and be taken up in his embrace.

From the crossroads to the Cross
It is at the crossroads of Golgotha we face our true condition: one so desperate, it is beyond our ability to fix. As German astronomer, Johann Hieronymus Schroeder, once wrote, "It has been the cross which has revealed to good men that their goodness has not been good enough." And that can be a hard message indeed.

For those who don't believe in God, feelings of guilt and

remorse are not the result of violating some divine code of morality, but are hang-ups to be overcome.

For others, God is a cosmic scorekeeper who keeps track of performance to determine our merit and worth. If the good done in this world outweighs the bad, then heaven awaits. If not, our destiny is either a purifying process of re-cycling or final removal. But since the criteria for a passing grade are unknown, our "worthiness quotient" is up to guesswork and uncertainty.

But for those who accept the divine call, God is the Savior who extends the gift of eternal life to all who receive him. Like Johnson's protagonist, they have come to the crossroads acknowledging both their need and debt. But unlike him, they move from the crossroads to the Cross. It's *there* they look up, fall to their knees, and ask the Lord above, "Save me if you please."

Instead of the restless uncertainty besetting the hero of *Crossroads*, these sojourners have the settled confidence spoken of by the apostle John: "I write these things to you who believe in the name of the Son of God so that you may *know* that you have eternal life."[6]

Now, to what that means.

The Life That is Truly Life

Is life nothing more than the sum-total of our personal experiences? Is there no higher purpose to human existence than to set goals, make them, and rest in the afterglow of our successes? Those are questions that haunt the human soul.

By 2005 Tom Brady had led New England Patriots to three Super Bowl victories. And he was only 28. During a *60 Minutes* interview, Steve Kroft asked the quarterback to reflect on his accomplishments. Brady obliged: "Why do I have three Super Bowl rings and still think there's something greater out there for me? I mean maybe a lot of people would say, 'Hey man, this is what it is. I reached my goal, my dream, my life.' Me, I think, 'God, it's got to be more than this.' I mean this can't be what it's all cracked up to be."

"What's the answer?" Kroft pressed.

"I wish I knew...I wish I knew."[7]

Great Disappointments
One of life's great disappointments is to set goals that we never attain. But the greater disappointment is to attain them only to realize that they have no lasting significance; whether it is winning three Super Bowls (young athletes dallying with performance enhancement drugs, take notice) or making a financial fortune.

On the opening page of *The Call*, Os Guinness shares this from a troubled business man,

> "I've made a lot of money... far more than I could ever spend, far more than my family needs... To be

honest, one of my motives for making so much money was simple—to have money to hire people to do what I don't want to do. But there's one thing I've never been able to hire anyone to do for me; find my own sense of purpose and fulfillment. I'd give anything to discover that."[8]

The entrepreneur achieved success that most people only dream about, but it was not success that satisfies. Like Tom Brady, he is emblematic of go-getters who get what they're after, and discover that what they got has left them with an unfulfilled longing that is universal and unique to humankind: the soul-deep desire to know who we are and to find our niche, with the satisfaction that we and our labors matter in the grand scheme of things.

From Socrates to Sartre -- indeed, from the beginning of recorded history to the present, the puzzle of life's meaning has occupied the minds of philosophers, kings, and common folk alike, including those in the Bible.

God's servant Job, in the aftermath of his crushing losses, asks plaintively, "What is man that you make so much of him?"[2] With awe and wonder, David, the man after God's heart, echoes: "What is man that you are mindful of him?" Three times in as many chapters King Solomon, beset in existential angst, inquires "What does man gain from all his labor?"[9]

Such are the metaphysical questions of man's nature and purpose. Questions that press upon us, and we can't escape.

The Human Experience
In the documentary film, *The Human Experience* (2008), 20 year-old Jeffery Aziz and his older brother Clifford set out on a philosophical quest. Raised in a broken home with no one to help them wrestle with the great mysteries of life, the brothers decide to immerse themselves in the

lives of the least and the last. Their goal: to discover the purpose of life by broadening their "human experience."

Their journey takes them to New York City where they spend a week on the streets with the homeless during the coldest week of the year; to Peru where they volunteer at a hospital for abandoned children; and, finally, to Ghana Africa where they live with lepers.

Among the destitute, abandoned, and diseased the brothers are surprised to find optimism, confidence, and even joy. Individuals tell them that, despite their physical circumstances, they know they are here for a reason. To a person, they are at a loss to say what the reason is; but *that* it is, they have no doubt. The hope and certainty of significance by people on the margins of society leave an impact on the brothers.

At the film's end, after a poignant reunion with his estranged father, Jeffery reflects on what the human experience has taught him. Life's meaning, while still a mystery, is at least one for which he knows there is an answer, an answer that he will continue to pursue. I'd like to recommend that he resume his quest with the book of Ecclesiastes.

Fleshing out the answer
Solomon, after posing his existential question for the third time, writes: "God has set eternity in the hearts of men."[10] Therein lies a profound teaching about us. Eternity is woven into our design, our desires. We are made for eternity. Eternity is our destiny, the end of our earthly strivings. Of course, that begs the question: What is eternity?

A millennium later, Jesus, in his most eloquent recorded prayer, explained, "Now this is eternal life: that they may know you, the only true God and Jesus Christ, whom you have sent."[11]

There it is. Our purpose, the point of our earthly existence, is "eternity", and "eternity" is knowing God. This is not some Gnostic notion of knowledge reserved for the spiritual in-crowd. Neither is it about information transfer nor, foremost, about intellectual understanding. The "knowing" that Jesus is referring to is a relational experience of intimacy and submission.

There is perhaps no more vivid picture of this relationship than in John chapter 15.

In the last of his famous "I am" statements, Jesus tells his disciples: "I am the vine; you are the branches. If a man remains in me and I in him, he will bear much fruit; apart from me you can do nothing."

In an unhealthy tree, the organic connection between vine and branch has broken down leading to fruitlessness. But in a healthy tree, there is a region where the branch is in the vine and the vine is in branch, making it difficult to determine where one stops and the other begins. The seamless bond results in fruit production.

When we are in relationship with Jesus, he is "in us"— through his divine imprint of heart, mind, and conscience, and by his indwelling Spirit who teaches, comforts, and gifts us -- and we are "in Him" as members of His Body, the Church, which he has entrusted the keys of his kingdom with authority to bind and loose.

Built to last
What this means is that eternity is not reserved for the hereafter, but starts in the here-and-now. Eternal life is loving God and loving neighbor by advancing His kingdom though the Great Commission and Cultural Commission.[12] It is life that aligns with our created

purpose and, in the end, satisfies the deepest longings of our heart. It is "life," Paul tells his spiritual son Timothy, "that is truly life."[13]

Yet sadly, when people are faced with choosing that life, all too often they temporize ("Lord, first let me go and bury my father"); or, sincerely wanting it, but considering its demands on their already full dance card, decide that they don't have enough time.

The truth is, they have plenty of time, we all do. There are 24 hours in a day, always have been, always will be. It is not that over-booked people don't have enough time; it is that they don't have enough eternity. In their frenzied pursuit for success, approval and happiness, they have filled their schedule with lists of have to's, got to's, need to's and want to's that have all but numbed them to the pangs of eternity, until one-by-one they check off their to-do's, only to experience a familiar gnawing: *God, it's got to be more than this.*

In all of creation, human beings are the only things, as a famous marketing slogan goes, that are "built to last." Is it any wonder, then, that things that aren't--whether they be Super Bowl rings, Grammies, Oscars, or a spread in Fortune 500—give us a fleeting moment of contentment, then leave us empty?

Two messages
Every person has a choice between two messages: that of the culture and that of the Cross. The message of the culture is to find yourself, follow your dreams (passions or heart), and carry American Express. The message of the Cross is to lose (and deny) yourself and follow Christ, carrying your cross and each other's burdens.

One leads to the life of unsatisfied yearnings, and the other, to life that is truly life.

———

306

"The truth that makes men free is for the most part the truth which men prefer not to hear." -- Herbert Agar

Back to Two Men

Few individuals have had as much impact on modern culture as Sigmund Freud. Freud came at a time when popular sentiment was being shaped by the theories of Isaac Newton, Charles Darwin and Karl Marx. Materialistic explanations for the physical world, biological world, and socio-politics formed the first musical bars of the "God is Dead" elegy penned by Frederick Nietzsche. But it was Freud who completed the score by unpacking the mysteries of the human psyche and behavior.

In the decades that followed, Freud's influence expanded beyond psychology and psychotherapy to fields as diverse as literary criticism and ethics, writes Dr. Armand Nicholi in *The Question of God*.[14]

While Freud was arguably the most significant scientific materialist of the 20th century, C.S. Lewis was the most influential voice for the spiritual worldview of the last hundred years. An uncommon Christian apologist, Lewis spoke with clarity to the contemporary truth-seeker. His apologetic writings and Christian fiction communicated theological truths to the "person on the street" without the use of *churchspeak* or academic jargon.

Proficiently and presciently, he presented a robust challenge to materialism. With armor-piercing logic, Lewis showed that faith had its reasons and reason had its faith. Religious belief was not a matter of faith versus reason, but a matter of good faith versus bad faith.

308

In chapter 1 we reviewed the worldviews of Lewis and Freud. Now we will examine what practical effect their belief systems had on their lives.

Life's purpose

At the heart of worldview is the question of purpose. For Freud, life's purpose was happiness, a human condition he attributed to pleasure, particularly that derived from sexual satisfaction. Anything restraining man's sexual impulse (like religious mores), he insisted, are harmful because they lead to repression, anxiety, and guilt which inhibit the experience of pleasure and, hence, happiness.

While Freud's views adrenalized the sexual revolution and privacy "rights" evolution, Freud himself remained tethered to a traditional moral code—a fact that even mystified him. Not only was Freud a faithful husband and devoted father throughout his life, he admitted to a strong inclination to treat others kindly, even when it meant his own discomfort.

As to why he felt bound to a virtuous life, Freud was puzzled. "When I ask myself why I have always behaved honorably," he wrote a colleague, "...I have no answer. Sensible it certainly was not."

Lewis, on the other hand, came to understand that the good life was not one directed toward pleasure, but one directed toward a Person. He acknowledged that while some happiness is permitted us now, our happiness will always be incomplete, because Earth, in its present form, is not our home. How did that translate in his life?

In an interview in *Christianity Today*, Lewis's stepson, Douglas Gresham, said that Lewis gave away about two-thirds of his income, despite having grown up with a "pathological fear" of poverty. In one instance, his friend J.R.R. Tolkien chided him for giving a panhandler all the money in his pocket, insisting the man was only going to spend it on drink. Lewis replied, "Well, if I had kept it, I would have only spent it on drink." In his yearning for the "yet-to-come," Lewis did not neglect needs in the "here-and-now."[15]

View of man

Lewis held high view of humanity. He once said that "You have never talked to a mere mortal."
Organizations, nations, and civilizations all pass away, but people endure for eternity -- the lowliest, of which, is so glorious, that if we were to encounter one in its eternal state, we would be tempted to fall prostrate and worship it. That was a big turnaround for Lewis.

Prior to his conversion, Lewis's grim views led him to guard the interior of his life. Deeming nothing riskier than human relationships, Lewis refused to let his happiness depend on something he might lose. Personal conceit and distrust of others convinced him that "safety" was to be found by turning inward.

After conversion, his outward inclination couldn't have been starker. Lewis extended himself to an increasing circle of friends. He was one, according to Gresham, who would converse equally with plumbers or professors while drawing a crowd by his infectious laughter and storytelling.

Freud, by comparison, maintained a low valuation of humanity throughout his life: "The unworthiness of human beings...has always made a deep impression in me." This extended to his patients, for whom he maintained a "level of contempt."

This low view of man made the *Golden Rule* absurd. In Freud's opinion, love was something to be given only to those worthy of it; in other words, "love my neighbor, as my neighbor loves me." It is little wonder that Freud experienced a life-long pattern of strained and conflicted relationships.

Views of God and beyond

Both Freud and Lewis had problems with authority, traceable to the ambivalent relationship each had with his father. While Freud despised his father for weakness, Lewis despised his for capricious behavior and emotional detachment. Paternal ambivalence played a significant role in the negative attitudes both men developed for God. Yet, the lives of both men were riddled with contradictions.

Freud considered the Bible a fairy tale full of wishful thinking. But in his autobiography, he attributes his understanding of the Bible with the direction of his life. Letters written by this unapologetic atheist are rife with terms like "the good Lord," "if God so wills," "with God's help," and "my secret prayer." Freud considered religion a mass delusion accepted by those of "weak intellect," yet he had the highest praise for Isaac Newton, St. Paul, and Oskar Pfister (a close friend who was a pastor and psychoanalyst)—ironically, all men of faith.

Supposedly, Freud settled the question of God as a young man but, as Nicholi observes, Freud "remained preoccupied [with it] throughout his life." Even the subject of his last book, *Moses and Monotheism*, suggests that the question was not been as settled as Freud would lead us to believe.

Freud criticized the superstitious faith of believers, despite his own superstitious obsession with death. As early as the age of 38, Freud obsessed that certain numbers, like 61 or 62, or time markers, like the age his father or mother died, pointed to when he would die. Dr. Nicholi notes that even at the age of 80, Freud's superstition about death "gave him no peace."

After advising others of their need to resolve the question

of death in order to endure life, Freud never resolved the issue for himself. Instead, he wrestled with clinical depression for years, seeking relief with prolonged use of cocaine.

Lewis also experienced a "whirl of contradictions" during his atheistic period. While denying that God existed, he found himself both mad that God didn't exist, and angry that he created a sorrowful world in which creatures were forced to exist. But just who was he mad at? As Lewis later realized, it was Him who lived and died and rose again, as foreshadowed in myth, revealed in the Bible, and recounted in Nature's pattern of life, death and re-birth.

In contrast to Freud, who lived in gloom and pessimism until death, Lewis awakened to a new morning: "How true it is: the SEEING ONE walks out into joy and happiness unthinkable, where the dull, senseless eyes of the world see only death and destruction."

The lives of Freud and Lewis have much to say about the credibility of their respective worldviews. While Freud's worldview left him longing for a happiness he never enjoyed, Lewis's brought him a joy more desirable than any other longing: life that is truly life.

The power of conversion
Realizing that such anecdotal evidence could be exceptional, Dr. Nicholi included a study of Harvard students having had a "religious conversion"-- many of whom, with a history of depression.

Nicholi found a decrease in substance abuse and existential despair in the students after conversion; combined with improved academic performance, enhanced self-image, and increased capacity for satisfying relationships.

His study, published in the *American Journal of Psychiatry*, also revealed that the students had a new sense of joy and forgiveness that led to reduced feelings of self-hatred, helping them feel more tolerant and loving toward others.

Freud contended that religious belief was a pathological escape from reality. But as the lives of Lewis and the Harvard students indicate, it is a rational response to what one really knows to be real—that, contrary to the sentiments of Richard Dawkins and his ilk, there *is* a God.

Thus, it is those embracing the materialistic worldview, with its vortex of contradictions, who attempt escape from reality. The attempt plunged Freud ever deeper into an emotional darkness he was never able to resolve; for, as Lewis came to realize, "We may ignore, but we can nowhere evade, the presence of God."[16]

Epilogue

The most important question we will ever ask ourselves is whether God exists. If there is no God, the Woodstock generation has it right: we are stardust children, cosmic happenstances of fleeting existence and no ultimate meaning. If, on the other hand, there is a God and Jesus was right about him, then we are God's children, special beings created for intimacy with him and entrusted with shaping the world according to his will.

In the Introduction I said that the problem with unbelief is not that the evidence for God has been heard and found wanting, but that it has been unheard and ignored. This book has been my attempt to address that by presenting the rational bases for belief in God and the serious rational and existential problems with unbelief.

If I've succeeded, believing readers will feel better prepared, in the words of St. Peter, "to give an answer to everyone who asks you to give the reason for the hope that you have," and unbelievers, having been exposed to the evidence for God against the faith of religious skepticism, will begin reconsidering the answer to life's most important question.

Soli Deo Gloria
Regis Nicoll
January 2017

References and Endnotes

Note: All scripture references from the *New International Version* (1984)

Preface
[1] Gallup poll on religion
http://www.gallup.com/poll/1690/religion.aspx

Introduction
[1] The God Delusion, Richard Dawkins, *Mariner Books*, 2008. pp. 111-159
[2] Occam's Razor, a cardinal principle of science which holds that when various solutions are offered to a problem, the simplest is the preferred.
[3] The Brights' website: http://www.the-brights.net/index.html

Chapter 1
[1] Cross-National Correlations of Quantifiable Societal Health with Popular Religiosity and Secularism in the Prosperous Democracies, Gregory S. Paul, *Journal of Religion & Society*, Vol. 7 (2005)
[2] *The Question Of God: C.S. Lewis And Sigmund Freud Debate God, Love, Sex, And The Meaning Of Life*, Armand Nicholi, *Free Press*, 2003
[3] "Scientific materialism" or "scientism" holds that the material world is all that exists and that true knowledge is available only through the natural sciences.
[4] Letter to Mary Willis Shelburne on June 17, 1963. It's available in *The Collected Letters of C.S. Lewis, Volume 3*.
[5] Loose Change: Conspiracy film rewrites Sept. 11, William Welch, *USA Today,* April 29, 2007 http://tinyurl.com/pcumd3l
[6] The Problems of Philosophy, Bertrand Russell, *Arc Manor*, 2008, p. 85
[7] In 1964 physicist Peter Higgs conjectured that mass was caused by an invisible field that pervades the entire universe. Comprised of what were later dubbed, "Higgs particles," this field can be thought of as a kind of cosmic molasses that preferentially inhibits the motion of certain particle types. Because of its importance in understanding the nature of the universe, the Higgs has been referred to as the "God Particle." But after the existence of the Higgs was verified in 2013, questions have turned to where *it* comes from, why *it* has the properties it has, and why it acts on different particles

differently. Such questions signal that materialistic science has approached the edge of an ever-receding black hole of inquiry.

[8] In the Book of Acts chapter 17, the Apostle Paul engages a group of Greek philosophers, quoting Epimenides, a Cretan poet who lived six centuries earlier in Athens. According to Greek historian Diogenes Laertius, Epimenides was summoned to Athens by an Athenian named Nicias because a plague had broken out in Athens and Epimenides was the wisest man around. Epimenides noticed that the Athenians were worshipping hundreds of gods. He surmised that there must be an unknown god who the Athenians had overlooked, and this god was not pleased. He suggested that the Athenians release an entire flock of sheep at their hungriest time of the day. If one of the sheep chose to sit and rest in the grass instead of graze, the citizens were to build an altar there and sacrifice to this unknown god. They did, and sure enough, several of the sheep laid down even though it was at their normal grazing hour. The Athenians did as Epimenides suggested, and built an altar and sacrificed to this unknown god. The plague lifted. They asked Epimenides whose name should they carve on the altar. Epimenides said, "agnosto theo". The unknown god. The hill the sheep were grazing on was Mars Hill.

[9] Under the Influence: How Christianity Transformed Civilization, Alvin J. Schmidt, *Zondervan*, 2001

[10] Science of Mechanics, trans. Thomas J. McCormick (La Salle, Illinois: Open Court, Ernst Mach 1960), p.549

[11] Truth Decay: Defending Christianity against the Challenges of Postmodernism, Douglas Groothius, *IVP Books*, 2000

[12] Stellar parallax is a nearby star's apparent movement against the background of more distant stars as the Earth revolves around the Sun. ref: http://tinyurl.com/nemn8gk

[13] Intelligent design (ID) is the proposition that certain features in nature are best explained, scientifically, as products of intelligence.

[14] "Losing My Faith: If I'm So Done with Religion, Why Do I Still Feel It's Loss?", Margaret Johnson, December 29, 2011, *The Huffington Post*.
http://tinyurl.com/8molutv

[15] "Getting Religion," Mark Lilla, *The New York Times*, September 18, 2005,
http://tinyurl.com/98qwghp

[16] In 1929 Edwin Hubble discovered redshifts in the light emissions from stars, indicating that the universe was not static, but expanding. Nearly seventy years later, light spectra measurements of supernovae indicated that the universe is not only expanding, but accelerating! Mystified by this unknown cosmic power source, physicists dubbed it, "dark energy." Subsequent measurements revealed that dark energy accounts for 70 percent of all the stuff in

the universe. What's more, gravitational anomalies observed in stellar objects indicated a sizeable source of invisible ("dark") matter affecting their movements. When "dark matter" is added to dark energy, it turns out that dark stuff makes up 95 percent of the cosmos. But *what* it is, no one knows; and the answer is as elusive as ever. For that reason, a number of leading physicists, including Krauss, have called it the biggest mystery in physics.

[17] ENCODE Project Writes Eulogy for Junk DNA, *Science,* September 7, 2012, http://tinyurl.com/c5u9p8c

[18] An Agnostic Manifesto, Ron Rosenbaum, *Slate,* June 28, 2010, http://tinyurl.com/7atez8o

[19] Quantum theorist, David Bohm depicts the *quantum potential* as a kind of a ubiquitous cosmic substrate of "potentiality" that is neither matter nor energy, but gives rise to such things through "disturbances" in the quantum field.

[20] Finding Darwin's God, Kenneth R. Miller, *HarperCollins*, 1999, p. 186

[21] Imponderables Complicate Hunt For Intelligent Life Beyond Earth, Yudhijit Bhattacharjee, *Science*, 23 April 2010, Vol. 328 no. 5977 p. 421

[22] *The Last Word*, Thomas Nagel, *Oxford University Press*: 1997. pp 130-131.

[23] Proverbs 1:7

[24] Hopkins' poem, "The Grandeur of God," begins with "The world is charged with the grandeur of God."

[25] 1 Corinthians 13:9

[26] Stepping Up: A call to courageous manhood, Dennis Rainey, *Family Life*, 2011, p. 129.

[27] 1 Corinthians 2:9

[28] Belief in God Far Lower in Western U.S. Overall, Frank Newport, *Gallup*, July 28, 2008, http://tinyurl.com/5hxkyr

[29] Scientists and Belief, *Pew Research*, November 5, 2009, http://tinyurl.com/q5os5zk

[30] Leading scientists still reject God, Larson, Edward J.; Larry Witham (1998). *Nature*, vol. 394., No. 6691

[31] Intelligent people 'less likely to believe in God', Graeme Patterson, *The Telegraph*, June 11, 2008, http://tinyurl.com/3m8o9z

[32] Intelligence: Knowns and Unknowns, Report of a Task Force established by the Board of Scientific Affairs of the American Psychological Association, August 1, 1995

[33] Mainstream science on intelligence: An editorial with 52 signatories, history, and bibliography, Gottfredson, L. S. (1997). *Intelligence*, 24, 13–23

[34] A Brief History of Time, Stephen Hawking, *Bantam Books*, 1988, p.

[35] A.N. Wilson: Why I believe again, A. N. Wilson, *New Statesman,*

Chapter 2: The Nature of Reality
[1] Ephesians 1:23, 4:6
[2] In the 17th century, while Isaac Newton and most scientists believed light was composed of a stream of corpuscles, Dutch physicist Christiaan Huygens thought it was a wave vibrating in some sort of ether. However, in 1801, Thomas Young devised the now-famous double-slit experiment to demonstrate the interference of light waves, providing solid evidence that light was a wave, not a particle. Ref. : http://tinyurl.com/omfg8jm
[3] Broken Arrow of Time: Rethinking the Revolution in Modern Physics, James Galen Bloyd, Writers Cub Press, 2001
[4] 186,282 miles per second.
[5] Miracles, C.S. Lewis, *The Macmillan Co.*, 1947. p. 112
[6] Wholeness and the Implicate Order" David Bohm, *Routledge Classics*, 1980, p. 242
[7] The Development of the Space-Time View of Quantum Electrodynamics, Nobel Lecture, Richard Feynman, December 11, 1965
[8] Dancing Wu Li Masters, Gary Zukav, *Bantam Books*, 1991, p.328

Chapter 3: The Holy Grail of Science
[1] Job 38:33
[2] A Brief History of Time, Stephen Hawking, *Bantam Books*, 1988, p. 129
[3] Field theory, or quantum field theory, treats subatomic entities not as vanishingly small point particles, but as excited states of a ubiquitous quantum field.
[4] Einstein's theory of special relativity describes the equivalence of matter and energy in the famous equation $E=mc^2$
[5] Romans 11:34
[6] Einstein: A Biography (1954), Antonina Vallentin, p. 24
[7] Habakkuk 3:3-4
[8] Miracles, C.S. Lewis, *The Macmillan Co.*, 1947, p. 19
[9] *Pensées*, Blaise Pascal, E.P. Dutton &Co., 1958, p. 18,
[10] Antimatter is comprised of particles which have the same mass as particles of ordinary matter but have opposite properties: electronic charge, spin, quantum number, etc.
[11] Hyperspace: A Scientific Odyssey through the 10th Dimension, Michio Kaku, *Oxford University Press*, 1994 p. 99
[12] The Whole Shebang, Timothy Ferris, Simon and Shuster, 1997, p. 224
[13] Hyperspace: A Scientific Odyssey through the 10th Dinension, Michio Kaku, *Oxford University Press*, 1994 p. 157
[14] Desperately Seeking Superstrings? Paul Ginsparg and Sheldon

Glashow, *Physics Today*, May 1986:
http://arxiv.org/pdf/physics/9403001.pdf
[15] Taking Science on Faith, Paul Davies, *New York Times*, Nov. 24, 2007, http://tinyurl.com/kv4vsbh
[16] The Beginning of Time, Stephen Hawking lecture, http://www.hawking.org.uk/the-beginning-of-time.html
[17] Science and Christianity: Conflict or Coherence?, Henry F. Schaefer III, *The Apollos Trust*, 2004, p.73
[18] Essays on Physics, Death and the Mind, edited by Ingrid Fredriksson, *McFarland and Co.*, 2012, p. 171

Chapter 4: In the Beginning
[1] Evidence of the Universe's First Instant, Peter N. Spotts, *The Christian Science Monitor*, March 17, 2006, http://tinyurl.com/nldc5h3
[2] 'Smoking Gun' Found in Big Bang Theory, Matt Crenson (AP), March 16, 2006, http://tinyurl.com/nu84vr3
[3] John 1:1-3
[4] *The Fabric Of The Cosmos: Space, Time, And The Texture Of Reality,* Brian Greene, *Knopf Doubleday*, 2005, p. 308
[5] Einstein's theory of General Relativity predicts that the inward pull of gravity will lead to the eventual collapse (and end) of the universe. Logically, if the universe will end, it must have begun and, as Einstein and everyone else "knew," the universe was eternal and unchanging. It is one of science's great ironies that Einstein modified his original theory of general relativity by including a small repulsive force to counteract the attractive force of gravity. But with the discoveries of stellar redshifts, universe expansion, and the "Big Bang," Einstein had to retract his modification and, in doing so, called it his "biggest blunder." But this "blunder" would re-emerge some 70 years later to become a leading contender for dark energy -- the strange force behind cosmic expansion.
[6] A Brief History of Time, Stephen Hawking, *Bantam Books*, 1988, p. 129
[7] A "Just Right" Universe: Chapter Fourteen, The Creator and the Cosmos, Dr. Hugh Ross, Ph.D., http://tinyurl.com/p2f3ml6
[8] Leadership and the New Science: Discovering Order in a Chaotic World, By Margaret J. Wheatley, *Berrett-Koehler Publishers*, 1999, p. 96
[9] The Road Ahead, Bill Gates, *Penguin*: London, Revised, 1996 p. 228
[10] Stephen C. Meyer, "The Signature in the Cell," Harper One, 2009, pg. 213.
[11] The Intelligent Universe, F. Hoyle, New York, *Holt Rinehart and Winston*, 1984
[12] The Cosmic Blueprint, Paul Davies, *Templeton Press,* 2004

[13] God (or Not), Physics and, of Course, Love: Scientists Take a Leap, *New York Times*, January 4, 2005, http://tinyurl.com/pey6ay5
[14] Our Cosmic Habitat, Martin Rees, *Princeton Univ. Press*, 2001, p. 162
[15] The Universe: Past and Present Reflections, Fred Hoyle, *Engineering and Science*, Nov. 1981, p8-12
[16] 60 Seconds: Marcus Chown, Graeme Green, Metro, Jan 18, 2007, http://tinyurl.com/ngrcwqm
[17] Particle Physics and Inflationary Cosmology, Andrei Linde, *Contemp.Concepts Phys.* 5 (2005)
[18] Hawking unveils new thinking on black holes, *Associated Press,* July 21, 2004, http://tinyurl.com/pmjj2of
[19] Is string theory in trouble?, Amanda Gefter, *New Scientist*, Dec. 17, 2005, http://tinyurl.com/oo5e2ru
[20] Science's Alternative to an Intelligent Creator: the Multiverse Theory, Tim Folger, Discover, November 10, 2008, http://tinyurl.com/5qwd7x
[21] Is speculation in multiverses as immoral as speculation in subprime mortgages?, John Horgan, *Scientific American*, January 28, 2011, http://tinyurl.com/keh8h8q
[22] Does God So Love the Multiverse? Don N. Page, Institute for Theoretical Physics Department of Physics, University of Alberta Room 238 CEB, 11322 – 89 Avenue Edmonton, Alberta, Canada T6G 2G7, http://arxiv.org/pdf/0801.0246.pdf
[23] Living in the Multiverse Opening Talk at the Symposium "Expectations of a Final Theory" at Trinity College, Cambridge, September 2, 2005, ed. B. Carr (Cambridge University Press). Steven Weinberg Physics Department, University of Texas at Austin, http://arxiv.org/pdf/hep-th/0511037.pdf
[24] BICEP2 Experiment's Big-Bang Controversy Highlights Challenges for Modern Science, Joel Achenbach, *Washington Post*, July 23, 2014, http://tinyurl.com/mdyuqd5
[25] Paul Davies, "Be Warned Matrix, This Could be the Matrix," July 22, 2004, *The Sydney Morning Herald*, http://tinyurl.com/nu63tzh
[26] Brian Whitworth, "10 Reasons Our Universe Might Actually Be Virtual Reality," Dec. 2, 2014, *Gizmodo*, http://tinyurl.com/pkrnahc
[27] Ibid
[28] Brian Whitworth, "Quantum Realism FAQ," http://brianwhitworth.com/QRFAQ.pdf
[29] The Black Hole at the Beginning of Time --We may have Emerged from a Black Hole in a Higher-Dimensional Universe," August 10, 2014, *The Daily Galaxy*, http://tinyurl.com/ptocv4y
[30] Zeeya Merali, "Stephen Hawking: 'There are no black holes,'" January 24, 2014, *Nature*, http://tinyurl.com/k5n6qm6
[31] Thania Benios, "Researcher Shows That Black Holes Do Not Exist," September 24, 2014, *Phys. Org*, http://phys.org/news/2014-

09-black-holes.html

[32] Romans 1:20

[33] Genesis Chapter 1

[34] In 1964 physicist Peter Higgs conjectured that mass was caused by an invisible field that pervades the entire universe. Comprised of what were later dubbed, "Higgs particles," this field can be thought of as a kind of cosmic molasses that preferentially inhibits the motion of certain particle types. Because of its ubiquity and its importance to the Standard Model of physics, many pundits refer to Higgs as the "God Particle."

[35] 2 Timothy 4:3-4

[36] Join the SETI Search, Jill Tarter, *TED Talk*, February 2009, http://tinyurl.com/mnv4gkq

[37] Imponderables Complicate Hunt For Intelligent Life Beyond Earth, Yudhijit Bhattacharjee, *Science*, 23 April 2010, Vol. 328 no. 5977 p. 421

[38] SETI Website, http://www.seti.org/seti-educators

[39] Stephen Hawking Thinks these Three Things Could Destroy Humanity, Tanya Lewis, *LiveScience.com*, February 23, 2015, http://tinyurl.com/kh9ahzr

[40] Genesis Chapter 1

Chapter 5: Breaking the Spell of Materialism

[41] Physics and Philosophy, Werner Heisenberg, *Harper Classics,* 1952, p. 186

[42] Ibid

[43] The Dancing Wu Li Masters, Gary Zukav, *Bantam Books*, 1979, p. 314

[44] The Ghost Particle, *NOVA,* PBS, Feb. 21, 2006, http://tinyurl.com/pc7ux3f

[45] The Greatest Story Ever Told, *The Edge*, Carolyn Porco, http://tinyurl.com/pjm3xg9

[46] Why Humanity Needs a God of Creativity, *New Scientist*, Stuart Kauffman, http://tinyurl.com/kjjvwg

[47] Darwinists for Jesus, Yudhijit Bhattacharjee, *The New York Times*, June 15, 2008.

[48] Thoughts on the Existence of God, Paul Johnson, *Forbes*, June 6, 2005, http://tinyurl.com/p3wrpsz

[49] By Their Creator: How a Belief in a Creator Shapes the American Conscience, Philip Eveland, Writers Club Press, 2002 , p. 226

[50] Ornithologist and Evolutionary Biologist Alan Feduccia— Plucking Apart the Dino-Birds, Saturday, Kathy A. Svitil, *Discover*, February 2003

[51] Darwin's Doubt, Stephen Meyer, *Harper Collins*, 2013, p. 12

[52] Ibid, p. 31

[53] Ibid, p. 13-14

[54] Ibid, p. 86

[55] Ibid, p. 17

[56] Ibid, p. 57-58

[57] Ibid, p. 262

[58] Wrong-way evolution of the creationist movement, Patrick Chisholm, *Christian Sci. Monitor*, February 23, 2005, http://tinyurl.com/okl3awg

[59] Ongoing Evolution Among Darwin's Finches, *Teaching About Evolution And The Nature Of Science,* National Academy Press, Washington, DC

[60] There is a God: How The World's Most Notorious Atheist Changed His Mind, Antony Flew with Roy Varghese, *Harper Collins*, 2008, p. 155

[61] Four in 10 Americans Believe in Strict Creationism, Gallup, December 17, 2010, http://tinyurl.com/38zk54d

[62] Homunculi rule: Reflections on Darwinian populations and natural selection by Peter Godfrey Smith, Daniel C. Dennett, *Oxford University Press*, 2009, http://tinyurl.com/q86am8e

[63] Nothing in Biology Makes Sense except in the Light of Evolution, Theodosius Dobzhansky Source: *The American Biology Teacher*, Vol. 35, No. 3 (Mar., 1973), pp. 125-129

[64] 'Death anxiety' prompts people to believe in intelligent design, reject evolution, study suggests, *ScienceDaily*, 23 May 2011, http://tinyurl.com/4ng7sqk

[65] Frontiers Profile: Daniel Dennett, *PBS* web feature, http://tinyurl.com/ozsh96o

[66] Psalm 42:1

[67] The Question of God: Nine Conversations -- Love thy neighbor, *PBS*, 2004, http://tinyurl.com/pyxujjx

[68] The Question of God, C.S. Lewis and Sigmund Freud Debate God, Love Sex, and the Meaning of Life, Dr. Armand Nicholi, *Free Press*, 2002

[69] Are There Secular Reasons?, Stanley Fish*, New York Times*, Feb. 22, 2010, http://tinyurl.com/yg46fte

[70] Exodus 19:15, 17 "You shall not steal." "You shall not covet your neighbor's house. You shall not covet your neighbor's wife, or his male or female servant, his ox or donkey, or anything that belongs to your neighbor."

[71] Morality: We can send religion to the scrap heap, Sam Harris, *New Scientist*, Oct. 20, 2010, http://tinyurl.com/kflgt36

[72] In God's Name, John Micklethwait, *The Economist,* Nov. 1, 2007, http://tinyurl.com/o9hcmkm

[73] The Future of World Religions: Population Growth Projections, 2010-2050, *Pew Research Center*, April 5, 2015, http://tinyurl.com/o97tdzz

[74] Is Man the Measure? An evaluation of contemporary humanism,

Norman Geisler, *Baker*, 1983, p. 46-47

[75] Science and Religion: Incompatible?, Michael Shermer, *HuffPost Blog*, May 1, 2012, http://tinyurl.com/mbq2kja

[76] Anomalous Events That Can Shake One's Skepticism to the Core, Michael Shermer, *Scientific American*, September 16, 2014, http://tinyurl.com/pq9426z

[77] Why I am and Atheist, Michael Shermer website, June 2005, http://tinyurl.com/6v7wjy

[78] Science and Religion: Incompatible?, Michael Shermer, *HuffPost Blog*, May 1, 2012, http://tinyurl.com/mbq2kja

Chapter 6: An Intelligent Proposition

[1] Tammy KITZMILLER, et al., Plaintiffs v. DOVER AREA SCHOOL DISTRICT, No. 04cv2688. United States District Court, M.D. Pennsylvania. Dec. 20, 2005.

[2] Four in 10 Americans Believe in Strict Creationism, *Gallup*, December 17, 2010, http://tinyurl.com/38zk54d

[3] When Evolutionists Attack, Andrew Brown, *The Guardian,* March 5, 2006, http://tinyurl.com/oyua3l5

[4] Does Medical Science Need Evolutionary Science? Casey Luskin, *Evolution News and Views*, May 28, 2015, http://tinyurl.com/p5rnksu

[5] The Signature in the Cell, Stephen Meyer, *Harper One*, 2009.

[6] Ibid, p. 136-140

[7] The Design Inference, William Dembski, *Cambridge Univ. Press*, 2006, p. 36

[8] Out of Eden, Richard Dawkins, *Harper Collins*, 1995, p. 17

[9] The Signature in the Cell, Stephen Meyer, *Harper One*, 2009. App. B

[10] Ibid, Chapter 18

[11] Ibid,. App. A

[12] The Music of Life, Denis Noble, *Oxford Univ. Press,* 2006, p. 66

Chapter 7: The Designer behind the Design

[1] Discovering God, Rodney Stark, *HarperOne*, 2007

[2] David Brooks: We Need to Start Talking about Sin and Righteousness Again, Jeffery Haanen, *Christianity Today*, May 13, 2015

[3] Miracles, C.S. Lewis, *HarperCollins*, 1947, p. 222

[4] Romans 10:17

[5] 2 Timothy 3:16

[6] Psalm 33:6

[7] A Footnote to All Prayers, C.S. Lewis, http://liturgy.co.nz/a-footnote-to-all-prayers

[8] Romans 8:26

[9] Psalm 19:1-2

[10] Genesis 1:26

[11] The Gospel of John 1:9

[12] 2 Timothy 3:16-17

[13] The Gospel of John 1:14-18

[14] The Gospel of John 14:26

[15] Ephesians 3:9-10

[16] Romans 1:20

[17] Dancing Wu Li Masters, Gary Zukav, *Bantam Books*, 1991, p.328

[18] Ephesians 4:6

[19] The Gospel of John 1:3

[20] The Creator and the Cosmos, Hugh Ross, *NavPress*, 2001

[21] Isaiah 45:18

[22] What Mad Pursuit: A Personal View of Scientific Discovery, Francis Crick, 1990, p 138

[23] Debating Design: from Darwin to DNA, edited by William Dembski and Michael Ruse, *Cambridge University Press*, 2004, p. 324

[24] The Blind Watchmaker, Richard Dawkins, *W.W. Norton & Co.*, 1996, p.1

[25] Life Itself: Its Origin and Nature, Francis Crick, *Simon and Shuster*, 1982

[26] "Information, physics, quantum: the search for links", Wheeler, J. A.: Proceedings III International Symposium on Foundations of Quantum Mechanics, Tokyo, 1989, p. 354-368

[27] Psalm 19:1-4

[28] Facing Up: Science and its Cultural Adversaries, *Harvard University Press*, Steven Weinberg, 2001 P. 47

[29] Intelligent Design: the bridge between Science and theology, William Dembski, *Intervarsity Press*, 1999, p. 230

[30] Psalm 8:4

[31] Religion: Is God in Our Genes?, Jeffery Kluger, *Time,* October 24, 2004

[32] Job 32:8

[33] Eudaemonia, The Good Life - A Talk With Martin Seligman, http://tinyurl.com/m7mquq9

[34] Evolution and Ethics, Thomas Huxley, In *Collected Essays* (1894), Vol. 9, p. 81-22.

[35] 2 Peter 1:20-21

[36] God in the Dock, C.S. Lewis, *Eerdman's Publishing Co.*, 1972, p. 159

[37] 1 Corinthians, Chapter 15

[38] The Gospel of Luke, Chapter 1

[39] 2 Peter 3:15-16

[40] Why the "Lost Gospels" Lost Out, Ben Witherington III, *Christianity Today*, June 1, 2004

[41] Daniel 9:25-26

[42] The Story of the Bible, F.G. Kenyon, 1936, p. 144
[43] Colossians 2:2-3
[44] C.S. Lewis' liar, lunatic, Lord Trilemma: "I am trying here to prevent anyone saying the really foolish thing that people often say about Him: "I'm ready to accept Jesus as a great moral teacher, but I don't accept His claim to be God." That is the one thing we must not say. A man who said the sort of things Jesus said would not be a great moral teacher. He would either be a lunatic--on a level with the man who says he is a poached egg--or else he would be the Devil of Hell. You must make your choice. Either this man was, and is, the Son of God: or else a madman or something worse. You can shut Him up for a fool, you can spit at Him and kill Him as a demon; or you can fall at His feet and call Him Lord and God. But let us not come with any patronizing nonsense about His being a great human teacher. He has not left that open to us. He did not intend to." From Mere Christianity, C.S. Lewis, New York, *Macmillan/Collier*, 1952, p. 55
[45] Jesus: An Historian's Review of the Gospels, Michael Grant, *Scribner's,* 1977, p. 200
[46] Colossians 1:15, 2:9
[47] The Gospel of John 1:14-18
[48] The Everlasting Man, G.K. Chesterton, 1925, p.106
[49] The Gospel of John 13:34-35
[50] The Gospel of John 14:19-20
[51] Paul Copan, "True for You, But Not for Me: Overcoming Objections to Christian Faith," *Bethany House Publishers*, (2009), p.174
[52] In Josh McDowell, Evidence that Demands a Verdict, *Here's Life Publishers*, rev. ed. 1979), p. 373
[53] The Gospel of Matthew 16:18
[54] Evangelism in the Early Church, Michael Green, *Eerdman's Publishing Co.*, 2003, p. 427
[55] A Godward Life: Savoring the Supremacy of God in All of Life, John Piper, *Multnomah Publishers Inc.,* 1997, p. 253
[56] 1 Peter 2:11-13
[57] The Rise of Christianity, Rodney Stark, *HarperCollins,* 1997, Chapters 1-3
[58] Faith Does Breed Charity, Roy Hattersley, *The Guardian*, Sept. 11, 2005, http://tinyurl.com/okcuebf
[59] Michael A. Shea, "Napoleon: On the Divinity of Jesus Christ at Saint Helena, 1820," http://tinyurl.com/mw9aez5
[60] Acts of the Apostles 5:29-39
[61] Genesis 1:26; Job 33:4
[62] The Gospel of Mark 10:27
[63] 2 Peter 1:19-21
[64] 1 Corinthians 12:1-7

[65] The Gospel of John 15:26, 16:8; 1 Corinthians 12:3
[66] 1 Corinthians 6:19
[67] Ephesians 5:18
[68] Colossians 2:9

Chapter 8: Some Objections
[1] Job 13:24
[2] Till We Have Faces, C.S. Lewis, *Harcourt Brace & Company*, 1980
[3] 1 Corinthians 13:12
[4] Job 42:1-5
[5] 2 Corinthians 3:18; Colossians 3:4
[6] Joshua Chapter 6
[7] Ezekiel 18:20
[8] Romans 8:18
[9] The Gospel of John 12:48
[10] The Holiness of God, R.C. Sproul, *Tyndale House Publishers*, 2000
[11] 2 Corinthians 4:17
[12] 2 Corinthians Chapters 11-12
[13] Does Death Exist?: Life is Forever, says Theory, Robert Lanza, *Huff Post Blog,* Jan. 4, 2010, http://tinyurl.com/y8n6kwx
[14] Romans 8:20
[15] PhysLink.com, Physics and Astronomy online, http://tinyurl.com/75vfm
[16] Romans 8:19-23, 2 Corinthians 5:4
[17] Ecclesiastes 7:15
[18] Religion and Human Rights: An Introduction, edited by John Witte, M. Christian Green, *Oxford University Press*, 2012, p. 276
[19] The Gospel of Luke 13:1-5
[20] Ecclesiastes 7:2, The Gospel of John 5:24
[21] Romans 9:14-16
[22] 1 Corinthians 5:1-5
[23] Jude 1:24
[24] The World's Last Night and other Essays, C.S. Lewis, *A Harvest Book*, 1960, p. 10
[25] God Bless Ted Turner, Rod Dreher, *National Review Online*, Feb. 11, 2003, http://tinyurl.com/8k5jd7d
[26] When Bad Things Happen to Good People, Harold S. Kushner, *Anchor,* 2004

Chapter 9: Between Two Messages
[1] Death on a Friday Afternoon: Meditations on the Last Words of Jesus from the Cross, Richard John Neuhaus, *Basic Books,* 2000, p. 209-210.
[2] Hebrews 4:14-16

[3] Cross Purposes: Discovering the Great Love of God for You, Dr. D. James Kennedy, et al, *Multnomah Publishers*, 2007, p. 128

[4] The Gospel of John 10:9

[5] Galatians 4:4-5

[6] 1 John 5:13

[7] Tom Brady Talks to Steve Croft, *60 Minutes*, http://tinyurl.com/nh4bzlw

[8] The Call: Finding and Fulfilling the Central Purpose of Your Life, *W Publishing Group*, 2003, Os Guinness, p. 1

[9] Psalms 8:4, Ecclesiastes Chapters 1-3

[10] Ecclesiastes 3:11

[11] The Gospel of John 17:3

[12] The Cultural Commission, given to Adam and Eve in the garden *and* to the Apostles through Jesus' command to make disciples "of all nations," is our mission to flourish creation by creating culture in a way that restrains evil, upholds justice, inspires virtue, and promotes the common good until that day when what God wills done is done, on earth as it is in heaven. Ref. Genesis 1:26, The Gospel of Matthew 28:19-20

[13] 1 Timothy 6:19

[14] *The Question Of God: C.S. Lewis And Sigmund Freud Debate God, Love, Sex, And The Meaning Of Life*, Armand Nicholi, Free Press, 2003

[15] The Man Behind the Wardrobe, Mark Moring, *Christianity Today*, October 31, 2005.

[16] C.S.Lewis, Letters to Malcolm: Chiefly on Prayer, *A Harvest Book,* 1963, p. 75